Database Design Using Entity-Relationship Diagrams

Second Edition

Sikha Bagui and **Richard Earp**

CRC Press
Taylor & Francis Group
Boca Raton London New York

CRC Press is an imprint of the
Taylor & Francis Group, an **informa** business
AN AUERBACH BOOK

CRC Press
Taylor & Francis Group
6000 Broken Sound Parkway NW, Suite 300
Boca Raton, FL 33487-2742

© 2012 by Taylor & Francis Group, LLC
CRC Press is an imprint of Taylor & Francis Group, an Informa business

No claim to original U.S. Government works

Version Date: 20110510

International Standard Book Number: 978-1-4398-6176-9 (Hardback)

Library of Congress Cataloging-in-Publication Data

Bagui, Sikha, 1964-
        Database design using entity-relationship diagrams / Sikha Bagui and Richard
        Earp. -- 2nd ed.
        p. cm.
    Includes bibliographical references and index.
        ISBN 978-1-4398-6176-9 (alk. paper)
        1. Database design. 2. Relational databases. I. Earp, Richard, 1940- II. Title.

QA76.9.D26B35 2012
005.74--dc23   2011012482

Visit the Taylor & Francis Web site at
http://www.taylorandfrancis.com

and the CRC Press Web site at
http://www.crcpress.com

Dedicated to my late father-in-law, Paresh C. Bagui; late mother-in-law, Khodan B. Bagui; father, Santosh Saha; mother, Ranu Saha, and husband, Subhash Bagui

S.B.

Dedicated to my wife, Brenda, and my children, Beryl, Rich, Gen, and Mary Jo

R.E.

Contents

Preface

Data modeling and database design have undergone significant evolution in recent years. Today, the relational data model and the relational database system dominate business applications. The relational model has allowed the database designer to focus on the logical and physical characteristics of a database separately. In this book, we concentrate on techniques for database design with a very strong bias for relational database systems, using the ER (entity relationship) approach for conceptual modeling (solely a logical implementation).

INTENDED AUDIENCE

This book is intended to be used for data modeling by database practitioners and students. It is also intended to be used as a supplemental text in database courses, systems analysis and design courses, and other courses that design and implement databases. Many present-day database and systems analysis and design books limit their coverage of data modeling. This book not only increases the exposure to data modeling concepts, but also presents a step-by-step approach to designing an ER diagram and developing a relational database from it.

BOOK HIGHLIGHTS

This book focuses on presenting (a) an *ER design methodology* for developing an ER diagram; (b) a *grammar* for the ER diagrams that can be presented back to the user; and (c) *mapping rules* to map the ER diagram to a relational database. The steps for the ER design methodology, the grammar for the ER diagrams, as well as the mapping rules are developed and presented in a systematic step-by-step manner throughout the book. Also, several examples of "sample data" have been included with relational database mappings to give a "realistic" feeling.

This book is divided into 12 chapters. The first three chapters are background material. The first chapter introduces the concept of data, the database, and software engineering. Chapter 2 presents the different database models. Chapter 3 introduces the relational model and discusses functional dependencies used to generate third normal form databases.

From Chapter 4, we start presenting the concept of ER diagrams. Chapter 4 introduces the concept of the entity, attributes, relationships, and the "one-entity" ER diagram. Steps 1, 2, and 3 of the ER design methodology are developed in this chapter. The one-entity grammar and mapping rules for the one-entity diagram are presented.

Chapter 5 extends the one-entity diagram to include a second entity. The concept of testing attributes for entities is discussed, and relationships between the entities are developed. Steps 3a, 3b, 4, 5, and 6 of the ER Design Methodology are developed, and grammar for the ER diagrams developed up to this point is presented.

Chapter 6 discusses structural constraints in relationships. Several examples are given of 1:1, 1:M, and N:M relationships. Step 6 of the ER design methodology is revised, and step 7 is developed. A grammar for the structural constraints and the mapping rules is also presented.

Chapter 7 develops the concept of the weak entity. This chapter revisits and revises steps 3 and 4 of the ER design methodology to include the weak entity. Again, a grammar and the mapping rules for the weak entity are presented.

Chapter 8 discusses and extends different aspects of binary relationships in ER diagrams. This chapter revises step 5 to include the concept of more than one relationship and revises step 6b to include derived and redundant relationships. The concept of the recursive relationship is introduced in this chapter. The grammar and mapping rules for recursive relationships are presented.

Chapter 9 discusses ternary and other "higher-order" relationships. Step 6 of the ER design methodology is again revised to include ternary and other higher-order relationships. Several examples are given, and the grammar and mapping rules are developed and presented.

Chapter 10 discusses enhanced entity relationships (EERs): generalizations and specializations, shared subclasses, and categories or union types. Once again, step 6 of the ER design methodology is modified to include generalizations and specializations, and the grammar and mapping rules for mapping the EER are presented.

Chapter 11 gives a summary of the mapping rules and reverse engineering from a relational database to an ER diagram.

Chapters 4–11 present ER and EER diagrams using a Chen-like model. In Chapter 12, we discuss the Barker/Oracle-like models, highlighting the main similarities and differences between the Chen-like model and the Barker/Oracle-like model.

In every chapter, we present several examples. "Checkpoint" sections within the chapters and end-of-chapter exercises are presented in every chapter to be worked out by the students to obtain a better understanding of the material within the respective sections and chapters. At the end of Chapters 4–10, there is a running case study, with the solution (that is, the ER/EER diagram and the relational database with some sample data).

Acknowledgments

Our special thanks are due to our editors, John Wyzalek, Amy Blalock, and Judith Simon at CRC Press.

We would also like to thank President Judy Bense, Provost Chula King, and Dean Jane Halonen for their inspiration, encouragement, support, and true leadership quality.

Our sincere thanks also go to Dr. Leo Ter Haar, chair, Computer Science Department, for his advice, guidance, and support and for encouraging us to complete this book, and Dr. Norman Wilde and Dr. Ed Rodgers for their continuing support and encouragement throughout past years. And, last but not least, we would like to thank our fellow faculty members, Diana Walker and Michelle Lockhart for their continuous support and encouragement.

Introduction

This book was written to aid students in database classes and to help database practitioners in understanding how to arrive at a definite, clear database design using an entity relationship (ER) diagram. In designing a database with an ER diagram, we recognize that this is but one way to arrive at the objective: the database. There are other design methodologies that also produce databases, but an ER diagram is the most common. The ER diagram is a subset of what are called "semantic models." As we go through this material, we occasionally point out where other models differ from the ER model.

The ER model is one of the best-known tools for logical database design. Within the database community, it is considered a natural and easy-to-understand way of conceptualizing the structure of a database. Claims that have been made for it include the following: It is simple and easily understood by nonspecialists, it is easily conceptualized, the basic constructs (entities and relationships) are highly intuitive and thus provide a natural way of representing a user's information requirements, and it is a model that describes a world in terms of entities and attributes that is most suitable for computer-naïve end users. In contrast, many educators have reported that students in database courses have difficulty grasping the concepts of the ER approach, particularly in applying them to real-world problems.

We took the approach of starting with an entity and then developing from it an "inside-out strategy" (as mentioned in Elmasri and Navathe, 2007). Software engineering involves eliciting from a (perhaps) "naïve" user what the user would like to have stored in an information system. The process we present follows the software engineering paradigm of requirements/specifications, with the ER diagram being the core of the specification. Designing a software solution depends on correct elicitation. In most software engineering paradigms, the process starts with a requirements elicitation followed by a specification and then a feedback loop. In plain English, the idea is (a) "tell me what you want" (requirements), then (b) "this is what I think you want" (specification). This process of requirements/specification may (and probably should) be iterative so that the user understands what he or she will get from the system and the analyst understands what the user wants.

A methodology for producing an ER diagram is presented. The process leads to an ER diagram that is then translated into plain (but meant to be precise) English that a user can understand. The iterative mechanism then takes over to arrive at a specification (a revised ER diagram and English) that both the user and analyst understand. The mapping of the ER diagram into a relational database is presented; mapping to other logical database models is not covered. We feel that the relational database is the most appropriate to demonstrate mappings as it is the most used contemporary database model. Actually, the idea behind the ER diagram is to produce a high-level database model that has no particular logical model (relational, hierarchical, object oriented, or network) implied.

We have a strong bias toward the relational model. The "goodness" of the final relational model is testable via the ideas of normal forms. The goodness of the relational model produced by a mapping from an ER diagram theoretically should be guaranteed by the mapping process. If a diagram is "good enough," then the mapping to a "good" relational model should happen almost automatically. In practice, the scenario will be to produce as good an ER diagram as possible, map it to a relational model, and then shift the discussion to discussion of "Is this a good relational model or not?" by using the theory of normal forms and other associated criteria of "relational goodness."

The approach we take to database design is intuitive and informal. We do not deal with precise definitions of set relations. We use the intuitive "one/many" for cardinality and "may/must" for participation constraints. The intent is to provide a mechanism to produce an ER diagram that can be presented to a user in English and to polish the diagram into a specification that can then be mapped into a database. We then suggest testing the produced database by the theory of normal forms and other criteria (i.e., referential integrity constraints). We also suggest a reverse-mapping paradigm for mapping a relational database back to an ER diagram for the purpose of documentation.

THE ER MODELS WE CHOSE

We begin our venture into ER diagrams with a "Chen-like" model, and most of this book is written using the Chen-like model. Why did we choose this model? Chen (1976) introduced the idea of the ER diagrams (Elmasri and Navathe 2007), and most database texts use some variant of the Chen model. Chen and others have improved the ER process over the years, and while there is no standard ER diagram model, the Chen-like model and variants thereof are common, particularly in comprehensive database texts. In the last chapter, we briefly introduce the "Barker/Oracle-like" model. As with the Chen model, we do not follow the Barker or Oracle models precisely and hence use the term *Barker/Oracle-like* models in this text.

There are also other reasons for choosing the Chen-like model over the other models. With the Chen-like model, one need not consider how the database will be implemented. The Barker-like model is more intimately tied to the relational database paradigm. Oracle Corporation uses an ER diagram that is closer to the Barker model. Also, in the Barker-like and Oracle-like ER diagram there is no accommodation for some of the features we present in the Chen-like model. For example, multivalued attributes, many-to-many relationships, and weak entities are not part of the Barker- or Oracle-like design process.

The process of database design follows the software engineering paradigm, and during the requirements and specifications phase, sketches of ER diagrams are made and remade. It is not at all unusual to arrive at a design and then revise it. In developing ER models, one needs to realize that the Chen model is developed to be independent of implementation. The Chen-like model is used almost exclusively by universities in database instruction. The mapping rules of the Chen model to a relational database are relatively straightforward, but the model itself does not represent any particular logical model. Although the Barker/Oracle-like model is popular, it is implementation dependent on knowledge of the relational database. The Barker/Oracle-like model maps directly to a relational database; there are no real mapping rules for that model.

BIBLIOGRAPHY

Chen, P. P. 1976. The entity relationship model-toward a unified view of data, *ACM Transactions on Database Systems,* 1(1).

Elmasri, R., and Navathe, S. B. 2007. *Fundamentals of Database Systems,* 5th ed. Addison Wesley, Reading, MA.

1

Data, Databases, and the
Software Engineering Process

1.1 INTRODUCTION

In this chapter, we introduce some concepts and ideas that are fundamental to our presentation of the design of a database. We define *data*,
describe the notion of a database, and explore a process of how to design
a database.

1.2 DATA

Data, as we use the term, are facts about something or someone. For
example, a person has a name, an address, and a gender. Some data
(facts) about a specific person might be "Mary Smith," "123 4th St.,"
"female." If we had a list of several people's names, addresses, and gen-
ders, we would have a set of facts about several people. A *database* is a
collection of *related* data. For this "set of facts about several people" to
be a database, we would expect that the people in the database had something in common—that they were "related" in some way. Here *related*
does not imply a familial relationship, but rather something more like
"people who play golf," "people who have dogs," or "people I interviewed
on the street today." In a "database of people," one expects the people to
have some common characteristic that ties them together. A "set of facts
about some people" is not a database until the common characteristic is
also defined. To put it another way: Why are these people's names and
addresses being kept in one list?

CHECKPOINT 1.1

1. A tree is classified as a "large oak tree about 100 years old." What are three facts about this tree?
2. Another tree has the following characteristics: pine, small, 15 years old. If I write about the two trees and their facts on a piece of paper, what do I have?
3. Why is the piece of paper not a database of trees?

1.3 BUILDING A DATABASE

How do we construct a database? Suppose you were asked to put together a database of items one keeps in a pantry. How would you go about doing this? You might grab a piece of paper and begin listing items that you see. When you are done, you would have a database of items in the pantry. Simple enough, but is it a good database or a poor one? Was your approach to database construction a good methodology or not-so-good methodology? The answer to these questions would depend on why you constructed the list—who will use the list and for what. If you are more methodical, you might first ask yourself how best to construct this database before you grab the paper and begin a list of items. A bit of prethinking might save time in the long run because you might think about how the list was to be used and by whom.

When dealing with software and computer-related activity like databases, we have a science of "how to" called software engineering (SE). SE is a process of specifying systems and writing software. To design a good database, we will use ideas from SE. By being aware of SE and respecting its known systematic approach, we can see *why* we handle database design the way we do. In this chapter, we present a brief outline of SE. After this brief background/overview of SE in this chapter, we explore database models, in particular the relational database model, in subsequent chapters. While there are many kinds of database models, most of the databases in use today are relational. Our focus in this book is to put forward a methodology based on SE to design a sound relational database (as opposed to other database models).

CHECKPOINT 1.2

You have a set of books on bookshelves in your house. Your mother asks you to create a list of all the books she has.

1. Who is going to use this list?
2. When the list is completed, is it a database?
3. What questions should be asked before you begin?
4. What is the question-and-answer procedure in question 3 going to accomplish?

1.4 WHAT IS THE SOFTWARE ENGINEERING PROCESS?

The term *software engineering* refers to a process of specifying, designing, writing, delivering, maintaining, and finally retiring software. Software engineers often refer to the "life cycle" of software; software has a beginning and an ending. There are many excellent references on the topic of SE (Schach, 2011). Some authors use the term *software engineering* synonymously with "systems analysis and design," but the underlying point is that any information system requires some process to develop it correctly. SE spans a wide range of information system tasks. The task we are primarily interested in here is that of specifying and designing a database. "Specifying a database" means that we will decide on and document what the database is supposed to contain and how we will go about the overall task itself.

A basic idea in SE is to build software correctly, a series of steps or phases is required to progress through a life cycle. These steps ensure that a process of thinking precedes action—thinking through "what is needed" *precedes* "what software is written." Further, the "thinking before action" necessitates that all parties involved in software development understand and communicate with one another. One common version of presenting the thinking before acting scenario is referred to as a "waterfall" model (Schach, 2011); the software development process is supposed to flow in a directional way without retracing.

Generally, the first step in the SE process involves formally specifying what is to be done. We actually break this first step down into two steps: requirement elucidation and actually writing of the specification document. The waterfall model implies that once the specification of the software is written and accepted by a user, it is not changed, but rather it is used as a basis for design. One may liken the overall SE exercise to building a house. The specification is the phase of "what you want in your house." Once agreed on, the next step is to design the house to the specification. As the house is designed and the blueprint is drawn, it is not acceptable to revisit the specification except for minor alterations. There has to be a "meeting of the minds" at the end of the specification phase to move along with the design (the blueprint) of the house to be constructed. So it is with software and database development. Software production is a life-cycle process—software (a database) is created, used, and eventually retired.

The "players" in the software development life cycle may be placed into two camps, often referred to as the *user* and the *analyst*. Software is designed by the analyst for the user according to the user's specification. In our presentation, we will think of ourselves as the analyst trying to enunciate what the users think they want. Recall the example in this chapter in which your mother asked you to draw up a list of items in a home library. Here, the mother is the user; the person drawing up the list of objects is the analyst.

There is no general agreement among software engineers regarding the exact number of steps or phases in the waterfall-type software development model. Models vary depending on the interest of the SE-researcher in one part or another in the process. A very brief description of the software process goes like this (*software* in the following may be taken to mean *a database*):

Step 1 (or Phase 1): Requirements. Find out what the user wants/needs. The "finding-out procedure" is often called "elucidation."

Step 2: Specification. Write out the user wants/needs as precisely as possible. In this step, the user and analyst document not only what is desired but also how much it will cost and how long it will take. A credo of SE is to generate software on time and on budget.

Step 2a: Feed back the specification to the user. A formal review of the specification document is performed to see if the analyst (you) has it right.

Step 2b: Redo the specification as necessary and return to step 2a until the analyst and the user both understand one another and agree to move on.

Step 3: Design—software is designed to meet the specification from step 2. As in house building, now that the analyst knows what is required, the plan for the software is formalized—the blueprint is drawn up.

Step 3a: Software design is independently checked against the specification. If it is necessary, the design is repaired or redone until the analyst has clearly met the specification. Note the sense of agreement in step 2 and the use of step 2 as a basis for further action. When step 3 begins, going back up the waterfall is difficult; it is supposed to be that way. Perhaps minor specification details might be revisited, but the idea is to move on once each step is finished. Once step 3a is completed, both the user and the analyst know what is to be done. In the building-a-house analogy, the blueprint is now drawn up.

One final point here: In the specification, a budget and timeline are proposed by the analyst and accepted by the user. In the design, this budgetary part of the overall design is sometimes refined. All SE takes money and time and not only is it vital to correctly produce a given product, but also the ancillary items of time and money must be clear to all parties.

Step 4: Development. Software is written; a database is created.

Step 4a: In the development phase, software, as written, is checked against the design until the analyst has clearly met the design. Note that the specification in step 2 is long past, and only minor modifications of the design would be tolerated here. The point of step 4 is to build the software according to the design (the blueprint, if you will) from step 3. In our case, the database is actually created and populated in this phase.

Step 5: Implementation. Software is turned over to the user to be used in the application.

Step 5a: User tests the software and accepts it or rejects it until it is written correctly (that is, until it meets the specification and design). In our case, the database is queried, data are added or deleted, and the user uses what was created. A person may think that this is the end of the software life cycle, but there are two more important steps.

Step 6: Maintenance. Maintenance is performed on the software until it is retired. No matter how well specified, designed, and written, some parts of the software may fail. Some parts may need to be modified over time to suit the user. Times change; demands and needs change. Maintenance is a very time-consuming and expensive part of the software process—particularly if the SE process has not been done well. Maintenance involves correcting hidden software faults as well as enhancing the functionality of the software.

In databases, new data are often required; some old data may no longer be needed. Hardware changes. Operating systems change. The database engine itself, which is software, is often upgraded— new versions are imposed on the market. The data in the database must conform to change, and a system of changing the data in the database has to be in place.

Step 7: Retirement. Eventually, whatever software is written becomes outdated. Database engines, computers, and technology in general are all evolving. Think of the old software package you used on some old personal computer. It does not work any longer because the operating system has been updated, the computer is obsolete, and the old software has to be retired. Basically, the SE process has to start all over with new specifications. The same is true with databases and designed systems. At times, the most cost-effective thing to do is to start anew.

CHECKPOINT 1.3
1. In what phase is the database actually created?
2. Which person tests the database?
3. Where does the user say what is wanted in the database?

1.5 ENTITY RELATIONSHIP DIAGRAMS AND THE SOFTWARE ENGINEERING LIFE CYCLE

This text concentrates on steps 1 through 3 of the software life cycle for databases. A database is a collection of related data. The concept of *related data* means that a database stores information about one enterprise: a business, an organization, a grouping of related people or processes. For example, a database might contain data about Acme Plumbing and involve customers and service calls. A different database might be about the members and activities of the Over 55 Club in town. It would be inappropriate to have data about the Over 55 Club and Acme Plumbing in the same database because the two organizations are not related. Again, a database is a collection of *related* data. To keep a database about each of the above entities is fine, but not in the same database.

Database systems are often modeled using an entity relationship (ER) diagram as the blueprint from which the actual data are stored; the blueprint is the output of the design phase. The ER diagram is an analyst's tool to diagram the data to be stored in a database system. Phase 1, the requirements phase, can be quite frustrating as the analyst has to elicit needs and wants from the user. The user may or may not be computer sophisticated and may or may not know the capabilities of a software system. The analyst often has a difficult time deciphering a user's needs and wants to create a specification that (a) makes sense to both parties (user and analyst) and (b) allows the analyst to do design efficiently.

In the real world, the user and the analyst may each be committees of professionals, but the idea is that users (or user groups) must convey their ideas to an analyst (or team of analysts)—users have to express what they want and what they think they need; analysts have to elicit these desires, document them, and create a plan to realize the user's desires.

User descriptions may seem vague and unstructured. Typically, users are successful at a business. They know the business; they understand the business model. The computer person is typically ignorant of the business but understands the computer end of the problem. To the computer-oriented person, the user's description of the business is as new to the analyst as the computer jargon is to the user. We present a methodology that is designed to make the analyst's language precise enough so that the user is comfortable with the to-be-designed database and still provide the analyst with a tool that can be mapped directly into a database.

In brief, we next review the early steps in the SE life cycle as it applies to database design.

1.5.1 Phase 1: Get the Requirements for the Database

In phase 1, we listen and ask questions about what facts (data) the user wants to organize into a database retrieval system. This step often involves letting users describe how they intend to use the data. You, the analyst, will eventually provide a process for loading data into and retrieving data from a database. There is often a "learning curve" necessary for the analyst as the user explains the system he or she knows so well to a person who may be uninformed of their specific business.

1.5.2 Phase 2: Specify the Database

Phase 2 involves grammatical descriptions and diagrams of what the analyst thinks the user wants. Database design is usually accomplished with an ER diagram that functions as the blueprint for the to-be-designed database. Since most users are unfamiliar with the notion of an ER diagram, our methodology will supplement the ER diagram with grammatical descriptions of what the database is supposed to contain and how the parts of the database relate to one another. The technical description of a database can be dry and uninteresting to a user; however, when the analysts put what they think they heard into English statements, the users and the analysts have a better meeting of the minds. For example, if the analyst makes statements like, "All employees must generate invoices," the user may then affirm, deny, or modify the declaration to fit what is actually the case. To continue the example, it makes a big difference in the database if "*all* employees *must* generate invoices" versus "*some* employees *may* generate invoices."

1.5.3 Phase 3: Design the Database

Once the database has been diagrammed and agreed to, the ER diagram becomes the finalized blueprint for construction of the database in phase 3. Moving from the ER diagram to the actual database is akin to asking a builder of houses to take a blueprint and commence construction.

As we have seen, there are more steps in the SE process, but also as stated, this book is about design and hence the remaining steps of the waterfall model are not emphasized.

> **CHECKPOINT 1.4**
> 1. Briefly describe the major steps of the SE life cycle as it applies to databases.
> 2. Who are the two main players in the software development life cycle?
> 3. Why is written communication between the parties in the design process important?

1.6 CHAPTER SUMMARY

This chapter serves as a background chapter. The chapter briefly describes data, databases, and the SE process. The SE process is presented as it applies to ER diagrams—the database design blueprint.

CHAPTER 1 EXERCISES

Fred Jones operates a golf shop. He has golf equipment and customers, and his primary business is selling retail to customers. Fred has so many customers that he wants to keep track of them on a computer. He approaches Sally Smith, who is knowledgeable about computers, and asks her what to do.

1. In our context, Fred is a _____; Sally is a _____.
2. When Fred explains to Sally what he wants, Sally begins writing what?
3. When Fred says, "Sally, this specification is all wrong," what happens next?
4. If Fred says, "Sally, this specification is acceptable," what happens next?
5. If, during the design, Sally finds out that Fred forgot to tell her about something he wants, what is Sally to do?
6. How does Sally get Fred's specifications in the first place?
7. Step 3a says: "Software design is independently checked against the specification." What does this mean?

BIBLIOGRAPHY

Schach, S. R. 2011. *Object-Oriented and Classical Software Engineering*. New York: McGraw-Hill.

2

Data and Data Models

2.1 INTRODUCTION

In this chapter, we introduce more concepts that are essential to our presentation of the design of a database. We defined a database as a collection of related facts (related data). In this chapter, we explore database models and introduce the relational database model. While there are many kinds of database models, most of the databases in use today are relational; our focus in this book is to design a good relational database. In the next chapter, we introduce the concept of functional dependencies to define what is a good (and a not-so-good) relational database. The purpose of this chapter is mostly historical; it engenders an appreciation for the simplicity and power of the relational model.

2.2 FILES, RECORDS, AND DATA ITEMS

Data has to be stored in some fashion in a file to be useful. Suppose there were no computers—think back to a time when files were paper documents. A business kept track of its customers and products. A doctor's office kept track of patients. A sports team kept statistics on its players. In all of these cases, data was recorded on paper. The files with data in them could be referred to as a "database." A database is most simply a repository of data about some specific entity. A customer file might be as plain and minimal as a list of people that did business with a merchant. There are two aspects to filing: storage and retrieval. Some method of storing data that will facilitate retrieval is most desirable.

Suppose we have a file of customer records. The whole file might be called the customer file, whereas the individual customer's information is kept in a customer record. Files consist of records. More than likely, more information than a list of just customer's names would be stored. Most likely, at the very least a customer's name, address, and phone number would constitute a customer record. Each of these components of the record is called a data item or field. The customer file contains customer records that consist of fields of data.

Here is an example of some data (you can imagine each line as a 3 × 5 card, with the three cards making up a file):

CUSTOMER File

Record 1:	Jones, J	123 4th St	Mobile, AL
Record 2:	Smith, S	452 Main St	Pensacola, FL
Record 3:	Harris, H	92 Adams Lane	Elberta, AL

This file contains three records. There is one record for each customer. The records each consist of four fields: record number, name, address, city. As more customers are added, they also are assigned a 3 × 5 card, and these records are placed in the file. Several interesting questions and observations arise:

1. The merchant who keeps this file may well want to add information in the future. Suppose that the merchant wanted to add a telephone number. Would the merchant add a number to all 3 × 5 cards, or would the adding be done "as necessary"? If it were done as necessary, then some customers would have telephone numbers, and some would not. If a customer had no phone number, then the phone number for that customer would be "null" (unknown).

2. How will the file be organized? Imagine not three customers, but 300 or 3,000. Would the 3 × 5 cards be put in alphabetical order? Perhaps, but what happens if you get another J. Jones or S. Smith? The field on which the file is organized is called a *key*. Perhaps the file should be organized by telephone number, which might not have a duplicate value?

3. Suppose the file were organized by telephone number. What if the telephone number for some customer was not recorded? If there were no telephone number, the common terminology is that we say the telephone field for that record is null. It would make no sense to have the file organized by telephone number if some values were null. Clearly, the key of a file cannot be null. Also, if telephone number were the key, then the person finding a record in the file would have to know the phone number to find the appropriate record efficiently.

4. The format of the file given is

CUSTOMER(record_number, name, address, city)

The format of the file dictates the order of the fields in any record. In this record, record_number is first, followed by a name, and so on. The file design could have the fields in some other order, but once defined, the order of the fields stays constant.

If a telephone number field were added, then the file format could be

CUSTOMER (record_number, name, address, city, telephone)

This shorthand format notation is referred to as the *file design*. If the file were set up to find data by name and name were the key, then the name would be underlined, as follows:

CUSTOMER (record_number, name, address, city, telephone)

5. You might ask, "Why not use the record number to organize the file?" On one hand, it is unique (which is desirable for a key), but on the other hand, you would have to know the record number to find a customer. The example is organized by record number; however, imagine 300 or more customers. You want to find Smith's address— you would have to know the record number. It makes more sense to organize this file of 3 × 5 cards by name. Taking some of these points into consideration, here is an enhanced version of the customer file in which each line represents a 3 × 5 card:

CUSTOMER File

Record 1:	Adams, A	77 A St	Pensacola FL	555-5847
Record 2:	Charles, X	365 Broad St	Mobile AL	555-8214
Record 3:	Harris, H	92 Adams Lane	Elberta, AL	555-1234
Record 4:	Jones, A	22 Pine Forest	Pensacola FL	null
Record 5:	Jones, J	123 4th St	Mobile, AL	555-9978
Record 6:	Morris, M	932 Dracena Way	Gulf Breeze FL	555 1111
Record 7:	Smith, S	452 Main St	Pensacola, FL	555-0003

CHECKPOINT 2.1
1. What does it mean to say a field has unique values?
2. Why is it desirable to have a key be unique?
3. Why does a file have to be organized by a key field?
4. What does *null* mean?
5. Consider this customer file:

```
Record 1:    77 A St     Adams, A      Pensacola    555-5847
                                       FL
Record 2:    Charles,    365 Broad     555-8214     Mobile AL
             X           St
Record 3:    555-1234    Harris, H     92 Adams     Elberta,
                                       Lane         AL
```

What is wrong here?

2.3 MOVING FROM 3 × 5 CARDS TO COMPUTERS

Let us return to our example of a merchant who kept his customer file on 3 × 5 cards. As time passed, the customer base grew and the merchant probably desired to keep more information about customers. From a data-processing standpoint, we would say that the techniques for storing and retrieval led to enhanced forms or cards, more fields, and perhaps better ways to store and find individual records. Were customer records kept in alphabetical order? Were they stored by telephone number or record number (which might be a customer number)? What happened if a new field was required that was not on existing forms or cards? Such was a data-processing dilemma of the past.

When computers began to be used for businesses, data was stored on magnetic media. The magnetic media were mostly disks and tapes. The way data was stored and retrieved on a computer started out like the 3 × 5 cards, but the data was virtual; it did not physically exist where you could touch it or see it without some kind of software to load and find records and some kind of display device to see what the "3 × 5 card" had on it. The most common way data was fed into a computer was via punched cards. Punched card systems for handling data were in use as early as the 1930s; sorters were capable of scanning and arranging a pile of cards. Using punched cards to input data into computers did not blossom until the 1960s. The output or "display device" was typically a line printer.

As data was placed on a computer, and software could be developed to handle the data, filing techniques evolved. In the very early days of databases, the files kept on computers basically replicated the 3 × 5 cards. There were many problems with computers and databases in the "early days." (Generally, *early days* in terms of computers and databases means roughly early to mid-1960s.) Some problems involved input (how the data got into the computer), output (how the data was to be displayed), and file maintenance (for example, how the data was to be stored and kept up to date; how records were to be added and deleted; how fields were to be added, deleted, or changed). A person using a computer for keeping track of data could buy a computer and hire programmers, operators, and data entry personnel. In the early days, computers were expensive and large. Most small businesses did not have the resources to obtain a computer, much less hire people whose jobs were solely "on the computer." Early attempts at filing data and retrieving them were the purview of large businesses and large organizations. One thing was clear: Many more virtual customer records than the 300 or so we envisioned were possible.

In the early days, imagine that some company had a computer, and the departments within the company wanted to keep files on the computer. Suppose further that the company made some product and had several departments (e.g., sales, accounting, production). Now, suppose that each department wanted to keep data about customers. Each department had a different view of customers. The sales department wanted to know the name, address, telephone number, and some data related to the propensity to buy the product. The accounting department wanted to know roughly the same information, but wanted to keep track of billing and payments. Production also wanted some of the same information, but wanted to know what the customer wanted in the product and how many they should make. Each department wanted about the same thing, but each approached the problem in a different way. What actually happened in the early days was that each department shared the expensive computer but hired its own programming staff to keep "their database." While the sense of sharing the expensive computer was there, the sense of sharing data was not. The idea of a "software package" to store and retrieve data was not there either. Programmers used computer languages like COBOL, RPG, ALGOL, PL/1, and FORTRAN to store and retrieve data. Each department created its own records and its own storage and retrieval methods, kept its own programs, and had its own data entry groups.

The earliest databases were filing systems maintained by some computer language. For example, a programmer wrote a COBOL program to gather input data on punched cards and to store the data in a computer file. Then, the programmer wrote another set of programs to retrieve the data and display it in whatever way a user wanted to see it. Early computer filing systems were simple sequential files. The data on punched cards was read and stored. Reconsider the customer file we introduced previously:

CUSTOMER File

Record 1:	Adams, A	77 A St	Pensacola FL	555-5847
Record 2:	Charles, X	365 Broad St	Mobile AL	555-8214
Record 3:	Harris, H	92 Adams Lane	Elberta, AL	555-1234
Record 4:	Jones, A	22 Pine Forest	Pensacola FL	null
Record 5:	Jones, J	123 4th St	Mobile, AL	555-9978
Record 6:	Morris, M	932 Dracena Way	Gulf Breeze FL	555-1111
Record 7:	Smith, S	452 Main St	Pensacola, FL	555-0003

If you could look at the data on a disk, it might look like this:

Adams, A	77 A St	Pensacola FL	555-5847
Charles, X	365 Broad St	Mobile AL	555-8214
Harris, H	92 Adams Lane	Elberta, AL	555-1234
Jones, A	22 Pine Forest	Pensacola FL	null
Jones, J	123 4th St	Mobile, AL	555-9978
Morris, M	932 Dracena Way	Gulf Breeze FL	555-1111
Smith, S	452 Main St	Pensacola, FL	555-0003

The records as addressed by COBOL had a structure like this:

```
01 CUSTOMER
        05 NAME          CHARACTER(20)
        05 ADDRESS       CHARACTER(20)
        05 CITY-STATE    CHARACTER(25)
        05 PHONE         CHARACTER(7)
```

The file was referred to as a "sequential file." If a person wanted to see a listing of data by address rather than name, the file had to be sorted and the data redisplayed. If data was added to the file, it had to be put in its proper place according to the sequential key, which in this example is the name field.

Two other principal filing systems evolved in the 1960s: indexed and the direct access filing systems. Indexed systems were based on the maintenance of indexes for records rather than a strict sequential ordering of the records themselves. Look again at the customer example in a different light:

CUSTOMER File

```
Record 1:   Adams, A     77 A St.    Pensacola   555-5847
                                      FL
Record 2:   Charles, X   365 Broad   Mobile AL   555-8214
                          St
. . .
```

In this case, suppose that Record 1 were not a numerical record but rather a disk address. Then, suppose there was an index to the records themselves that consisted of names and disk addresses like this:

Name	Disk address
Adams, A	1
Charles, X	2
Harris, H	3
and so forth.	

Now, suppose you added a customer called Baker, B. In a sequential filing system, you would have to put Baker between Adams and Charles, but in an indexed system, you could put Baker anywhere on the disk and simply change the index to find Baker:

```
Name              Disk address
Adams, A          1
Baker, B          8
Charles, X        2
Harris, H         3
```

Disks were arranged by their geometry. A disk usually consisted of an arrangement of platters that looked like flat, brown phonograph records with a spindle in the center. The disk rapidly rotated, and data was arranged on the plate concentrically and written and read magnetically. If all of this sounds like an old phonograph system, that is likely where the idea of stacking disks originated. If you could look at the data on a specific plate, it would be arranged in a circle, and there would be many circles, getting larger as you moved out on the plate. Each circle was called a *track*. Data on a disk was thought to be located in a relative position on some track and imaginary overlaid tracks called *cylinders*. Here is a simplified example: If the tracks were designated as 1, 2, 3, … starting from the data circle nearest the spindle, and the cylinders were designated 1, 2, 3, … starting from the top of the disk, then a data address would be referenced as follows, for example: cylinder 4, track 3, record 24. This would mean that the data was on the 4th plate from the top, on the 3rd track from the spindle, and in the 24th position on that track.

The indexed systems became quite elaborate. The one illustrated was called a *relative record indexed system*. In the relative record system, one needed to know only which cylinders a file occupied, and then the position of the record could be calculated relative to the starting position of the file. Originally, relative record systems were not popular, whereas there was a common indexed system used primarily on IBM computers that was based on disk geometry (cylinders, tracks, and records) called an *indexed-sequential* system.

Whatever the index system, one had to keep indexes to store and find records. Imagine not 30 or 300 customers, but 300,000. Now, suppose that someone wanted to find customers by their address rather than their name. You would have to have another index, or you would have to look at each record in the filing system until you found the address you needed. One other less-common way to manage early data access and retrieval was to base the index on an exact location of data on a disk: the direct access filing system. The popular indexed-sequential system was probably the best amalgamation of the properties of all filing systems in that it efficiently handled record additions, deletions, and updating as well as providing reasonable data access speeds. Early filing systems involved choices: elaborate indexes or elaborate programs to sort and find data (or both). Regardless of the choice of index, there were always problems with maintaining the index (or indexes); adding, updating, or deleting records; finding and displaying records and reprogramming all of these items for new applications or hardware.

In the late 1960s, software packages called database systems began to emerge. *Database systems* were purchasable programs that stored and retrieved data as well as performed maintenance (adding, deleting, and modifying fields and records). With a database system, one did not have to write COBOL programs to handle data directly but rather relied on the database program to handle data. With these systems, each department could share data and resources. Instead of each department having its own programmers and perhaps its own computer, there could be one central computer to store data, one programming staff, and one database software package. Data could be shared, with each department having its own view of the data. All this sounds great, but in reality it took several years to break away from the "my data" mold. In addition, there were hybrid systems that emerged that focused mainly on retrieval of data that delayed the move to a totally relational environment because of the investment companies had in software and programmers.

Why was sharing data a good thing? It not only used expensive resources more efficiently but also reduced redundancy. *Redundancy* means storing the same information in different places. If each department stored its own version of data, its own view of customers, then the customer name, address, telephone number, and so on were recorded by each department. Suppose the customer moved. Then, each department changed its data when it found out the customer moved, and at some point the customer's address could be stored inconsistently: The accounting department had one address, the sales department had another. The root problem here is the lack of data sharing, and sharing was a central goal of the early database systems.

The early database software evolved into two main data models: the hierarchical and the network models. Although the relational model for a database was recognized as a desirable technique in the early 1970s, the relational model was treated as a really good theoretical technique for which computers were not fast enough to implement.

The database models (hierarchical, network, and relational) were *logical models*—ways of logically perceiving the arrangement of data in a file structure. One perceived how the data was to be logically stored, and the database physically implemented the logical model. As we shall see, there is a close relationship between the logical and physical implementations of the hierarchical and network models. Since there were no practical relational implementations on other than what was then supercomputers at research centers, the world of commercial databases in the 1970s involved choosing between the hierarchical and network models. The next sections give a little insight into each of these three main models and an introduction to the relational model.

CHECKPOINT 2.2
1. What is a sequential file?
2. What is COBOL?
3. Why is ordering important in a sequential filing system?
4. What is a database program?
5. In the early days, how was data put into a file?

2.4 DATABASE MODELS

We now take a look back at database models as they were before the relational database was practical. The look back shows why the "old systems" are considered obsolete and why the relational model is the de facto standard in databases today. The old systems were classified as two main types: hierarchical and network. These two models defined a database before the 1980s. Although they might be considered "old fashioned," there are systems still in use today that depend on these models.

2.4.1 The Hierarchical Model

In hierarchical database models, all data are arranged in a top-down fashion in which some records have one or more "dependent" or "child" records, and each child record is tied to one and only one "parent." The parent-child relationship is not meant to infer a human familial relationship. The terms *parent* and *child* are historical and are meant to conjure up a picture of one type of data as dependent on another. As is illustrated here, the child will be sports played by a parent-person. Another terminology for the parent-child relationship is *owner* and *objects owned*, but parent-child is more common.

In this section, we present some versions of the hierarchical model for several reasons: (a) to illustrate how older models were constructed from file systems; (b) to show why file-based databases became outdated when relational databases became practical; and (c) to see the evolution of file-based systems.

We begin with an example of a hierarchical file situation. Suppose you have a database of people who play a sport at some location. A sample record might consist of *Brenda* who plays *tennis at city courts* and who plays *golf at the municipal links*. The person, Brenda, would be at the top of the hierarchy, and the sport-location would be the second layer of the hierarchy. Usually, the connection between the layers of the hierarchy is referred to as a parent-child relationship.

Each parent person may be related to *many* child sport-locations, but each sport-location (each child) is tied back to the *one* person (one parent) it "is played by." You may be thinking, "Suppose the same sport is played by two people at the same location?" That is a good question, but it is not a situation that can be handled by hierarchical file systems in a direct way. If, for example, Richard also plays *golf at the municipal links*, then *golf at municipal links* will be recorded twice as a child for each parent. If the same sport-location occurs, then it is recorded redundantly.

The *one* person, *many* sports tie may be called a *one-to-many* relationship. Some more data might look like the following, with a person's name followed by the sport and location:

The model:
```
Person: sport, location; sport, location; sport,
    location ...
```

The data itself:
```
Brenda: tennis, city courts; golf, municipal links
Richard: golf, municipal links; snorkeling, Pensacola
    bay; running, UWF track
Abbie: downhill skiing, Ski Beech
```

Now this data could be stored in a database in many ways. You could imagine information on each person on a 3 × 5 card with the person's data. You could also store the data on separate cards in a sequential file like this:

```
Brenda
tennis, city courts
golf, municipal links
```

```
Richard
golf, municipal links
snorkeling, Pensacola bay
running, UWF track
Abbie
downhill skiing, Ski Beech
```

The first thing you notice is that there is a series of text records (or 3 × 5 cards), but it is hard to distinguish between person and sports without semantics (you can tell the difference between person and sports by looking at the entry, but the computer cannot do this unless you give the line of text a meaning: semantics). For the computer, it is helpful to identify whether a record is a person (P) or a sport (S). Hence, the sequential file could be

```
P     Brenda
S     tennis, city courts
S     golf, municipal links
P     Richard
S     golf, municipal links
S     snorkeling, Pensacola bay
S     running, UWF track
P     Abbie
S     downhill skiing, Ski Beech
```

In actuality, this sequential file would be useful only if a person wanted to list all the people followed by the sport-locations for that person. Furthermore, the relationship of person to sport-location is one of position in the file. The arrangement was sometimes called a *header-trailer format*; persons are header records, sports are trailer records. If one wanted to know all the people who played golf, they would have to read the entire file and pick out those individuals. A better organization of the data would be to have two files, one for person, one file for sport-locations. For the two-file model to make sense (i.e., to have the files "related"), there would have to be pointers or references of some kind from one file to the other. One way to implement a pointer scheme would be a pointer from the sport (child) to the person (parent) like this:

PERSON(record_number, name)
With data:

```
1. Brenda
2. Richard
3. Abbie
```

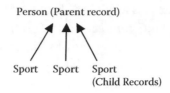

Person (Parent record)

Sport   Sport   Sport
                  (Child Records)

FIGURE 2.1
A hierarchy of persons and sports with parent pointers.

SPORTS(sport, location, reference to person)
With data:
```
tennis, city courts, 1
golf, municipal links,1
golf, municipal links, 2
snorkeling, Pensacola bay, 2
running, UWF track, 2
downhill skiing, Ski Beech, 3
```

A diagram of this relationship is shown in Figure 2.1.

The actual location of the records on a disk could be arbitrary. The sense of the data is not lost if the locations are disk addresses and if you imagine that there are thousands of persons and sports:

PERSON(record address, name)
With data:
```
A45C. Brenda
C333. Abbie
B259. Richard
```

SPORTS(sport, location, reference to person)
With data:
```
golf, municipal links, B259
running, UWF track, B259
downhill skiing, Ski Beech, C333
snorkeling, Pensacola bay, B259
tennis, city courts, A45C
golf, municipal links, A45C
```

This system has a parent-child link. Here, we assume that the primary key of the person file is the record_number. The "reference to person" in the sports file refers to the primary key of the person file and is called a *foreign key* (FK) because it is a primary key of another file. The FK references a primary key, hence completing the essential relationship of one file to the other. If there were no relationship, then you would have two independent files with no connection—the system would make no sense.

While we have established the relationship of child to parent in the discussion, the database has some drawbacks. To answer a question like, "Who plays golf at municipal links?" you start looking at the Sports file, look for "golf at municipal links," and see what parent records there are. If your question were, "What sports does Richard play?" you would first find Richard in the Person file, then look through the Sports file to find links back to Richard.

If you were actually implementing this model, you could enhance the system a bit. An improvement to this model would be to reference each sport from within each parent record (let us go back to simple numbers for this):

PERSON(record address, name, (sport address))
With data:
```
    1. Brenda,  (101,  102)
    2. Richard  (103,  104,  105)
    3. Abbie  (106)
```

SPORTS(sport, location, reference to person)
With data:
```
    101,  tennis,  city courts,  1
    102,  golf,  municipal links,  1
    103,  golf,  municipal links,  2
    104,  snorkeling,  Pensacola bay,  2
    105,  running,  UWF track,  2
    106,  downhill skiing,  Ski Beech,  3
```

Figure 2.2 depicts the relationship between parent and child records in both directions. When viewed from the parent, this link is called a multiple-child pointer (MCP). When viewed from the child the link is called a parent pointer.

In this model, the relationship between parent and child records is done two ways. The "reference to person" in the Sports file is a link (the FK) from child to parent. The reference to multiple children in the parent records is called an MCP scheme. While it is true that the MCP is redundant to the relationship, it does two practical things: (a) It allows questions to be asked

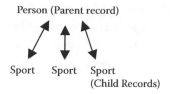

FIGURE 2.2
A hierarchy of persons and sports with parent and child pointers.

of the system that are easier to answer than with just parent pointers; and
(b) it allows the file system to be audited with a computer program. For
example, if you want to ask the system, "How many sports does Richard
play?" you need only look at the person file and count MCP references.

We have illustrated two ways to construct a relationship between two
files: the FK parent pointer and the MCP. Both of the linking techniques
are viable relationship implementations. The second one, the MCP system,
was actually implemented more often than the FK system. This is perhaps
because from a hierarchical standpoint it is easier to see the hierarchy.
You could implement either (or both) relationships to make this a hierarchical database. Please remember that this illustration is just skeletal. In
real life, there would likely be far more fields in the records for the person
and for the sport or location. Also in real databases, one expects thousands, if not millions, of records. If you could implement the relationship
between person and sports only one way, which of these systems (MCP or
FK) would work best if there were 1 million person-sport combinations?
The answer to this would likely depend on how many sports each person
played and how variable the number of sports was. For example, if no person played more than five sports, the MCP system would work quite well.
If, on the other hand, the number of sports played was highly variable
(one person plays 1 or 2 sports, and some play 100), then the FK system
might be better because the FK system only keeps a parent reference, and
the MCP system with this high variability of pointers in the parent might
become cumbersome.

2.4.1.1 The Hierarchical Model with a Linked List

Having used the MCP/FK system to construct a hierarchical set of data,
we now present a second hierarchical model. The MCP system has some
drawbacks regardless of which direction one approaches the relationship

(as MCP, FK, or both). For example, suppose you implemented the system with the child pointers in the parent record (MCP), and there were more child records than were planned. Suppose the system was not person and sports, but students at a school and absences. The student would be the parent, and the absence records would be the child. Now, suppose you designed this system with an MCP relationship so that a student could have up to 20 absences. What happens when the student is absent for the 21st time? One of two things has to happen: (a) The MCP system would have to be modified to include some kind of overflow; or (b) some other hierarchical system would have to be used. We could, of course, implement this as an FK system and ignore the MCP part entirely. Or, we could implement a different system, and that is what we illustrate now.

The following file system uses a "linked list" or "chain" system to implement the relationship between parent and child. This system is similar to both of the schemes discussed. With the same data, the records would set up like this:

```
Parent (link to 1st child)
```

and within the child records:

```
Child (link to next child)
```

Here is the data from above with this type of arrangement:

PERSON(record address, name, first sport)
With data:

```
1. Brenda (101)
2. Richard (103)
3. Abbie (106)
```

SPORTS(sport, location, link to next sport for that person)
With data:

```
101, tennis, city courts, 102
102, golf, municipal links, 999
103, golf, municipal links, 104
104, snorkeling, Pensacola bay, 105
105, running, UWF track, 999
106, downhill skiing, Ski Beech, 999
```

Here, 999 means "no next link."

Figure 2.3 illustrates a linked list parent-to-child pointing scheme. In this system, we have a link from parent to child that we did not have with the FK system alone. Furthermore, the records in both the parent and the

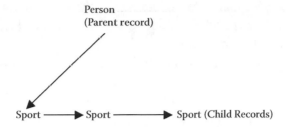

FIGURE 2.3
A hierarchy of persons and sports with a parent-to-child linked list.

child are uniform. Both the parent and the child records contain only one pointer. Also in this system, it would not matter whether a person played 1 sport or 100—the system works well if the number of child records is unknown or highly variable. If you would argue that finding a specific child record among 200,000 sport records might be time consuming, you are 100% correct. If you argue that the system is fragile and that if one link is lost the whole thing goes down, you are correct again. While this linked list system may look somewhat fragile, it formed the basis for several of the most successful commercial databases. As you might expect, enhancements to the basic linked list included things like direct links back to the parent, forward and backward links, links that skipped along the chain in one direction and not in the other (coral rings). All these enhancements were the fodder of databases in the 1970s.

2.4.1.2 Relationship Terminology

Having seen how to implement relationships in hierarchical databases, we need to tighten some language about how relationships are formed. Relationships in all database models have what are called *structural constraints*. A structural constraint consists of two notions: cardinality and optionality. *Cardinality* is a description of how many of one record type relate to the other and vice versa. Suppose we implement a database about the personnel of a company. We have an employee (parent) and the employee's dependents (child). In our company, if an employee can have multiple dependents and the dependent can have only one employee parent, we would say the cardinality of the relationship is one to many: One employee relates to many dependents, abbreviated 1:M. If the company were such that employees might have multiple dependents and a dependent might be claimed by more than one employee, then the cardinality would be many to many: Many employees relate to many dependents, abbreviated M:N (as in M of one side relates to N on the other side, and M and N are generally not equal).

Optionality refers to whether one record *may* or *must* have a corresponding record in the other file. If the employee may or may not have dependents, then the optionality of the employee-to-dependent relationship is *optional* or *partial*. If the dependents *must* be "related to" employee(s) (and every employee must have dependents), then the optionality of dependent to employee is *mandatory* or *full*.

Further, relationships are always stated in both directions in a database description. We would say

Employees may have zero or more dependents,

and

Dependents must be associated with one and only one employee.

Note the employee-to-dependent, one-to-many cardinality and the optional/mandatory nature of the relationship. We return to this language, but it is easy to see that the way a database is designed depends on the description of it. If the description is clear and unambiguous, then the likely outcome of database design is far more predictable.

2.4.1.3 Drawbacks of the Hierarchical Model

All relationships between records in a hierarchical model have a cardinality of one to many or one to one, but never many to one or many to many. So, for a hierarchical model of employee and dependent, we can only have the employee-to-dependent relationship as one to many or one to one; an employee may have zero or more dependents. In the hierarchical model, you could not have dependents with multiple parent-employees (unless we introduce redundant recording of dependents).

As we illustrated, the original way hierarchical databases were implemented involved choosing some way of physically "connecting" the parent and the child records. Imagine you have looked up information on an employee in an employee filing cabinet and you want to find the dependent records for that employee in a dependent filing cabinet. One way to implement the employee-dependent relationship would be to have an employee record point to a dependent record and have that dependent record point to the next dependent (a linked list of child records). For example, you find employee Jones. In Jones's record there is a notation that Jones's first dependent is found in the dependent filing cabinet, file drawer 2, record 17. The "file drawer 2, record 17" is called a *pointer* and is the connection or relationship between the employee and the dependent. Now, to take this example further, suppose the record of the dependent in file drawer 2, record 17, points to the next dependent in file drawer 3, record 38, then that dependent points to the next dependent in file drawer 1, record 82.

As we pointed out in the person-sports model, the linked list approach to connecting parent and child records has advantages and disadvantages. For example, some advantages would be that each employee has to maintain only one pointer, and that the size of the linked list of dependents is theoretically unbounded. Drawbacks would include the fragility of the system in that if one dependent record is destroyed, then the chain is broken. Further, if you wanted information about only one of the child records, you might have to look through many records before you found the one you were looking for.

There are, of course, several other ways of implementing the parent-child link. The point here is that some system has to be chosen to be implemented in the underlying database software. Once the linking system is chosen, it is fixed by the software implementation; the way the link is done has to be used to link all child records to parents regardless of how inefficient it might be for one situation.

There are three major drawbacks to the hierarchical model:

1. Not all situations fall into the one-to-many, parent-child format.
2. The choice of the way in which the files are linked has an impact on performance both positively and negatively.
3. The linking of parents and child records is done physically. If the dependent file were reorganized, then all pointers would have to be reset.

2.5 THE NETWORK MODEL

Each of the methods presented for the hierarchical database has advantages and disadvantages. Since the network model allows M:N relationships, we want to implement a system of pointers for multiple parents for each child record. How would this be handled? You would most likely have to have multiple child-forward links with either a linked list or an MCP system in the parent, parent pointers in the child records (perhaps more than one), and possibly some other enhancement to a pointer scheme. The network model alleviated a major concern of the hierarchical model because in the network model, one was not restricted to having one parent per child; a many-to-many relationship or a many-to-one relationship was acceptable. To give an example of a network approach, let us revisit the Person-Sports example but now allow a sports record to be connected to more than one person. Here is some sample data like those presented with more persons and more sports and using an MCP system in both directions:

First, the data:

```
Brenda: tennis, city courts; golf, municipal links
Richard: golf, municipal links; snorkeling, Pensacola
   bay; running, UWF track
Abbie: downhill skiing, Ski Beech
David: snorkeling, Pensacola bay; golf, municipal
   links
Kaitlyn: curling, Joe's skating rink; downhill skiing,
   Ski Beech
Chrissy: cheerleading, Mountain Breeze High; running,
   UWF track
```

Now, suppose we diagram this conglomeration of data with pointers (we use record numbers in each "file"):

PERSON(record_number, name, (sports))
SPORTS(record_number, sport, location, (who plays))

In each case, the part of the file description in parentheses that looks like (who plays) is called a *repeating group*, meaning that it can have multiple values. Our small, albeit perplexing, database looks like this:

PERSON (record_number, name, (sports))
With data:

```
1. Kaitlyn (107, 106)
2. Abbie (106)
3. Brenda (102, 101)
4. Chrissy (108, 105)
5. Richard (103, 104, 105)
6. David (104, 102)
```

SPORTS (record_number, sport, location, (who plays))
With data:

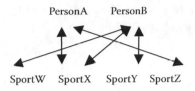

FIGURE 2.4
A network of persons and sports with MCP and parent pointers.

```
101      tennis, city courts (3)
102      golf, municipal links (3, 6)
103      golf, municipal links (5)
104      snorkeling, Pensacola bay (5, 6)
105      running, UWF track (4, 5)
106      downhill skiing, Ski Beech (2, 1)
107      curling, Joe's skating rink (1)
108      cheerleading, Mountain Breeze High (4)
```

The network with pointers in both directions is illustrated in Figure 2.4.

The complexity of the network database is exponentially greater than that of the hierarchical one. The database just illustrated could have been implemented as a series of linked child/parents or some other combination of links and pointers. The second and third drawbacks of hierarchical databases spill over to network databases. If one were to design a file-based database system from scratch, one would have to choose some method of physically connecting or linking records. This choice of record connection then locks us into the same problem as before: a hardware-implemented connection that has an impact on performance both positively and negatively. Further, as the database becomes more complicated, the paths of connections and the maintenance problems become exponentially more difficult to manage.

As a project, you could create the Person-Sports database with a few more records than given in the example using linked lists. At first, you might think this to be a daunting exercise, but one of the most popular database systems in the 1970s used a variant of this system. The parent and child records were all linked with linked lists going in two directions—forward and backward. The forward/backward idea was to speed up finding child records such that one could search for children by going either way. An enhancement of this system would be to use forward-pointing linked lists with a backward-pointing chain of links, but with the backward chain skipping every *n* records, where the optimal *n* turns out to be the square root of the number of entries in the chain.

2.6 THE RELATIONAL MODEL

Codd (1970) introduced the relational model to describe a database that did not suffer the drawbacks of the hierarchical and network models (i.e., physical links and hardware-bound restrictions). Codd's premise was that if we ignore the way data files are connected and arrange our data into simple two-dimensional, unordered tables, then we can develop a calculus for queries (questions posed to the database), and we can focus on the data as data, not as a physical realization of a logical model. Codd's idea was truly logical in that one was no longer concerned with how data was physically stored. Rather, data sets were simply unordered, two-dimensional tables of data. To arrive at a workable way of deciding which pieces of data went into which table, Codd proposed "normal forms." To understand normal forms, we must first introduce the notion of *functional dependencies*. After we understand functional dependences, normal forms follow.

As a historical note, when Codd introduced his relational model, it was deemed by most people as "theoretical only." At the time, a typical mainframe computer might have 64K of internal memory, and a good set of hard disks might have as much as several megabytes of storage. To top that off, the computer typically took up a large room that required separate air handling, special architectural features like raised floors, and enhanced power grids. Remember that all the "computing power" was shared by everyone who had to have computing. In a company, users might include accounting, purchasing, personnel, finance, and so on. For even one of those units to be able to run the relational model in the early 1970s would have required vast dedicated resources. As computers became more ubiquitous, less expensive, smaller, and so on, the amount of memory available both internally and externally became cheaper and had far greater capacity. The relational model "grew up" with the evolution of computers in the 1980s. We expand the notion of relational database in the next chapter.

CHECKPOINT 2.3

1. What are the three main data models we have discussed?
2. Which data model is mostly used today? Why?
3. What are some of the disadvantages of the hierarchical data model?
4. What are some of the disadvantages of the network data model?
5. How are all relationships (mainly the cardinalities) described in the hierarchical data model? How can these be a disadvantage of the hierarchical data model?
6. How are all relationships (mainly the cardinalities) described in the network data model? Would you treat these as advantages or disadvantages of the network data model?
7. What are structural constraints?
8. Why was Codd's promise of the relational model better?

2.7 CHAPTER SUMMARY

In this chapter, we covered concepts that are essential to the understanding and design of a database. We also covered data models from a historical perspective—the hierarchical and network models and then introduction of the relational model. This chapter should serve more as background to the material for the rest of the book.

BIBLIOGRAPHY

Codd, E. F. 1970. A relational model of data for large shared data banks. *Communications of the ACM,* 13(6): 377–387.

3

The Relational Model and Functional Dependencies

3.1 INTRODUCTION

As discussed in Chapter 2, Edgar Codd's premise for the relational database was that data should be arranged in simple two-dimensional, unordered tables. By properly arranging data in this fashion, we can ask questions about the contents of the database (generate queries) in a straightforward way; we essentially ignore the physical way data is actually stored. To begin, we explore the "proper table" idea and then look at functional dependencies (FDs). As Codd suggested, we will not create our database with physically linked records but rather just ensure that our data is in a suitable form. The suitable form means that data is normalized, and normalization is achieved by following the notion of FDs.

3.2 FUNDAMENTAL RELATIONAL DATABASE

We begin our discussion of the relational database with the most fundamental idea: the two-dimensional table. The two-dimensional table means that data is arranged in rows and columns with one piece of data in each cell:

	column1	column2	column3	...
row1	data-cell	data-cell	data-cell	
row2	data-cell	data-cell	data-cell	
row3	data-cell	data-cell	data-cell	

Here is an example of a CUSTOMER table:

Name	Phone_no	Address
Jones	222-3333	123 4th St
Smith	333-2154	55 Main St
Adams	555-8888	3145 Euclid Ct

The columns are given titles: Name, Phone_no, Address.

The rows are horizontal arrangements of data cells under each column. Row 1 contains

```
Jones 222-3333    123 4th St
```

Often, when discussing a row in a table, it is denoted like this:

```
<Jones, 222-3333, 123 4th St>
```

The data cells contain facts, for example, you have a customer named Smith, Smith's address is 55 Main Street, and so on. In the two-dimensional table, each column of data contains the same kind of data—the same data type with the same semantics (same meaning). The following is a two-dimensional arrangement, but it violates the sense of "each column contains the same kind of data":

Name	Phone_no	Address
Jones	222-3333	123 4th St
55 Main St	Smith	333-2154
Adams 3145	Euclid Ct	555-8888

All the same data is there, but it is jumbled around, and the column headings make no sense. In an arrangement like this, we would say the data was "inconsistent."

In relational databases, the data cell is supposed to be *atomic*. The characteristic of atomicity means that the cell contains one fact and only one fact. If Adams had two phone numbers and if they were entered on the same row, it would not be a valid table of data for a relational database. You would have to design the tables some other way.

Name	Phone_no	Address
Jones	222-3333	123 4th St
Smith	333-2154	55 Main St
Adams	555-8888, 555-8889	3145 Euclid Ct

The Phone_no for Adams is nonatomic. The data cell that contains the two phone numbers is said to contain a *repeating group*. If a two-dimensional arrangement of data cells contains only atomic data, it is said to be a *table*. This data arrangement with a nonatomic cell is not a table, unlike the previous example with all atomic cells. In Codd's terminology of database, if you have a table (i.e., a two-dimensional arrangement of atomic data), then your data is in the first normal form (1NF).

In relational database theory, there is a shorthand notation for talking about rows and columns in tables. We will call populated tables *relations*, and we will call columns *attributes*. Relations are generally abbreviated with a capital letter like R and the attributes as A, B, C, ... We can say that

R(A, B, C, D)

is in 1NF, whereas

R(A, B, C, {D})

is not 1NF as {D} represents a repeating group.

CHECKPOINT 3.1

1. Is the following arrangement of data a table?

License_no	Make	Color
12345	Honda	Grey
54321	Ford	Green, White

2. Is the following arrangement of data a table?

License_no	Make	Color
12345	Honda	Grey
54321	Green	Ford

3. Is the following arrangement of data a table?

License_no	Make	Color
12345	Honda	Grey
54321	Ford	Green

4. Is the following arrangement of data a table?

Make	License_no	Color
Honda	12345	Grey
Ford	54321	Ford

5. Is the following arrangement of data a table?

License_no	Make	Color
12345	null	Grey
54321	Green	null

6. What does R(A,B,C,D,E,F) mean?

3.3 RELATIONAL DATABASE AND SETS

In mathematics, we define sets as an unordered collection of unique objects. Codd viewed and defined a relational database such that (a) all data was atomic in two-dimensional tables, and (b) all tables contained sets of rows. The notion of "sets of rows" is a powerful one in that it implies two things: (a) there are no duplicate rows, and (b) there is no order among the rows (rows are not presumed to be sorted in any way). Mathematical sets do not have sorted order and do not contain duplicates. If I had a set of apparel, it might contain shoes, socks, shirt, pants, and hats. The same set could be written as (pants, shirt, socks, hats, shoes). The order of the items in the set is not defined. An item either is in the set or not in the set. As far as the set is concerned, the set (pants, shirt, socks, hat, pants, shirt, shoes, socks, hats) is the same as before. The duplication of items makes no sense in sets.

When we look at some rows of data in a relational database, we think of the tables (the relation) as sets of rows. Consider the following table:

Name	Job
Rich	Carpenter
Beryl	Dentist
Mary Jo	Programmer

Setwise, here is the same table:

Name	Job
Beryl	Dentist
Mary Jo	Programmer
Rich	Carpenter

The order of the rows is unimportant. If we had a duplicate row like this

Name	Job
Rich	Carpenter
Beryl	Dentist
Mary Jo	Programmer
Rich	Carpenter

we would not have a valid relational table. Since a relational database is a "set of rows," the extra row is unnecessary for the extraction of information in the database. Also, from a practical standpoint the duplicate row would violate the sense of being able to identify one and only one row from a primary key.

As with sets, we may ask a question like, "Is <Lindsey, Cook> in the database?" In this case, Lindsey is not there. The point is that the particular row is either there or not—it is in the set of rows or it is not.

3.4 FUNCTIONAL DEPENDENCY

A functional dependency (FD) is a relationship of one attribute in a relation to another (according to the old terminology, one "field" in a "record" has a relationship to another "field"). In a database, we often have the case for which one attribute *defines* the other. For example, we can say that Social Security Number (SSN) defines or identifies a name. What does this mean? It means that if I have a database with SSNs and names, and if I know someone's SSN, then I can find the person's name. Further, since we used the word *defines*, we are saying that for every SSN we will have one and only one name. We will say that we have classified name as *functionally dependent* on SSN.

The idea of a FD is to define one field as an anchor from which one can always find a single value for another field. If this sounds familiar, it is this is the idea of a primary key we discussed previously. The main idea in FDs is to find primary keys such that all data in a record depends on the primary key alone.

In a database, the designer makes choices defining data with FDs. Recall that it is the designer's responsibility to elicit FD information from the user. The user tells us that a project has one location or multiple locations. The user tells us that a person can have one and only one phone number or not. Also, working backward from data, one cannot examine a database and "prove" that some attribute is functionally dependent on another. The sense of FD is one of definition, and it goes with the table design just like the definition of column order and data type.

As another example, suppose that a company assigned each employee a unique employee number. Just consider the employee number and name for a moment. Each employee has one employee number and one name. Names might be the same for two different employees, but for two employees their employee numbers would always be different and unique because the company defined them that way. It would be inconsistent in the database if there were two occurrences of the same employee number with different names.

We write an FD with an arrow like this:

SSN → Name

or

EmpNo → Name

The expression EmpNo → Name is read "Empno defines Name" or "Empno implies Name."

CHECKPOINT 3.2

1. In the following table, does all the data conform to EmpNo → Name?

Empno	Name
123	Beryl
456	Mary Jo

2. Does the fact that the data conforms to the proposed FD prove that the FD is in fact true?

3. In the following table, does all the data conform to EmpNo → Name?

Empno	Name
123	Beryl
456	Mary Jo, Mary, MJ

4. In the following database, does all the data conform to EmpNo → Name?

```
<123, Beryl>
<MJ, 456>
```

5. In the following database, does EmpNo → Name?

Empno	Name
123	Beryl
456	Mary Jo

3.5 NON-1NF TO 1NF

Let us consider this arrangement of data:

CUSTOMER

Customer_no	Name	Phone_no	Address
101	Jones	222-3333	123 4th St
102	Smith	333-2154	55 Main St
107	Adams	555-8888, 555-8889	3145 Euclid Ct

The Customer_no is likely to be unique, but the Phone_no for Adams is nonatomic. The data cell that contains the two phone numbers is said to contain a "repeating group." This arrangement of data makes sense to us, but it needs to be rearranged to conform to the definition of a 1NF table. Symbolically, R(A, B, {C}, D) is not 1NF as {C} represents a repeating group.

Before handling the non-1NF problem, it is best to define a primary key in R if possible. Recall that a primary key is an attribute that always uniquely identifies a row in a table. Suppose the primary key is attribute A (Customer_no), which we will assume is unique for each customer. Then, the way the repeating group is handled is through a process called *decomposition*. The original table, R(A, B, {C}, D), will be decomposed into two tables:

R1(A, B, D)   (the key is A)

and

R2(A,C)   (the key is both A and C—a concatenated key)

Going back to the CUSTOMER example, we defined Customer_no as the primary key; the decomposition would go like this:

CUSTOMER (Customer no, Name, {Phone_no}, Address)

will become

CUSTOMER1 (Customer no, Name, Address)(Key is Customer_no)

and

CUSTOMER2 (Customer no, Phone no)   (key is Customer_no + Phone_no)

The new populated tables will look like this:

CUSTOMER1

Customer_no	Name	Address
101	Jones	123 4th St
102	Smith	55 Main St
107	Adams	3145 Euclid Ct

CUSTOMER2

Customer_no	Phone_no
101	222-3333
102	333-2154
107	555-8888
107	555-8889

All data is now atomic in both tables—both tables are in 1NF. The primary key of the first table, Customer_no in CUSTOMER1, is referenced in the second table. Customer_no in CUSTOMER2 is called a foreign key as it references a primary key in another table. In CUSTOMER1, the key is Customer_no, which is unique and hence serves to identify a row. In CUSTOMER2, there is no one attribute that identifies a row; hence, the entire row is considered a primary key.

Let us consider another example. Suppose there were no customer number, no obvious key. Suppose the original data looked like this:

CUSTOMER

Name	Phone_no	Address
Jones	222-3333	123 4th St
Smith	333-2154	55 Main St
Adams	555-8888, 555-8889	3145 Euclid Ct

Neither Name nor Address would be considered a reliable row identifier; now, we have no obvious key, and we have a repeating group. What do we do? We take the repeating group values and combine them with all the other attributes and call the whole row a key. Is this the best key you can choose? Perhaps; ways to determine the worth of all attributes concatenated together as a key are determined further in this chapter as we define the other normal forms. Here, we have taken a non-1NF arrangement of data and made it 1NF. Further, this technique always works because you end up with atomic data in a two-dimensional table (1NF). Here is the decomposition in which we have no obvious primary key:

CUSTOMER (Name, {Phone_no}, Address)

Name	Phone_no	Address
Jones	222-3333	123 4th St
Smith	333-2154	55 Main St
Adams	555-8888, 555-8889	3145 Euclid Ct

is made into one table like this with Name and Phone_no as the key:

CUSTOMER (Name, Phone_no, Address)

Name	Phone_no	Address
Jones	222-3333	123 4th St
Smith	333-2154	55 Main St
Adams	555-8888	3145 Euclid Ct
Adams	555-8889	3145 Euclid Ct

In this transformed table, we now have 1NF, unique rows, and a primary key. We can proceed to see whether we are in the other normal forms. Notice in the case of CUSTOMER with Customer_no just given, it could be resolved to 1NF like this:

CUSTOMER (Customer_no, Name, Phone_no, Address, City)

Customer_no	Name	Phone_no	Address	City
101	Jones	222-3333	123 4th St	Pensacola
102	Smith	333-2154	55 Main St	Alpharetta
107	Adams	555-8888	3145 Euclid Ct	Two Egg
107	Adams	555-8889	3145 Euclid Ct	Two Egg

But, since we have a primary key in Customer_no, this decomposition is a bit severe. As we take up other normal forms, this problem will be resolved.

CHECKPOINT 3.3

1. What would you suppose is the key of this table?

Color	Make	Year
Red	Honda	2005
Green	Ford	2007
Blue	Ford	2005
Red	Buick	2008

2. Put this arrangement of data into 1NF:

Name	HomePhone	CellPhone
Jones	111-1111,222-2222	333-3333
Smith	444-4444	555-5555,666-6666
Adams	777-7777,888-8888	112-1212,113-1313

3.6 THE SECOND NORMAL FORM

The second normal form (2NF) can only be addressed when we have a table and data is in the first normal form (1NF). If you look at a table for the first time, you must first decide whether it is in fact a table (i.e., in 1NF) and, beyond the data in the table, ask what the design is. Consider the following arrangement of data:

License_no	Make	Color
12345	Honda	Grey
54321	Green	Ford

The data looks like it is in the 1NF, so we must ask, "What is the table design?" The small amount of data shown seems to contain atomic data and no duplicate rows. But, what is not stated are the intended FDs. The appropriate question is, "Are Make and Color functionally dependent on License_no?" Semantically, they appear to be, but whoever produced this table of data should also furnish an accompanying table design.

Now, let us consider this table of data with no FD defined as yet:

EMPLOYEE

EmpNo	Name
101	Kaitlyn
102	Brenda
103	Beryl
104	Fred
105	Fred

Does it appear to be a valid table? Yes, it is consistent. and it contains atomic data and no duplicate rows. Now, suppose we define the data like this: The table name is EMPLOYEE. EMPLOYEE has two attributes, EmpNo and Name. The data types of the attributes are as follows:

EMPLOYEE [Empno NUMERIC(3), Name VARCHAR(20)]

VARCHAR is a very common database type meaning variable number of characters, and the *VARCHAR(20)* means that data will be from zero to 20 characters. So far, so good, but is anything missing? We have stated nothing about FDs. If no FDs are defined with the table, the only ones we may assume are reflexive:

Empno → Empno,
Name → Name,

and

Empno, Name → Empno, Name

These reflexive FDs are always true; they exist for the sense of mathematical completeness. If you put these FDs in words, they would say, "If I know a person's name, I can tell you their name." Also note that combinations of attributes can be FDs. The expression Empno, Name → Empno,

Name means that if I know an Empno and Name combination, I can tell you the Empno and Name (a reflexive FD).

As we look at the table, it appears that we have the FD, Empno → Name, but unless it is explicitly defined as such, we can only say, "It appears that … ." Wait! There are two people named Fred. Is this a problem with FDs? Not at all. You expect that Name will not be unique, and it is common-place for two people to have the same first name. However, no two people have the same EmpNo, and for each EmpNo, there is one and only one name value.

A proper definition for this table would be

EMPLOYEE (<u>Empno</u> NUMERIC(3), Name VARCHAR(20))

given

Empno → Name

The underline under Empno indicates that Empno is the primary key in this table. If a primary key is defined, it is always on the left-hand side (LHS) of an FD. Primary keys imply FDs. Primary keys are defined. The primary key does not have to be the first column in the table, but it is conventional to put it there. FDs do not necessarily define primary keys, but as we shall see, a command of the FD calculus will lead us to conclude what may be a primary key and what may not.

Let us look at another example. Suppose you are given this relation with Empno defined as the primary key:

EMPLOYEE1 (<u>Empno</u> NUMERIC(3), Job VARCHAR(20), Name VARCHAR(20))

What does this tell us? The table definition tells us that the first column will be Empno, the second column is Job, and the third column is Name. It says all the Empnos will be numbers up to 3 digits long. Job and Name will be character strings of up to 20 characters each. The underline under Empno tells us that Empno is a primary key; hence, two FDs are defined, Empno → Job and Empno → Name. The FDs say that if you know the Empno, you can find the Job and the Name for that Empno; Job and Name are functionally defined by Empno. Here is some sample data:

EmpNo	Job	Name
101	President	Kaitlyn
104	Programmer	Fred
103	Designer	Beryl

Every time we find Empno = 104, we find the name Fred. Every time we find Empno 103, we know that the job of 103 is Designer.

Let us now consider another example. Consider this table:

TAXI (Cab_no NUMERIC(4), DateDriven(DATE), Driver VARCHAR(20))

FDs are forthcoming.

Here is some sample data:

Cab_no	DateDriven	Driver
101	2/4/2010	Rich
102	2/4/2010	Gen
103	2/5/2010	John
102	2/5/2010	Steph

While we cannot define FDs by looking at the data, we can eliminate them. Can we say that Cab_no → Driver? Clearly, we cannot because Cab_no 102 has two different drivers; we have two rows with data that contradicts the FD, Cab_no → Driver: <102,Gen>, <102, Steph>. Can we say that DateDriven → Driver? Again, the answer is no because we can find information to the contrary (see 2/4/2010). How about DateDriven → Cab_no? No. According to this table, it takes both the Cab_no and the DateDriven to define a Driver. Given this data, we can ask the table designer whether the combination of Cab_no and DateDriven will form the FD, Cab_no, DateDriven → Driver? Assuming this is the intention, the complete definition of the table would be

TAXI (Cab_no NUMERIC(4), DateDriven (DATE), Driver VARCHAR(20))

given the FD

Cab_no, DateDriven → Driver

The Cab_no and DateDriven attributes are both underlined. It is the combination of these two attributes that defines a primary key for this relation. When we have two or more attributes as a key, we say the key is *concatenated*. Concatenated means "put together."

Now suppose we expand our TAXI table a little and include information about the Cab itself—the color of the cab. Let us propose this design

TAXI(Cab_no NUMERIC(4), DateDriven (DATE), Driver VARCHAR(20), Color VARCHAR(20))

with FD

Cab_no, DateDriven → Driver, Color

Suppose the data now looks like this:

Cab_no	DateDriven	Driver	Color
101	2/4/2010	Rich	Yellow
102	2/4/2010	Gen	Green
103	2/5/2010	John	Yellow
102	2/5/2010	Steph	Green

Now this table seems to be okay, but there is a hidden problem with it. The design says Cab_no, DateDriven is the primary key. It is true with this little bit of data—if we know the combination of Cab_no and DateDriven, we can identify the Driver and the Color of the cab. If I know (102, 2/4/2010), then I can find the driver (Gen) and the color of the cab (Green). You may detect a problem here, but let us keep going and see if you see it. To illustrate the problem, suppose Cab_no 102 is painted red. You can change the data in the table to reflect this, but notice what you have to do:

Cab_no	DateDriven	Driver	Color
101	2/4/2010	Rich	Yellow
102	2/4/2010	Gen	Red
103	2/5/2010	John	Yellow
102	2/5/2010	Steph	Red

You had to make two changes. Imagine this table is thousands of rows, and you change the color of a cab. You have to change each row to reflect the new cab color for that cab. The color of the cab is recorded redundantly. When such redundancy appears, it is a symptom of a design problem. Here, we say that the table is not in the 2NF.

3.6.1 Anomalies

The update we just proposed is called an *update anomaly* because the change of cab color is not a simple update to the table, but rather it requires multiple updates due to the redundancy. There are other problems with this table of data—other anomalies. Anomalies come in three forms: update, insert, and delete. An example of an insert anomaly in the preceding ill-designed table would be as follows: Suppose you wanted to insert cab and color data into the table without identifying a driver or a date driven. You cannot do this because you would have to include a row like this: <105, null, null, Blue>. This is an invalid row because you cannot have part of the primary key as null. In a relational database, there is a defined rule called the *entity integrity constraint* that applies to all relations and prohibits any part of a primary key from being null. This makes sense because if a primary key or any part of it is null, it means that you do not in fact need to know the primary key to identify a row, and hence your definition of a primary key is contradictory.

An example of a delete anomaly would be the following: Suppose you wanted to delete a cab from the database. Suppose Cab_no 102 was wrecked and taken out of the fleet. You cannot delete Cab_no 102 in the table without deleting all the rows where Cab_no 102 appears, and this deletion would also delete the other information, such as <102,2/5/2010,Steph,Red> where we know that Steph drove on 2/5/2010. A delete anomaly causes data to be deleted beyond that which was intended.

3.6.2 Non-2NF to 2NF

In terms of FDs, the problem in our non-2NF table is that the Color of cab depends on the Cab_no and not the DateDriven. The correct FDs in this table are as follows:

Cab_no, DateDriven → Driver
Cab_no → Color

You need only the Cab_no to identify the color. Since you have a concatenated key and you have an attribute in the table that is dependent on only part of the key, this is said to be a partial dependency. Tables with partial dependencies are said to be *not in the second normal form*. The second normal form (2NF) table has a primary key with no partial dependencies. For a table to not be in the 2NF, there has to be a concatenated key with some attribute not dependent on the whole key.

In this non-2NF Cab situation, the symbolic discussion of the problem would be like this:

We have a relation, R(A,B,C,D), with the FDs AB → C and A → D. Hence, the relation is not in the 2NF because you have a partial dependency, A → D, when AB is the key of the relation; attribute D depends on part of the key AB, not the whole key.

What are you supposed to do with tables that are not in 2NF? The answer is *decomposition*. The non-2NF table is decomposed into two tables; each table contains data dependent only on the primary key (the whole key and nothing but the key). Symbolically, R(A,B,C,D) with FDs AB → C and A → D (non-2NF) will be decomposed into two relations, R1(A,B,C) and R2(A,D), both of which are in 2NF because all nonkey attributes depend only on the primary key. Going back to the Cab problem, the original table will be decomposed into two tables:

TAXI (Cab_no NUMERIC(4), DateDriven(DATE), Driver VARCHAR(20), Color VARCHAR(20))

with FDs

Cab_no, DateDriven → Driver, Cab_no → Color

becomes ...

TAXI_1 (Cab_no NUMERIC(4), DateDriven(DATE), Driver VARCHAR(20))

with FD

Cab_no, DateDriven → Driver

with sample data

Cab_no	DateDriven	Driver
101	2/4/2010	Rich
102	2/4/2010	Gen
103	2/5/2010	John
102	2/5/2010	Steph

and

Cab (Cab_no NUMERIC(4), Color VARCHAR(20))

with FD

Cab_no → Color

With sample data

CAB

Cab_no	Color
101	Yellow
102	Green
103	Yellow

We give the new TAXI table a slightly different name (TAXI_1) to distinguish it from the original. Reconsider the update we proposed. With the decomposed tables, suppose Cab_no 102 got painted red. The only row that changed in this new decomposed table is the second row in the CAB table, which would now look like this:

CAB

Cab_no	Color
101	Yellow
102	Red
103	Yellow

There is one change, one row updated. With the tables in their decomposed 2NF form, there is no redundancy, and all data depends on the primary key of each table:

TAXI_1(Cab_no NUMERIC(4), DateDriven (DATE), Driver VARCHAR(20))

with FD:

Cab_no, DateDriven → Driver

And

CAB (Cab_no NUMERIC(4), Color VARCHAR(20))

with FD:

Cab_no → Color

Observe also that the other anomalies are gone when the tables are decomposed. You can insert a cab and color into the CAB table without disturbing TAXI_1. The Cab does not need a Driver or DateDriven to be added to the database. You can delete a Cab-Color combination with losing the information about the Driver or DataDriven. You will delete only the color of the cab.

CHECKPOINT 3.4
1. Given AB → CDE, is R(A,B,C,D,E) in 2NF?
2. Given B → ACDE, is R(A,B,C,D,E) in 2NF?
3. Given AB → CD and B → E, is R(A,B,C,D,E) in 2NF?
4. If a table is in the 1NF and you have no concatenated key, you do not have to worry about 2NF problems (True/False)?

3.7 THE THIRD NORMAL FORM

Let us now consider another example of a table with a defined key:

EMPLOYEE (Empno NUMERIC(3), Name VARCHAR(20), SkillID NUMERIC(3), SkillDesc VARCHAR(20)) with FD

Empno → Name, SkillID, SkillDesc

Or, in shorthand

R(A,B,C,D)

with FD

A → BCD

Here is some sample data:

EMPLOYEE

Empno	Name	SkillID	SkillDesc
101	Adams	Prog	Programmer
102	Baker	Brick	Bricklayer
103	Charles	PR	Public Relations
107	Davis	Prog	Programmer

Is this table in 1NF and 2NF? Yes, it is. It contains all atomic attributes, and there are no concatenated keys and hence no chance of partial dependencies. Yet, there is still a problem here. Can you see it? For SkillID = Prog, we have a SkillDesc = Programmer. Again, we have redundancy in the database.

As we illustrated, redundancy is a "red flag"—it suggests a design problem. We have a primary key in Empno; knowing that, the Empno allows us to identify a row. Since Empno is the primary key, it identifies all the contents of the row; hence, we can legally say that Empno → Name, SkillID, SkillDesc. The problem is that SkillDesc is better defined by SkillID than by Empno; because of this, we can deduce that SkillDesc is functionally dependent on SkillID more so than Empno. We have a transitive dependency of Empno → SkillID and SkillID → SkillDesc. This transitive dependency causes redundancy, which provokes anomalies (update, insert, and delete). What would be an update anomaly in the EMPLOYEE table? Suppose we wanted to change the description SkillDesc of SkillID = Prog to SkillDesc = Programmer/analyst? There would be two row changes in this small table of only four rows. An insert anomaly arises when we try to insert new data in the table. Suppose we wanted to put the fact that we have a SkillID = Cart and SkillDesc = Cartographer in the table. We would have to do the following:

EMPLOYEE

Empno	Name	SkillID	SkillDesc
101	Adams	Prog	Programmer
102	Baker	Brick	Bricklayer
103	Charles	PR	Public Relations
107	Davis	Prog	Programmer
null	null	Cart	Cartographer

But, this will not work because we violated the entity integrity rule. A delete anomaly would occur if we deleted a row and lost more information than we planned. Suppose we decided to delete the employee Charles. Charles has the SkillID of PR, and you not only lose the row with Charles, but also lose the fact that SkillID = PR means SkillDesc = Public Relations.

Now, let us return to the original EMPLOYEE table and resolve the problem:

EMPLOYEE (Empno NUMERIC(3), Name VARCHAR(20), SkillID NUMERIC(3), SkillDesc VARCHAR(20))

with FD

Empno → Name, SkillID, SkillDesc
or

R(A,B,C,D)

with FD

A → BCD

The problem is that the SkillDesc is functionally dependent on SkillID and not Empno. The corrected FDs should be

Empno → Name, SkillID

and

SkillID → SkillDesc

or

R(A,B,C,D)

with FDs:

A → BC, C → D

Again, this situation is called a *transitive dependency* as A → C and C → D. The third normal form (3NF) demands that you have no transitive dependencies like this. As with the partial dependencies in non-2NF, non-3NF arrangements cause anomalies:

1. Possible multiple changes when you change a SkillDesc (an update anomaly)
2. Inability to add a row with just a SkillID and its SkillDesc (an insert anomaly)
3. Losing information when deleting a row (remember losing a SkillID when Charles was deleted?)—a delete anomaly

All of these anomalies are caused by the transitive dependency. How do we fix this problem? As before, we decompose the non-3NF table into two tables in which the attributes will depend only on the key of the table:

R(A, B, C, D) with FDs R→ABC and C → D becomes
R1(A, B, C) and R2(C, D).

With our EMPLOYEE data, we decompose into two tables like this:

EMPLOYEE1 (Empno NUMERIC(3), Name VARCHAR(20), SkillID NUMERIC(3))

with FD
Empno → Name, SkillID
and

SKILL (SkillID NUMERIC(3), SkillDesc VARCHAR(20))
with FD
SkillID →SkillDesc
The populated tables will look like this:

EMPLOYEE1

Empno	Name	SkillID
101	Adams	Prog
102	Baker	Brick
103	Charles	PR
107	Davis	Prog

SKILL

SkillID	SkillDesc
Prog	Programmer
Brick	Bricklayer
PR	Public Relations

These two tables represent a database in 3NF. The redundancy is now gone. If you want to change a SkillDesc, you make one change. If you want to delete an employee, you do not lose the SkillID-SkillDesc, and if you want to insert a new SkillID with no employee yet defined, you can do so. The anomalies are gone.

> **CHECKPOINT 3.5**
> 1. Consider this table:
>
> EMPLOYEE (Emp_no, Name, Project_no, Project_location)
>
> with FDs
>
> Emp_no → Emp_no, Name, Project_no
>
> and
>
> Project_no → Project_location
>
> Is this table in 1NF, 2NF, 3NF? Decompose the table if necessary.
>
> 2. Consider this table:
>
> R(A, B, C, D, E, F)
>
> with FDs
>
> AB → CD, D → E, E → F
>
> Is this table in 1NF, 2NF, 3NF? Decompose the table if necessary.

3.8 THE EQUIJOIN OPERATION

In a relational database, we often decompose tables to move to the 3NF. Managers and users will complain that "My table of data has been spread all over the place," or "The normalization process removed my primary information table." While tables are decomposed, they can be reconstructed easily with the equijoin operation of relational calculus, which is realized in SQL (Structured Query Language), the de facto query language of the relational database. A discussion of relational calculus and SQL are beyond the scope of this chapter, and many excellent references to the query language exist (Bagui and Earp, 2009, 2011; Earp and Bagui, 2008). The point here is that while a normalized table may have been decomposed, the original table can be re-formed from the decomposed ones. Let us give an example. Suppose we have a table like this from the previous section:

EMPLOYEE (Emp_no, Name, Project_no, Project_location)

with FDs

Emp_no → Emp_no, Name, Project_no, Project_location

and

Project_no → Project_location

We recognize the transitive dependency and decompose EMPLOYEE into these two tables:

EMPLOYEE1 (Emp_no, Name, Project_no)
PROJECT (Project_no, Project_location)

The EMPLOYEE table can be reconstructed by joining EMPLOYEE1 and PROJECT by the common attribute, Project_no. Project_no is the primary key of PROJECT and is a foreign key referencing EMPLOYEE1. If R(A, B, C) is decomposed into S(A, B) and T(B, C), the equijoin operation can reconstruct R combining rows of S and T where the values of common attribute B are equal. If R = EMPLOYEE, S = EMPLOYEE1, T = PROJECT, and B = Project_no, the equijoin would proceed like this:

EMPLOYEE (Emp_no, Name, Project_no, Project_location)
with data

```
<101, Adams, P1, Pensacola>
<102, Baker, P1, Pensacola>
<103, Charles, P2, Mobile>
<104, Davis, P2, Mobile>
```

decomposes to

EMPLOYEE1 (Emp_no, Name, Project_no)

with data

```
<101, Adams, P1>
<102, Baker, P1>
<103, Charles, P2>
<104, Davis, P2>
```

and

PROJECT (<u>Project_no</u>, Project_location)

with data

```
<P1, Pensacola>
<P2, Mobile>
```

The equijoin operation J gives us Result = (EMPLOYEE1 J PROJECT) on Project_no, resulting in

- `<101, Adams, P1>` joins with `<P1, Pensacola>` to give `<101, Adams, P1, Pensacola>`
- `<102, Baker, P1>` joins with `<P1, Pensacola>` to give `<102, Baker, P1, Pensacola>`
- `<103, Charles, P2>` joins with `<P2, Mobile>` to give `<103, Charles, P2, Mobile>`
- `<104, Davis, P2>` joins with `<P2, Mobile>` to give `<104, Davis, P2, Mobile>`

The RESULT table contains the same data as the original EMPLOYEE table. The join operation can use operators other than equality, but the other join varieties are uncommon and beyond the scope of this book. The recombining of decomposed relations during the normalization process uses the equijoin operation.

3.9 SOME FUNCTIONAL DEPENDENCY RULES

Having introduced the normal forms, we would now like to introduce a set of FD rules to aid in finding normal forms. We do not approach this subject with great mathematical rigor, but rather appeal to common sense and logic. There are far more rigorous treatments of this subject (Elmasri and Navathe, 2007). Before we can determine normal forms, we deal with finding a minimal key in a relation and then work from that key to the normal forms. We designate a relation with letters R, S, or T (usually R). We depict attributes as A, B, C, ... For example, if we have a relation R with three attributes A, B, and C, we abbreviate this R(A, B, C). Now, let us consider a problem consisting of a set of attributes and some FDs and see how a set of FD rules will allow us to organize the database:

We are given some data, which we put in a table R(A, B, C, D), and we are given some FDs: A → BC, B → D. The process of bringing this data to 3NF goes like this: (a) Find a minimal key of R; (b) determine whether R is in 3NF, and if not, decompose it until it is.

To find the key, we want to propose some rules for dealing with the FDs we are given. If A → BC, we mean that the attribute A defines B and C, or put another way, B and C are functionally dependent on A. Here is an example: Let

R be EMPLOYEE
A be Employee_no
B be Name
C be City
D be State

If we say A → BCD in R, we are saying that if you know the Employee_ no, you then can find the Name, City, and State for a given Employee_no in the relation R. When writing FDs, we are dealing with *sets* of attributes. Sets have no order, and duplication of attributes on either side of an FD adds no information. Some of the notions about sets are often expressed as FD rules, and if we view the FD as a set relation among attributes, we can say that all of the following are the same as A → BCD:

A → DCB, A → CDB, AA → BCD, A → BBCCDDDD, AAAAA → BBBCDDDDDDDD.

In the EMPLOYEE relation, since A (Employee_no) defines the other attributes, we designate A as a primary key. Hence, writing the relation in shorthand looks like this: R(A,B,C,D), where the underlined A is the primary key. Now, here are some rules:

i. **The reflexive rule:** A → A. In this chapter, we proffered this rule, which is trivially obvious; it simply means that if I know A, then I can tell you A. Since we treat the attributes as sets, the reflexive rule also tells us that AA → A and A → AA.

ii. **The augmentation rule:** If A → B, then AC → B. If you are given that A → B, then this means that if you know a value for A, you can find a value for B. If A is Employee_no and B is a Name, A → B says if you give me a value for Employee_no, then I can find a Name for that Employee_no. The augmentation rule says that if I augment the

LHS of the defining expression (A), I can still correctly find the right-hand side (RHS). Adding information to the LHS really does nothing to enhance the FD. Suppose we take an example: Employee_no = 101, implies that Name is Jones. Now, if we add information to the LHS, like Employee_no = 101, Date of Birth = 21 Nov 1958, what is the name? It is Jones, and the added information of birthday on the LHS is superfluous. Still, the rule is valid, and it will help us when deriving a key.

iii. **The decomposition rule:** If A → BCD, then A → B, A → C, and A → D. (Please do not confuse this FD rule with the decomposition of relations to gain normal forms. Unfortunately, the names are the same, but the meaning is overloaded.) Again, we appeal to intuition to understand this rule. If Employee_no defines a Name, Address, and City, then it is valid to say Employee_no defines a name, Employee_no defines an Address, and Employee_no defines a City. If you give me a valid Employee_no I can tell you a person's name, the person's address, and the person's phone number as one unit or piece by piece.

iv. **The union rule:** If A → B and A → C, then A → BC. The reverse of the decomposition rule is the *union rule*, which says the same thing as the decomposition rule, backward. As an example, if Employee_no defines a Name and Employee_no defines a City, then Employee_no defines a Name and a City. Also regarding the set feature of FDs—it means the same thing to say

Employee_no → City, Name and Employee_no → Name, City

v. **The transitive rule:** If A → B and B → C, then A → C. This rule seems to fly in the face of the 3NF, but for finding keys in a jumble of attributes, it is quite useful. Think of the rule in terms of a table of Employee_no, Job, and JobDescriptions. You are given that Employee_no → Job. You are given that Job → JobDescription. The rule says that Employee_no → JobDescription. Give me an Employee_no, and I'll tell you the job that person does because I can look up the Job and then find the JobDescription.

vi. **The subset rule:** A is a subset of some group of attributes F, then F → A. For example, if F = AB, then A is a subset of AB and AB → A. If AB is Employee_no and Name, then given an Employee_no and Name, I can tell you either Name or Employee_no.

Example 3.1

Let us consider the following problem: We are given some data in a table: R(A, B, C, D, E) and we are given some FDs: A → BC, B → D, AC → E. What we want to find is one set of attributes that defines all the others, a key to this relation, R. After we find the key, we will work on normal forms.

Step 1. Find an LHS (of an FD) that is a minimal key for R. You can always start with the reflexive property and use all the attributes on the LHS. ABCDE → ABCDE. ABCDE is a key, but what we want to find is some subset of all attributes that will define the others—a minimal key (if it exists). A good way to find a minimal LHS is to first look for an FD that has a concatenated LHS (if there is one). If there is no concatenated key, then choose an attribute that defines as many other attributes as possible. Admittedly, this is a subjective choice, but if you choose incorrectly, you only need to try again with a different or enhanced LHS. After choosing some LHS, we look at the FD rules and see if we can define the other attributes from our chosen LHS. In this case, we have AC → E. We will see if we can show that AC → ABCDE and hence let AC be a minimal key of the original R. Notice that we start with the largest concatenated LHS because we will need at least AC to define whatever is functionally dependent on it.

Step 2. Use the rules to find as many RHS attributes as possible with the chosen LHS. Since AC → E, we know by the reflexive rule that AC → AC, and then by the union rule, we combine these two:

Union rule: AC → E (given), AC → AC (reflexive), then AC → ACE.

Use the other given FDs to find other attributes that depend on the chosen LHS from step 1.

We have established that AC → ACE. We were given that A → BC.

Subset rule: AC → ACE (derived previously), then AC → A.
Transitive rule: AC → A, A → BC (given), then AC → BC.
Union rule: AC → ACE, AC → BC, then AC → ACEBC, and since we are dealing with sets of attributes, AC → ABCE.

Step 3. Repeat step 2 as necessary to get all attributes on the RHS from the chosen LHS if you can.

We have all attributes on the RHS except D. The other FD we are given is B → D.

Using the same line of thought and that we have established AC → ABCE:

Subset rule: AC → ABCE, then AC → B.
Transitive rule: AC → B, B → D (given), then AC → D.
Union rule: AC → ABCE, AC → D, then AC → ABCDE.

The process of using FD rules to find a minimal key is not an exact algorithm. Some people will see a transitive rule first, then a union rule; others will see decomposition rules first. The order of rule application is not as important as clearly defining a path from an LHS that defines all attributes (ABCDE → ABCDE) to some minimal key (here, AC → ABCDE).

Since our LHS defines all the other attributes, we have a minimal key AC. Now, the question: Is this in 1NF, 2NF, or 3NF? No repeating groups were indicated; hence, we have 1NF with R (A,C,B,D,E). The best tactic here is to remove transitive dependencies first. We have B → D, so we can decompose R as follows:

R (A, C, B, D, E) becomes R1 (A, C, B, E) and R2 (B, D).

When all transitive FDs have been removed, look for partial dependencies. While AC is the key of R, we have an FD: A → BC (a partial dependency) because R1 has AC → BE.

R1 (A, C, B, E) decomposes to

R3 (A, B, C) and R4 (A, C, E)

The final version of the database is

R2 (B, D)
R3 (A, B, C)
R4 (A, C, E)

We suggested that the better technique in decomposing was to remove the transitive dependencies first. The decomposition could be done by removing the partial dependencies first, but the FD with the transitive dependency has to be kept with its LHS. Consider the following:

R (A, C, B, D, E) becomes R1 (A, B, C) (partial dependency removed) and R2 (A, C, D, E). But, now there is a problem. You still have B → D, and you do not have B and D together in either R1 or R2.

You have to keep B and D together and hence decompose like this:

R (A, C, B, D, E) becomes R3 (A, B, C, D) and R4 (A, C, E) and then handle the transitive dependency.

R3 (A, B, C, D) decomposes to R5 (A, B, C) and R6 (B, D).

The final version is

R4 (A, C, E)
R5 (A, B, C)
R6 (B, D)

Regardless of how the decomposition is done, the final result has to be checked to see if all FDs are still there. If so, then you should have a 3NF database.

Example 3.2

Let us give one more example of a decomposition and key choice that is a little less straightforward. Suppose we have R (A, B, C, D, E, F) and AB → CD and B → E. Your first mission is to find a minimal key for R. From the previous discussion, we suggested that you choose the largest LHS of a given FD and then see if you can use the rules to show that it is a key. Here, you would choose AB to start and then see if you can show that AB → ABCDEF. Using our rules, we can show that

1. AB → AB (reflexive rule)
2. AB → CD (given)
3. AB → ABCD (union rule of 1 and 2)
4. AB → B (subset rule)
5. B → E (given)
6. AB → E (transitive rule on 4 and 5)
7. AB → ABCDE (union rule on 6 and 3)

What about F? You may have recognized this as a problem already, but when you look at the given FDs, you see that F does not appear on either an LHS or a RHS. You can see that the choice of AB as a starting key was good, but not complete. To handle this, you can do this:

8. ABF → ABCDE (augmentation rule and 7)
9. ABF → F (subset rule)
10. ABF → ABCDEF (union rule of 8 and 9).

This last discussion and example suggest two things: (a) our basic algorithm of "start with the largest concatenated key as the LHS" is good, but the augmentation rule allows us to include attributes on the LHS as necessary to get to a minimal key; and (b) you can derive new FD rules. Our use of the rules in steps 8, 9, and 10 suggest we can proffer this rule:

> **vii. The double augmentation rule:** You are given or have derived AB → C, then ABD → CD. You can add an attribute to both the LHS and the RHS at the same time as we did to go from step 7 to step 10.

There are many theories and algorithms about how to decompose and how to choose minimal keys. For example, to find a minimal key, there are proposed algorithms that start with *all attributes →
all attributes* and then remove attributes from the LHS—a top-down approach. In terms of decomposition, it seems easier to attack transitive dependencies first. We have presented what we feel is a practical workable approach to going from a jumbled set of attributes to 3NF. Here is the summary of the approach we illustrated:

Find the minimal key (MK):
   MK1. Lump all attributes into one relation R and choose the largest LHS FD as the minimal key K.
   MK2. Use FD rules to find out whether K can in fact define all the attributes in R.
   MK3. If K cannot define all the attributes, then augment K with another "well-chosen" attribute and return to step MK2 with K now K′ (K plus some other attribute). With practice, the well-chosen attribute will be some attribute from the original set that defines whatever other attributes are missing in step MK2.

Decompose (D):
   D1. Remove all transitive dependencies to a separate relation.
   D2. Remove all partial dependencies to a separate relation.

Check to see if the final product still retains all given FDs.

CHECKPOINT 3.6
For each of the following, find a minimal key and decompose as necessary to reach the 3NF. Show decomposed relations with keys.

   1. R(A, B, C, D, E, F) and A → BCDEF
   2. R(A, B, C, D) and AB → CD, C → D

3. R(A,B,C,D) and AB → D, B →C
4. R(A,B,C,D,E) and ABC → D, D → E
5. R(A,B,C,D,E) and AB →C, B → D, D →E
6. R(A,B,C,D) and ABD → C
7. R(A,B,{C}) and A → B and A ⇸ C (A has multiple occurrences of C)
8. R(A,B,C,D,E) and C → ABDE

3.10 THE BOYCE CODD NORMAL FORM

We have suggested that all databases be placed in 3NF. When all the tables are in 3NF, there is likely to be no redundancy, no anomalies. There is one situation for which 3NF may not be "quite good enough." We placed this last in the chapter because it is somewhat unusual but possible, and database designers should be aware of it. Some authors suggest that this is a "stronger form than 3NF," but there is still a difficulty with tables normalized to Boyce Codd normal form (BCNF), as we discuss. Here is the problem:

Suppose you had a relation with three attributes, R (A, B, C). Suppose further that AB → C, but add the FD, C → B. The relation with its primary key would be R (A, B, C); it is in 3NF because there are no partial dependencies and no transitive dependencies of the type D → E, E → F. But, there is still a slight problem. There is that odd transitive FD, C → B; hence, there will be redundancy and anomalies.

Here is an example of this situation: Suppose we have a local ballpark where there are children who play sports. Some children play for more than one team. Each team may have multiple coaches, and a player is assigned a coach on each team. We have a database of players, teams, and coaches, and we omit some player, team, and coach details for simplicity.

PARK (Player, Team, Coach)
LaLaLand PARK

Player	Team	Coach
Walsh	Tigers	Adams
Smith	Pirates	Baker
Walsh	Spiders	Davis
Smith	Tigers	Edwards
Philips	Pirates	Baker

Player, Team → Coach. Note that Player does not → Team, Team does not → Coach (look at the data to disprove these FDs). On the other hand, Coach → Team. While this data is in 3NF, you have redundancy because Coach → Team.

The normalization to BCNF, which denies any transitive dependency, would work like this:

R (A, B, C), with FDs AB → C, C → B can be normalized into R1 (C, B) and R2(A, C). The problem is that one of the FDs has vanished (AB → C), but so have the anomalies. The ballpark example normalized to BCNF looks like this:

PC (Player, Coach)   CT (Coach, Team)
LaLaLand PARK

Player	Coach	Coach	Team
Walsh	Adams	Adams	Tigers
Smith	Baker	Baker	Pirates
Walsh	Davis	Davis	Spiders
Smith	Edwards	Edwards	Tigers
Philips	Baker		

In the PC table, both attributes are a concatenated key (Player, Coach → Player, Coach). Since there can be no partial or transitive dependencies, PC is in 3NF and BCNF. CT is also in 3NF and BCNF (Coach → Team). The decomposition problem is that we lost the FD: Player, Team → Coach. The original table can be reconstructed with an equijoin operation by joining PC and CT on Coach, but the BCNF version allows updates with no redundancy, whereas the original PARK table does not. Consider adding a coach to the original PARK table; it can only be done if a player is assigned, or else there would be a null in the key. In the BCNF version, a coach can be added to CT with no player assigned. The other anomalies will be left as exercises.

BCNF is a little more complicated than the 1NF, 2NF, and 3NF. In the first three normal forms, there is no issue regarding whether the decomposition is a "good idea." All databases should be reduced to at least 3NF. BCNF presents a quandary. What is more annoying to the person using the database? Is the loss of an FD worse than some anomalies? In a non-BCNF situation, if the occurrence of anomaly-producing redundancy is low, then it may well be better just to leave the tables as is—in 3NF but not BCNF. If the redundancy is pervasive, then normalization to BCNF may be in order. One option that is never acceptable is to keep both versions because that is total redundancy.

3.11 CHAPTER SUMMARY

This chapter was meant to give an introduction to the relational database. Relational tables are *sets of rows*. As sets, the rows have no implied order among them, and in a correct relation, there are no duplicate rows. Normal forms are introduced along with (a) why the normal forms are desirable; (b) why nonnormalized tables generate anomalies; and (c) how to move from nonnormalized tables to normal form tables. Anomalies are abnormal table maintenance operations (delete, insert, and update) that are abnormal because of redundancy and bad table design. The equijoin operation was introduced to show how decomposed tables can be reconstructed. An FD calculus was introduced to show how to determine keys and decompositions on an aggregate of data. Finally, BCNF was covered. Decomposing non-BCNF tables removes redundancies and anomalies but hides FDs.

CHAPTER 3 EXERCISES

Exercise 3.1

If X → Y, can you say Y → X? Why or why not ?

Exercise 3.2

Decompose the following data into 1NF tables:

Khanna, 123 4th St., Columbus, Ohio {Delhi University, Calcutta University, Ohio State}

Ray, 4 Moose Lane, Pensacola, Florida {Zambia University, University of West Florida}

Ali, 88 Tiger Circle, Gulf Breeze, Florida {University of South Alabama, University of West Florida}

Sahni, 283 Penny Street, North Canton, Ohio {Wooster College, Mount Union College}

Exercise 3.3

Consider this data:

Name	Address	City	State	Car	Color	Year
Smith	123 4th St	Pensacola	FL	Mazda	Blue	2012
Smith	123 4th St	Pensacola	FL	Nissan	Red	2011
Jones	4 Moose Lane	Santa Clive	CA	Lexus	Red	2012
Katie	5 Rain Circle	Fort Walton	FL	Taurus	White	2012

and the following FDs:

Name → Address, City, State, Car, Color, Year and Car → Color, Year

Decompose as necessary to achieve 3NF.

BIBLIOGRAPHY

Armstrong, W. 1974. Dependency structures of data base relationships. *Proceedings of the IFIP Congress,* Stockholm, Sweden, August 5–10, 1974.

Bagui, S., and Earp, R. 2009. *SQL Essentials in Access.* Deer Park, NY: Linus.

Bagui, S., and Earp, R. 2011. *Essential of SQL Using SQL Server 2008.* Jones and Bartlett.

Chen, P. P. 1976. The entity relationship model—toward a unified view of data. *ACM Transactions on Database Systems,* 1(1), 9–36.

Codd, E. 1970. A relational model for large shared data banks. Communications of the ACM, 13(6), 377–387.

Codd, E. 1972. *Further Normalization of the Data Base Relational Model.* Republished in Randall J. Rustin (ed.), *Database Systems: Courant Computer Science Symposia Series* 6, Prentice-Hall, 1972.

Codd, E. 1974. Recent investigations in relational database system. *Proceedings of the IFIP Congress,* Stockholm, Sweden, August 5–10, 1974.

Date, C. 2003. *An Introduction to Database Systems.* Reading, MA: Addison-Wesley.

Earp, R., and Bagui, S. 2008. *Practical Guide to Using SQL in Oracle.* Plano, Texas: Wordware.

Elmasri, R., and Navathe, S. B. 2007. *Fundamentals of Database Systems.* Reading, MA: Addison-Wesley.

Maier, D. 1983. *The Theory of Relational Databases.* New York, NY. Computer Science Press.

Norman, R. J. 1996. *Object-Oriented Systems Analysis and Design.* Upper Saddle River, NJ: Prentice Hall.

Schach, S. R. 2011. *Object-Oriented and Classical Software Engineering.* New York: McGraw-Hill.

4

The Basic ER Diagram
A Data Modeling Schema

4.1 INTRODUCTION

This chapter begins by describing a data modeling approach and then introduces entity relationship (ER) diagrams. The concepts of entities, attributes, relationships, and keys are introduced. The first three steps in an ER design methodology are developed. Step 1 begins by building a one-entity diagram. Step 2 concentrates on using structured English to describe a database. Step 3, the last section in this chapter, discusses mapping the ER diagram to a relational database. These concepts—the diagram, structured English, and mapping—evolve together as the book progresses. At the end of the chapter, we also begin a running case study, which is continued in the following chapters.

4.2 WHAT IS A DATA MODELING SCHEMA?

A *data modeling schema* is a method that allows us to model or illustrate a database. This is often in the form of a graphic diagram, but other means of communication are also desirable; people who are not in the computer field may or may not understand diagrams and graphics. The ER diagram is a graphic tool that facilitates data modeling. ER diagrams are a subset of "semantic models" in database parlance. Semantic models refer to models that intend to elicit meaning from data. ER diagrams are not the only semantic modeling tools, but are common and popular.

When we begin to discuss the contents of a database, the data model helps us to decide which piece of data goes with which other piece(s) of data on a conceptual level. An early concept concerning the database is to recognize that there are levels of abstraction we can use in discussing databases. For example, if we were to discuss the filing of "names," we could discuss (a) abstractly, that is, "We will file names of people we know"; or (b) concretely, that is, "We will file first, middle, and last names (20 characters each) of people we know, so that we can retrieve the names in alphabetical order by last name, and we will put this data in a spreadsheet format in package *x*."

If a person is designing a database, the first step is to abstract, then refine the abstraction. The longer one stays away from the concrete details of logical models (relational, hierarchical, network) and physical realizations (fields [how many characters, the data type, …] and files [relative, spreadsheet, …]), the easier it is to change the model and to decide how the data will eventually be physically realized (stored). When we use the term *field* or *file*, we will be referring to physical data as opposed to conceptual data.

Mapping is the process of choosing a logical model and then moving to a physical database file system from a conceptual model (the ER diagram). A physical file loaded with data is necessary to actually obtain data from a database. Mapping is the bridge between the design concept and physical reality. In this book, we concentrate on the relational database model due to its ubiquitousness in the contemporary database models.

4.2.1 So, What Is an Entity Relationship Diagram?

The **ER diagram** is a semantic data modeling **tool** used to accomplish the goal of abstractly describing or portraying data. Abstractly described data is called a **conceptual** model. Our conceptual model will lead us to a "schema." A **schema** implies a permanent, **fixed** description of the structure of the data. Therefore, when we agree that we have captured the correct depiction of reality within our conceptual model, our ER diagram, we can call it a schema.

An ER diagram could also be used to document an existing database by reverse engineering it, but in introducing the subject, we focus on the idea of using an ER diagram to model a to-be-created database, and we deal with reverse engineering in further discussion.

4.3 DEFINING A DATABASE— SOME DEFINITIONS: ENTITY, RELATIONSHIP, ATTRIBUTE

As the name implies, an entity relationship diagram models data as *entities* and *relationships*. An *entity* is a thing about which we store data (e.g., a person, a bank account, a building). In the original presentation, Chen (1976) described an entity as a "thing which can be distinctly identified." So an entity may be a person, place, object, event, or concept about which we wish to store data. A *relationship* is a connection between entities. An *attribute* is the category of data that describes an entity or relationship.

An entity represents a type or class of something and should be named accordingly. The following are some examples of entities:

- Examples of a person entity would be EMPLOYEE, VET, or STUDENT.
- Examples of a place entity would be STATE or COUNTRY.
- Examples of an object entity would be BUILDING, AUTO, or PRODUCT.
- An example of an event entity would be SALES, RETURNS, or REGISTRATION.
- An example of a concept entity would be ACCOUNT or DEPARTMENT.

The name of an entity should be generic. The name should be able to accommodate changes "over time." For example, if we were modeling a business and the business made donuts, we might consider creating an entity called DONUT. But, how long will it be before this business evolves into making more generic pastry? If it is anticipated that the business will involve pastry of all kinds rather than just donuts, perhaps it would be better to create an entity called PASTRY—it may be more applicable over time. In this case, an entity "business" is too generic because you want to record data about donuts or pastry—components of the business.

In older data-processing circles, we would have referred to an entity as a "record," but the term *record* is too physical and too confining; *record* gives us a mental picture of a physical thing, and to work at the conceptual level, we want to avoid device-oriented terms. In a database context, it is unusual to store information about one entity, so we think of storing collections of data about entities; such collections are called *entity sets*. Entity sets correspond to the older concept of "files," but a file usually connotes a physical thing, and hence we abstract the concept of the file (entity set) as well as the concept of a record (entity). As an example, suppose we have a company that has customers. You would imagine that the company had a customer entity set with individual customer entities in it.

An entity may be very broad (e.g., a person), or it may be narrowed by the application for which data is being prepared (like a student or a customer). "Broad" entities, which cover a whole class of objects, are sometimes called *generalizations* (e.g., person), and "narrower" entities are sometimes called *specializations* (e.g., student). In further diagrams (in this book), we revisit generalizations and specializations, but for now, we concern ourselves with an application level at which there are no subgroups (specializations) or supergroups (generalizations) of entities.

When we speak of capturing data about a particular entity, we refer to this as an *instance*. An entity instance is a single occurrence of an entity. For example, if we create an entity called TOOL, and if we choose to record data about a screwdriver, then the screwdriver "record" is an instance of TOOL. Each instance of an entity must be uniquely identifiable so that each instance is separate and distinctly identifiable from all other instances of that type of entity. In a customer entity set, you might imagine that the company would assign a unique customer number, for example. This unique identifier is called a **key**.

A **relationship** is a link or association between entities. Relationships are usually denoted by verb phrases. We begin by expanding the notion of an entity (in this chapter and the next), and then we come back to the notion of a relationship (in Chapter 6) once we have established the concept of an entity.

An **attribute** is a property or characteristic of an entity. For example, an entity, AUTOMOBILE, has attributes type, color, vehicle_id, and so on.

4.3.1 A Beginning Methodology

Database modeling begins with a description of "what is to be stored." Such a description may come from anyone; we will call the describer the "user." For example, Ms. Smith of Acme Parts Company comes to you asking that you design a database of parts for her company. Ms. Smith is the user. You are the database designer. What Ms. Smith tells you about the parts will be the database description.

As a starting point in dealing with a to-be-created database, we identify a central, "primary" entity—a category about which we will store data. For example, if we wanted to create a database about students and their environment, then one entity would be STUDENT (our characterization of an entity will always be in the singular). Having chosen one first primary entity, STUDENT, we then search for information to be recorded about our STUDENT (attributes). This methodology of selecting one primary entity from a data description is our first step in drawing an ER diagram and hence the beginning of the requirements phase of software engineering for our database.

Once the primary entity has been chosen, we then ask what information we want to record about our entity. In our STUDENT example, we add some details about the STUDENT—details that will qualify, identify, classify, or express the state of the entity (in this case, the STUDENT entity). These details or contents of entities are called *attributes*.* Some example attributes of STUDENT would be the student's name, student number, major, address, and so on—information about the student. Keep in mind that in this process of selecting attributes, the user should be able to tell you what data he or she wishes to keep.

4.3.2 ER Design Methodology

Step 1. Select one primary entity from the database requirements description and show attributes to be recorded for that entity.

Requirements definition is the first phase of software engineering in which the systems analyst tries to find out what a user wants. In the case of a database, an information-oriented system, the user will want to store data. Now that we have chosen a primary entity and some attributes, our task will be to (a) draw a diagram of our first impression entity (our primary entity), (b) translate the diagram into English, and (c) present the English (and the diagram) back to the user to see if we have it right and then progress from there.

Step c is called *feedback* in software engineering. The process of refining via feedback is a normal process in the requirements/specification phases. The feedback loop is essential in arriving at the reality of what one wants to depict from both the user and analyst viewpoints. First, we show how to draw the entity, and then we present guidelines on converting our diagram into English.

---

* C. J. Date (1995), *An Introduction to Database Systems*, 6th edition, preferred the word "property" to "attribute" because it is more generic and because attribute is used in other contexts. We use attribute because we believe it to be more commonly used.

CHECKPOINT 4.1

1. Of the following items, determine which could be an entity and state why: automobile, college class, student, name of student, book title, number of dependents.
2. Why are entities not called files or records?
3. What are entity sets?
4. Why do we need entity relationship diagrams?
5. What are attributes? List attributes of the entities you found in question 1?
6. What is a relationship?

4.4 A FIRST "ENTITY-ONLY" ER DIAGRAM: AN ENTITY WITH ATTRIBUTES

To recap our example, we have chosen an example with a primary entity from a student information database: the student. Again, note that "a student" is something that we want to store information about (the definition of an entity). In this chapter, we do not concern ourselves with any other entities.

Let us think about some attributes of the entity STUDENT. That is, what are some attributes a student might have? A student has a name, an address, and an educational connection. We call the educational connection a *school*. We have picked three attributes for the entity STUDENT, and we have also chosen a generic label for each: name, address, school.

We begin our first venture into ER diagrams with a "Chen-like" model. Chen (1976) introduced the idea of the ER diagrams. Chen and others have improved the ER process over the years, and while there is no standard ER diagram model, the Chen-like model and variants thereof are common. After the Chen-like model, we introduce other models. We briefly discuss the Barker/Oracle-like model in Chapter 12. Chen-like models have the advantage that one need not know the underlying logical model to understand the design. Barker models and some other models require a full understanding of the relational model, and the diagrams are affected by relational concepts.

To begin, in the Chen-like model, we will do as Chen originally did and put the entities in boxes and show attributes nearby. One way to depict attributes is to put them in circles or ovals appended to the boxes (refer to Figure 4.1a and Figure 4.1b). Figure 4.1c is an alternative style of depicting attributes. The alternative attribute style (Figure 4.1c) is not as descriptive but is more compact and may be used if Chen-like diagrams become cluttered.

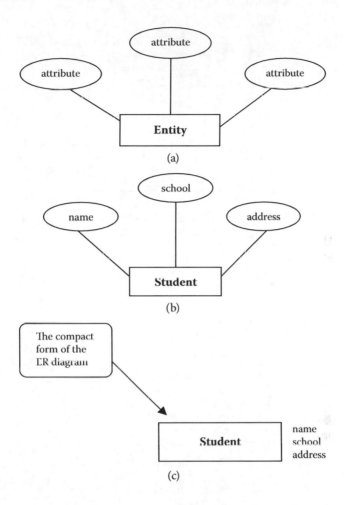

FIGURE 4.1
(a) Chen-like model: entity with attributes. (b) Student entity with three attributes. (c) Alternative ER model.

There are several ways of depicting attributes. We have illustrated the model of an "attribute in an oval" (Chen-like model) because it is common and useful. Refer to Figures 4.2a, 4.2b, and 4.2c for some alternate models for attributes. There are benefits to alternate forms for depicting attributes. The standard form of the Chen-like model with ovals and boxes is good for conceptualizing; it is easily changed and very clear regarding which attribute goes where. The concise forms (Figure 4.1c and other variants shown in Figures 4.2a, 4.2b, and 4.2c) are easily created from the standard form and are sometimes more useful for documentation when space is a concern.

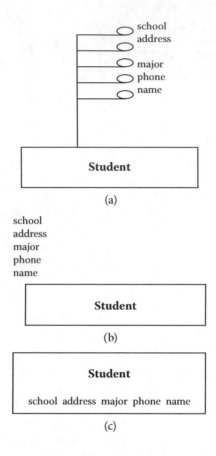

FIGURE 4.2

(a) Second alternative model for ER diagram. (b) Third alternative model for ER diagram. (c) Fourth alternative model for ER diagram.

Figures 4.1b and 4.1c show an ER diagram with one entity, **STUDENT**, and three attributes: name, address, and school. If more attributes were added to our conceptual model, such as phone and major, they would be appended to the entity (**STUDENT** is the only entity we have so far), as can be seen in Figure 4.3.

4.5 MORE ABOUT ATTRIBUTES

Attributes are characteristics of entities that provide descriptive detail about the entities. There are several different kinds of attributes: simple or atomic, composite, multivalued, and derived. The properties of an attribute

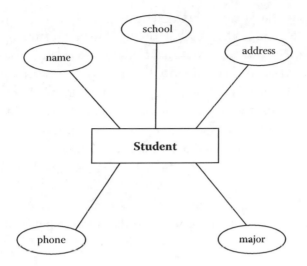

FIGURE 4.3
The STUDENT entity with five attributes.

are its name, description, format, and length, in addition to its atomicity. Some attributes may be considered as unique identifiers for an entity. In this section, we also introduce the idea of a key attribute, a unique identifier for an entity.

4.5.1 The Simple or Atomic Attribute

Simple or atomic attributes cannot be broken down further or subdivided, hence the notion "atomic." One may examine the domain of values* of an attribute to elicit whether an attribute is simple or not. An example of a simple or atomic attribute would be Social Security number; a person would be expected to have only one, undivided Social Security number.

Other tests of whether an attribute is simple or atomic will depend entirely on the circumstances that the database designer encounters—the desire of the user for which the database is being built. For example, a phone number attribute could be treated as simple in a particular database design, but in another scenario we may want to divide the phone number into two distinct parts, area code and the number. Another example of

---

* The domain of values is the set of values that a given attribute may take on. The domain consists of all the possible legal values that are permitted on an attribute. A data type is a broader term used to describe attributes, but data type includes the idea of which operations are allowable. Since people creating a database are usually more concerned about storage and retrieval, database data types usually just focus on the domain of values.

when the use of the attribute in the database will determine if the attribute is simple or atomic is a birthdate attribute. If we are setting up a database for a veterinary hospital, it may make sense to break a birthdate field up into month, day, and year since it will make a difference in treatment if a young animal is 5 days old versus if it is 5 months or 5 years old. Hence, in this case birthdate would be a composite attribute. For a RACE HORSE database, however, it may not be necessary to break up a birthdate field into month/day/year since all horses are dated only by the year in which they are born. In this case, birthdate, consisting of only the year, would be atomic.

If an attribute is nonatomic, it needs to be depicted as such on the ER diagram. The following sections deal with these more complicated, nonatomic attribute ideas: the composite attribute and the multivalued attribute.

4.5.2 The Composite Attribute

A *composite attribute*, sometimes called a *group attribute*, is an attribute that is formed by combining or aggregating related attributes. The names chosen for composite attributes should be descriptive and general. The concept of *name* is adequate for a general description, but it may be desirable to be more specific about the parts of this attribute. Most data-processing applications divide the name into component parts. Name, then, is called a *composite* attribute or an aggregate because it is usually composed of a first name, a last name, and a middle initial—subattributes, if you will. The way that composite attributes are shown in ER diagrams in the Chen-like model is illustrated in Figure 4.4. The subattributes, like first name, middle name, and last name, are called *simple*, *atomic*, or *elementary* attributes. The word *aggregate* is used in a different sense in some database query languages, and to avoid confusion, we do not call composite attributes aggregates; we use the word *composite*.

The test of whether an attribute will be composite (or not) will depend entirely on the circumstances that the database designer encounters—the desire of the user requesting the database be built. For example, in one database it may not be important to know exactly which city, state, or zip code a person comes from, so an address attribute in that database may not be broken up into its component parts; it may just be called *address*. In another database, it may be important to know which city and state a person is from, so in this second database we would have to break up the

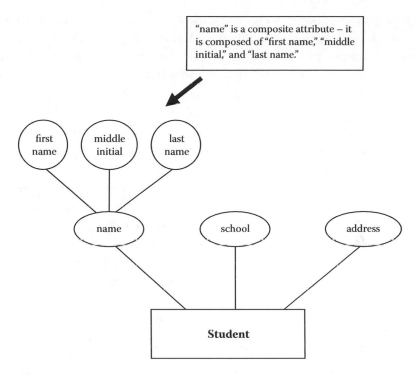

FIGURE 4.4
STUDENT entity with a composite attribute: name.

address attribute into street address, city, state, and zip code, making the address attribute a composite attribute.

4.5.3 The Multivalued Attribute

Another type of nonsimple attribute that has to be managed is called a *multivalued* attribute. The multivalued attribute, as the name implies, may take on more than one value for a given occurrence of an entity. For example, the attribute school could easily be multivalued if a person attends (or has attended, depending on the context of the database) more than one school. As a counter example, most people go by only one name; hence, the grouping name is not multivalued. The multivalued attribute called school is depicted in Figure 4.5 (Chen-like model) as a double oval, which illustrates the situation for which a database will store data about students who may have attended more than one school. Although we have chosen to illustrate school as a multivalued attribute, we do not mean to imply that this will always be the case in all databases. In fact, the attribute school may well be single valued in some databases. The idea of school may mean the current (or just previous) school as opposed to all schools attended. If the subjects about whom we are storing data can attend only one school at a time (and that is what we want to depict), then the attribute school may well be a single-valued attribute.

Again, the test of single versus multivalued will depend entirely on the circumstances that the database designer encounters—the desire of the user of the to-be-built database. It is recommended that if the sense of the database is that the attribute school means "current school," then the attribute should be called "current school" and illustrated as a single-valued attribute. We show a multivalued attribute in Figure 4.5. This diagram implies that multiple schools may be recorded for each student.

4.5.4 The Derived Attribute

Derived attributes are attributes that the user may envision but may not be recorded per se. These derived attributes may be calculated from other data in the database. An example of a derived attribute would be an age, which could be calculated once a student's birth date is entered. In the Chen-like model, a derived attribute is shown in a dashed oval (as shown in Figure 4.5b).

4.5.5 Keys

A database is used to store data for retrieval. An attribute that may be used to find a particular entity occurrence is called a *key*. As we model our database with the ER models, we may find that some attributes naturally seem to be keys. If an attribute may be thought of as a unique identifier for an entity, it is called a *candidate key*. When a candidate key is chosen to be *the* unique identifier, it becomes the *primary key* for the entity.

As an example of keys, suppose we add an attribute called student_number to our STUDENT entity example. We might well consider a student_number to be a unique identifier for the entity—a candidate key because of uniqueness. Name is often unique, but not necessarily so. Members of the same class often share last names. Address may or may not be a unique

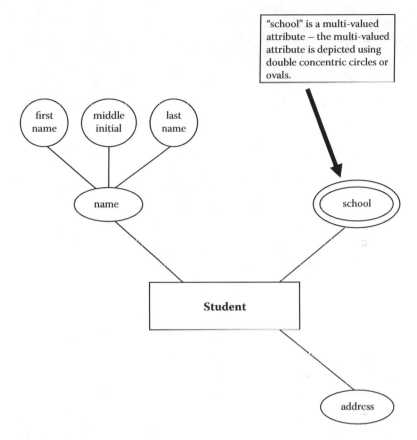

"school" is a multi-valued attribute – the multi-valued attribute is depicted using double concentric circles or ovals.

FIGURE 4.5
(a) STUDENT entity with a multivalued attribute.

identifier and hence is not a likely candidate key. Siblings who take classes together could easily have the same address. The point is that schools often choose to assign a unique student number to each student to be able to find student records—the idea of a key is to provide a unique way to find an entity instance (a particular record).

Some schools also choose to record a Social Security number (SSN) as an attribute. A SSN is also unique and hence a candidate key along with student_number. If both SSN and student_number were recorded, then the designer would have to choose which candidate key would be the primary key. In our case, we choose not to record a SSN. The STUDENT entity with the unique identifier student_number, added as a *key*, is depicted in Figure 4.6.

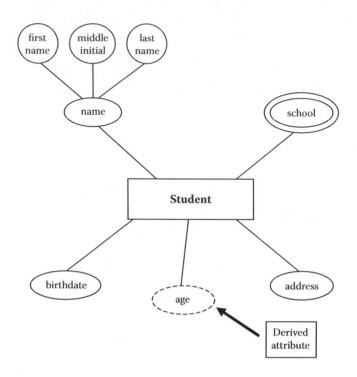

FIGURE 4.5
(b) STUDENT entity with a derived attribute: age.

In the Chen-like ER model, attributes, which are **unique identifiers** (candidate keys), are usually underlined (as shown in Figure 4.6). A unique identifier may be an attribute or a combination of attributes. It is not necessary to choose which candidate key will be the primary key at this point, but one could do so. When there is only one candidate key, we will generally speak of it as the primary key simply because it is obvious that the primary key is a candidate key. In Figure 4.6, we also depict the short form of the ER diagram (at the bottom of the figure) with composite attributes and multivalued attributes as well as primary keys. The composite attributes are listed with its component parts, and the multivalued attributes are enclosed in parentheses in the abbreviated form.

Finally, while on the subject of keys, we will have situations in the ER diagram (in the Chen-like model) for which no key is obvious or intended. Entities that have at least one identified key are called **strong** entities. In Chen's (1976) original article, strong entities were called **regular** entities. Some entities will be discovered that depend on other entities for their being

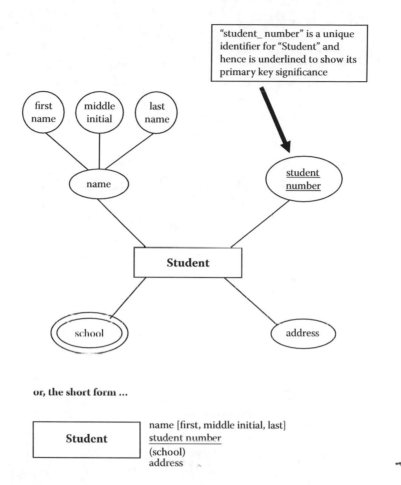

"student_ number" is a unique identifier for "Student" and hence is underlined to show its primary key significance

FIGURE 4.6
STUDENT entity with a primary key or unique identifier attribute.

(and hence their identification). Chen called those entities that rely on other entities for their existence *weak* entities.

We often are able to recognize these weak entities because they may not have candidate keys, although the actual meaning of a weak entity is "one that depends on another for existence." As Chen did, we follow the Chen-like ER notation and call such entities weak entities—weak because they will have to depend on some other entity to furnish a unique identifier to give the entity a reason to be recorded.

Although a weak entity may have a candidate key, it would not be a strong entity. We depict weak entities in the Chen-like ER diagrams with double boxes (see Figure 4.7). For now, we concentrate on those entities

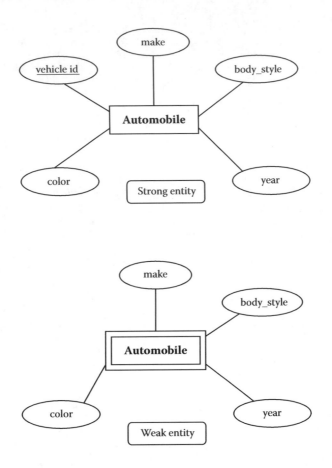

FIGURE 4.7
A strong and a weak AUTOMOBILE entity.

that have keys, the strong entities, and we will reconsider situations for which no key is obvious, the weak entities, later.

CHECKPOINT 4.2

1. Describe the basic types of data representation schemas used in ER modeling.
2. What notation is used to diagrammatically show an entity in the Chen-like ER model?
3. How do we diagrammatically show attributes in the Chen-like ER model?
4. How do we show composite attributes in the Chen-like ER model?
5. Draw an entity representation for the entity "building," with the following attributes: building name, occupancy, and whether or not it has an elevator (yes/no).

6. Embellish the building entity to include the building superinten-dent's name (first, middle, and last). Does this have to be a composite attribute? Why or why not?
7. Embellish the building entity to include the address of the building, which will be the primary key.
8. Again, embellish the building entity to include names (and only the names) of the janitorial staff.
9. Add a multivalued attribute to the building entity.
10. How many attributes can an entity have?

4.6 ENGLISH DESCRIPTION OF THE ENTITY

Now that we have an entity with attributes, we want to prepare the first feed-back to the user: the English description. Users will not likely want to study the entity diagram, but they might want to hear what you, the analyst, think you heard. For an English description, we use a "structured" English gram-mar and substitute the appropriate information from the entity diagram.

4.6.1 The Method

The template for the structured English for single entities is as follows: Let *Entity* be the name of the entity and *att(j)* be the attributes. The order of the attributes is not important, so $j = 1, 2, \ldots$ is assigned arbitrarily. Suppose that there are *n* attributes so far. The generalized English equiva-lent of our diagram is presented next.

4.6.1.1 The Entity

This database records data about *Entity*. For each *Entity* in the data-base, we record *att(1), att(2), att(3), … att(n)*.

4.6.1.2 The Attributes

For *atomic* attributes, *att(j)*:

For each *Entity*, there always will be one and only one *att(j)*. The value for *att(j)* will not be subdivided.

For *composite* attributes, *att(j)*:

For each *Entity*, we will record *att(j)*, which is composed of *x, y, z, …* (*x, y, z*) are the component parts of *att(j)*.

For *multivalued* attributes, *att(j)*:

> **For each *Entity*, we will record *att(j)*'s. There may be more than one *att(j)* recorded for each *Entity*.**

For *derived* attributes, *att(j)*:

> **For each *Entity*, there may exist *att(j)*'s, which will be derived from the database.**

4.6.1.3 The Keys

For the key(s):

(a) more than one candidate key (strong entity):

> **For each *Entity*, we will have the following candidate keys: *att(j)*, *att(k)*, ... (where *j*, *k* are candidate key attributes).**

(b) one candidate key (strong entity):

> **For each *Entity*, we will have the following primary key: *att(j)*.**

(c) no candidate keys (weak entity):

> **For each *Entity*, we do not assume that any attribute will be unique enough to identify individual entities without the accompanying reference to *Entity1* (i.e., some other entity), the owner Entity.**[*]

(d) no candidate keys (intersecting entity): This is discussed next.

4.6.2 ER Design Methodology

> **Step 2. Use structured English for entities, attributes, and keys to describe the database that has been elicited.**
> **Step 3. Show some sample data.**

Sample data also helps describe the database as it is perceived.

4.6.3 Examples

We now revisit each of our figures and add an English description to each.

4.6.3.1 Figure 4.3 Example

First, reconsider Figure 4.3. There are no multivalued or composite attributes. *Entity* = STUDENT, *att(1)* = name, *att(2)* = school, and so on (*j*

---

[*] The details of the weak entity/strong entity relationship will become clearer as we introduce relationships in Chapter 5.

assigned arbitrarily). The English "translation" of the entity diagram using the templates is discussed next.

4.6.3.1.1 The Entity

This database records data about STUDENTs. For each STUDENT in the database, we record a name, a school, an address, a phone number, and a major.

4.6.3.1.2 The Attributes

For each STUDENT, there will be one and only one name. The value for name will not be subdivided (note that in Figure 4.3 we did not divide name).

For each STUDENT, there will be one and only one major. The value for major will not be subdivided.

For each STUDENT, there will be one and only one address. The value for address will not be subdivided.

For each STUDENT, there will be one and only one school. The value for school will not be subdivided.

For each STUDENT, there will be one and only one phone. The value for phone will not be subdivided.

4.6.3.1.3 The Keys

For each STUDENT, we do not assume that any attribute will be unique enough to identify individual entities. (Remember that we are describing Figure 4.3.)

4.6.3.1.4 Sample Data

In addition to these descriptions, some sample data is often helpful in showing the user what you have proposed. Sample data for Figure 4.3 are as follows:

STUDENT

name	major	address	school	phone number
Smith	Cosc	123 4th St	St. Helens	222-2222
Jones	Acct	222 2nd St	PS 123	333-3333
Saha	Eng	284 3rd St	Canton	345-3546
Kapoor	Math	20 Living Cr	High	435-4534

4.6.3.2 Figure 4.4 Example

Now, consider Figure 4.4. This figure has a composite attribute, name. The English translation of this entity diagram would be as given next.

4.6.3.2.1 The Entity

This database records data about STUDENTs. For each STUDENT in the database, we record a name, a school, and an address.

4.6.3.2.2 The Attributes

For each STUDENT, there will be one and only one name. The value for name will be subdivided into first name, last name, and middle initial.

For each STUDENT, there will be one and only one address. The value for address will not be subdivided.

For each STUDENT, there will be one and only one school. The value of the school will not be subdivided.

4.6.3.2.3 The Keys

For each STUDENT, we do not assume that any attribute will be unique enough to identify individual entities.

4.6.3.2.4 Sample Data

STUDENT

name.first	name.last	name.mi	school	address
Richard	Earp	W	U. Alabama	222 2nd St
Boris	Backer		Heidleburg	333 Dreistrasse
Helga	Hogan	H	U. Hoover	88 Half Moon Ave
Arpan	Bagui	K	Northern School	33 Bloom Ave
Hema	Malini		South Bend	100 Livingstone

4.6.3.3 Figure 4.5a Example

Next consider Figure 4.5a. This figure has a composite as well as a multivalued attribute. The English translation of this entity diagram is given next.

4.6.3.3.1 The Entity

For the entity, this database records data about STUDENTs. For each STUDENT in the database, we record a name, schools, and an address.

4.6.3.3.2 The Attributes

For each STUDENT, there will be one and only one name. The value for name will be subdivided into first name, last name, and middle initial.

For each STUDENT, there will be one and only one address. The value for address will not be subdivided.

For each STUDENT, we will record schools. There may be more than one school recorded for each student.

4.6.3.3.3 The Keys

For each STUDENT, we do not assume that any attribute will be unique enough to identify individual entities.

4.6.3.3.4 Sample Data

STUDENT

name.first	name.last	name.mi	school	address
Richard	Earp	W	U. Alabama, Mountain	222 2nd St
Boris	Backer		Heidleburg, Volcano	333 Dreistrasse
Helga	Hogan	H	U. Hoover, St. Helens	88 Half Moon Ave
Arpan	Bagui	K	Northern School	33 Bloom Ave
Hema	Malini		South Bend	100 Livingstone

4.6.3.4 Figure 4.6 Example

Consider Figure 4.6. This figure has composite, multivalued, and key attributes. The English translation of this entity diagram is as follows.

4.6.3.4.1 The Entity

This database records data about STUDENTs. For each STUDENT in the database, we record a name, schools, an address, and a student_number.

4.6.3.4.2 The Attributes

For each STUDENT, there will be one and only one name. The value for name will be subdivided into first name, last name, and middle initial.

For each STUDENT, there will be one and only one address. The value for address will not be subdivided.

For each STUDENT, we will record schools. There may be more than one school recorded for each student.

4.6.3.4.3 The Keys

For each STUDENT, there is an attribute—student_number—that will be unique enough to identify individual entities.

4.6.3.5 Figure 4.7 Example

Finally, consider Figure 4.7 (top figure). This figure shows a strong entity. We combine the grammar a little to keep the methodology from being overly repetitive. The English translation of this entity diagram follows.

4.6.3.5.1 The Entity

This database records data about AUTOMOBILEs. For each AUTOMOBILE in the database, we record a make, body_style, year, color, and vehicle_id.

4.6.3.5.2 The Attributes

Each AUTOMOBILE will have one and only one make, body_style, year, color, and vehicle_id. None of these attributes will be subdivided.

4.6.3.5.3 The Keys

For each AUTOMOBILE, the attribute, vehicle_id, will be unique enough to identify individual entities.

The bottom of Figure 4.7 shows a weak entity. The only difference between the strong and weak entity description involves the key phrase, which may not exist in the weak entity.

Before leaving this introductory chapter on ER diagrams, we show the other major component of ER diagrams. Figure 4.8 shows a *relationship* between two entities, an AUTOMOBILE and a STUDENT. The concept of relationships is discussed elaborately in Chapter 6. A relationship adds action to the diagram. For example, the relationship in Figure 4.8 might be that STUDENTs *drive* AUTOMOBILEs.

Our ER design methodology has evolved to the following so far:

> **Step 1. Select one primary entity from the database requirements description and show attributes to be recorded for that entity. Label keys if appropriate.**
> **Step 2. Use structured English for entities, attributes, and keys to describe the database that has been elicited.**
> **Step 3. Show some sample data.**

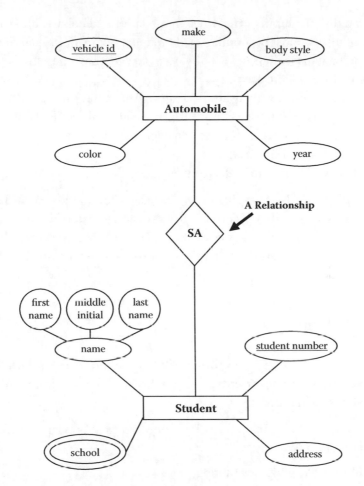

FIGURE 4.8
An ER diagram of a STUDENT-AUTOMOBILE database.

4.7 MAPPING THE ENTITY DIAGRAM TO A RELATIONAL DATABASE

Having illustrated the idea of the entity and the attribute, we now turn to a semiphysical realization of the concepts. We say *semiphysical* because we are really not concerned with the actual physical file that is stored in memory; rather, we are concerned with placing data into relational tables that we will visualize as a physical organization of data. Basically, a relational database is a database of two-dimensional tables called *relations*. The tables are composed of rows and columns. The rows are often called *tuples* and the columns *attributes*. In a relational database, all attributes (table columns) must be atomic, and keys must not be null. In addition, in relational databases, it is not usually necessary to know the actual physical location of the data in memory.

The process of converting an ER diagram into a database is called *mapping*. We concern ourselves only with the relational model; hence, as the chapters in this book develop, we consider mapping rules to map ER diagrams to relational databases.

We start with a rule to map strong entities.

> *Mapping rule 1—Mapping strong entities.* **Develop a new table (relation) for each strong entity and make the indicated key of the strong entity the primary key of the table. If more than one candidate key is indicated on the ER diagram, choose one for the primary key.**

Next, we have to map the attributes into the strong entity. Mapping rules are different for atomic attributes, composite attributes, and multi-valued attributes. First, we present the mapping rule for mapping atomic attributes.

> *Mapping rule 2—Mapping atomic attributes.* **For entities with atomic attributes, map the entities to a table and form columns for each atomic attribute.***

In discussing relational tables, it is common to abbreviate the diagram with a notation like this:

TABLENAME(attribute1, attribute2, ...)

A relational database realization of the entity diagram in Figure 4.3 would look like

STUDENT(name, phone, school, address, major)

And with some sample data:

STUDENT

name	phone	school	address	major
Jones	932-5100	U. Alabama	123 4th St	Chemistry
Smith	932-5101	U. Mississippi	123 5th St	Math

---

* These mapping rules are adapted from Elmasri and Navathe (2007).

Adams	932-5102	LSU	123 6th St	Agriculture
Sumon	435-0997	UWF	11000 Univ	Comp Sc
Mala	877-0982	Mount Union U	Alliance	History

The entity name **STUDENT** would be the name of the relation (table). The attributes in the entity diagram become the column headings. The actual table with data, a realization of a relation, is provided as an example of the type of data you might expect from such a relation. The ordering of the columns is irrelevant to the relational database as long as once the ordering is chosen, we stay with it. Recall that the point of this example is for you, the database analyst, to communicate to the user what you think the database should look like.

What about the composite and multivalued attributes? As we mentioned, it is an axiom of the relational database that all columns be atomic. If we have a nonatomic attribute on our diagram, we have to make it atomic for the mapping to the relational database. For composite attributes, we achieve atomicity by recording only the component parts of the attribute. Our next mapping rule maps composite attributes.

Mapping rule 3—Mapping composite attributes. **For entities with composite attributes, map entities to a table and form columns of each elementary (atomic) part of the composite attributes.**

Refer to Figure 4.4. A relational database, which corresponds to the entity diagram in Figure 4.4, would be

STUDENT(name.first, name.last, name.mi, school, address)

In this shorthand notation of a relational database, the composite attribute (name) is often included with a dot notation (e.g., name.first).

With some sample data,

STUDENT

name.first	name.last	name.mi	school	address
Richard	Earp	W	U. Alabama	222 2nd St
Boris	Backer		Heidleburg	333 Dreistrasse
Helga	Hogan	H	U. Hoover	88 Half Moon Ave

Arpan	Bagui	K	Cambridge	33 Bloom Ave
Hema	Malini		Fashion U	100 Livingstone

A multivalued attribute is depicted in Figure 4.5a. In this entity diagram, the STUDENT entity has a composite name attribute and a multivalued school attribute. This means that a student may have more than one school recorded for his or her row. Data, which would be represented by this diagram, might look like this:

STUDENT

name.first	name.last	name.mi	address	school
Richard	Earp	W	222 2nd St	U. Alabama, St Helens, Mountain, Volcano
Boris	Backer		333 Dreistrasse	Heidleburg, Manatee U. UCF, UWF
Helga	Hogan	H	88 Half Moon Ave	U. Hoover, Mount Union U, Manatee U
Arpan	Bagui	K	33 Bloom Ave	Cambridge, USF, Harvard
Hema	Malini		100 Livingstone	Fashion U, Milan U

Note that this is not considered a relational table because the school attribute is not atomic. To be a relational table, every attribute has to be atomic. To map this multivalued attribute atomically, we follow the following mapping rule:

> *Mapping rule 4—Mapping multivalued attributes.* **Form a separate table for the multivalued attribute. Record a row for each value of the multivalued attribute together with the key from the original table. The key of the new table will be the concatenation of the multivalued attribute plus the key of the owner entity. Remove the multivalued attribute from the original table.**

As per mapping rule 4, we require a key to map multivalued attributes; hence, we use Figure 4.6 to correctly map the multivalued attribute. Figure 4.6 would be mapped into the following two relations:

STUDENT(student_number, name.first, name.last, name.mi, address)

and

STUDENT_SCHOOL(student_number, school)

Some sample data would be

STUDENT

student_number	name.first	name.last	name.mi	address
111-11-2222	Richard	Earp	W	222 2nd St
222-11 2222	Boris	Backer		333 Dreistrasse
234-45-4567	Helga	Hogan	H	88 Half Moon Ave
888-77-9990	Arpan	Bagui	K	33 Bloom Ave
123-45-4321	Hema	Malini		100 Livingstone

STUDENT_SCHOOL

student_number	school
111-11-2222	U. Alabama
111-11-2222	St. Helens
111-11-2222	Mountain
111-11-2222	Volcano
222-11-2222	Heidleburg
222-11-2222	Manatee U
222-11-2222	UCF
222-11-2222	UWF
234-45-4567	U. Hoover
234-45-4567	Mount Union U
234-45-4567	Manatee U
888-77-9990	Cambridge
888-77-9990	USF
888-77-9990	Harvard
123-45-4321	Fashion U
123-45-4321	Milan U

In relational databases, every row of a table contains atomic attributes, and every row is unique. Therefore, a candidate key in any table is always *all* of the attributes. Usually, a subset of "all of the attributes" can be found to be a key, but since no two rows are ever the same, it is always true that one candidate key is the collection of all attributes.

> **CHECKPOINT 4.3**
>
> 1. How do you map multivalued attributes?
> 2. How do you map composite attributes?
> 3. What is a unique identifier? Is it a candidate key? Is it "the" primary key? Discuss.

4.8 CHAPTER SUMMARY

The main focus in this chapter was on developing the concept of the entity and developing a one-entity diagram using the Chen-like model. The concept of attributes was also discussed, and the last section focused on how a one-entity diagram could be mapped to a relational database. The grammar for a one-entity diagram and its attributes was also developed. This grammar is further developed in the following chapters. The next chapter discusses developing a second entity and the relationship between this second entity and the primary entity.

CHAPTER 4 EXERCISES

Note: The user should clarify the assumptions made when reporting the work.

Exercise 4.1

You want to create a database about businesses. Each business will have a name, address, the business phone number, the owner's phone number, and the first names of the employees who work at the business. Draw the ER diagram using the Chen-like model and then write the English description for your diagrams. Compare the English to your diagrams and state any assumptions you made when drawing the diagrams. Map your diagrams to a relational database.

Which attributes would you consider composite attributes in this database? Which attributes would you consider multivalued attributes in this database? Could there be any derived attributes? What would be good keys?

Exercise 4.2

You want to create a database about the books on your shelf. Each book has authors (assume that only the last name is needed), title, publisher, courses used in (course number only). Draw the ER diagram using the Chen-like model, and then write the English description for your diagrams. Compare the English to your diagrams and state any assumptions you made when drawing the diagrams.

Which attributes would you consider composite attributes in this database? Which attributes would you consider multivalued attributes in this database? Could there be any derived attributes? What would be good keys? Map your diagram to a relational database.

BIBLIOGRAPHY

Batini, C., Ceri, S., and Navathe, S. B. 1992. *Conceptual Database Design*. Redwood City, CA: Benjamin Cummings.

Chen, P. P. 1976. The entity relationship model—toward a unified view of data. *ACM Transactions on Database Systems*, 1(1):9–37

Chen, P. P. 1977. The entity-relationship model: a basis for the enterprise view of data. *Proceedings IFIPS NCC*, 46:76–84.

Codd, E. 1990. *Relational Model for Data Management—Version 2*. Reading, MA: Addison-Wesley.

Date, C. J. 1995. *An Introduction to Database Systems*, 6th ed., Reading, MA: Addison-Wesley.

Date, C. J. 2003. *An Introduction to Database Systems*. Reading, MA: Addison-Wesley.

Earp, R., and Bagui, S. 2000. Building an entity relationship diagram: a software engineering approach. *Database Management Journal*, 22–10 41:1–16.

Elmasri, R., and Navathe, S. B. 2007. *Fundamentals of Database Systems*. Reading, MA: Addison-Wesley.

Jeffry, A., Hoffer, V., and Heikki, T. 2011. *Modern Database Management*. Upper Saddle River, NJ: Prentice Hall.

Navathe, S., and Cheng, A. 1983. A methodology for database schema mapping from extended entity relationship models into the hierarchical model. In *The Entity-Relationship Approach to Software Engineering*, G. C. Davis et al. (editors). Amsterdam: Elsevier, North-Holland, 223–248.

Scheuermann, P., Scheffner, G., and Weber, H. 1980. Abstraction capabilities and invariant properties modeling within the entity-relationship approach. In *Entity-Relationship Approach to System Analysis and Design*, P. Chen (editor). Amsterdam: Elsevier, North-Holland, pp. 121–140.

Teorey, T. J., Yang, D., and Fry, J. P. 1986. A logical design methodology for relational databases using the extended entity-relationship model. *ACM Computing Surveys*, 18(2):197–222.

Valacich, J. S., George, J. F., and Hoffer, J. A. 2009. *Essentials of Systems Analysis and Design*. Upper Saddle River, NJ: Prentice Hall.

CASE STUDY

West Florida Mall

A new mall, West Florida Mall, just had its grand opening 3 weeks ago in Pensacola, Florida. This new mall is attracting a lot of customers and stores. West Florida Mall, which is part of a series of malls owned by a parent company, now needs a database to keep track of the management of the mall in terms of all its stores as well as the owners and workers of the stores. Before we build a database for this system of malls, the first step will be to design an ER diagram for the mall owner. We gathered the following initial user specifications about the mall, with which we can start creating the ER diagram:

1. We need to record information about the mall and each store in the mall. We need to record the mall's name and address. A mall, at any point in time, must contain one or more stores.
2. For each Store we will need to keep the following information: Store number (which will be unique), the name of the Store, location of store (Room number), departments, the owner of the store, and manager of the store. Each store may have more than one department, and each department is managed by a manager. Each store will have only one store manager. Each store is owned by only one owner. Each store is located in one and only one mall.
3. A Store manager can manage only one store. We have to record information on the store manager: the name, social security number, which store he or she is working for, and salary.
4. The store owner is a person. We have to record information about the store owner like name, address, and office phone number. A store owner has to own at least one store and may own more than one store.

DEVELOPING THE CASE STUDY

As per step 1 in designing the ER diagram, we have to select our primary entity and then the attributes for our primary entity (step 1 is shown next):

> ***Step 1. Select one primary entity from the database requirements description and show attributes to be recorded for that entity.***

We will choose MALL as our primary entity.

Our next step is to translate the diagram into English:

> ***Step 2. Use structured English for entities, attributes, and keys to describe the database that has been elicited.***

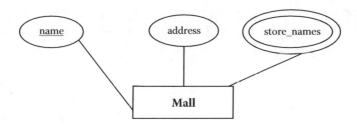

FIGURE 4.9
The MALL attribute.

The Entity

This database records data about a MALL.

For each MALL in the database, we record a name, an address, and store_names.

The Attributes for MALL

For each MALL, there will be one and only one name. The value for name will not be subdivided.

For each MALL, there will be one and only one address. The value for address will not be subdivided.

For each MALL, record store_names. There may be more than one store_name recorded for each MALL. The value of each store_name will not be subdivided.

The Keys

For each MALL, we assume that the mall name, name, will be unique.

The MALL entity is shown in Figure 4.9.

So far, for this case study, we selected one primary entity, MALL, showed its known attributes, and used structured English to describe the entity and its attributes. Next, we map this entity diagram to a relational database.

Mapping the Entity to a Relational Database

MALL is a strong entity, so we use mapping rule 1, which states

Develop a new table (relation) for each strong entity and make the indicated key of the strong entity the primary key of the table. If more than one candidate key is indicated on the ER diagram, choose one for the primary key.

We develop a new relation for the entity, MALL (as shown in Figure 4.9), and name will be our primary key. Data that would be represented by Figure 4.9 might look like this:

MALL

name	address	store_name
West Florida Mall	N Davis Hwy, Pensacola, FL	Penneys, Sears, Dollar Store, Rex
Cordova Mall	9th Avenue, Pensacola, FL	Dillards, Parisian, Circuit City
Navy Mall	Navy Blvd, Pensacola, FL	Belks, Wards, Pearl Vision
BelAir Mall	10th Avenue, Mobile, AL	Dillards, Sears, Penney's

We can see that MALL has a multivalued attribute, store_name. This does not make the table a relational table because store_name is not atomic; it is multivalued. For multivalued attributes, the mapping rule is

Form a separate table for the multivalued attribute. Record a row for each value of the multivalued attributes together with the key from the original table. The key of the new table will be the concatenation of the multivalued attribute plus the key of the owner entity. Remove the multivalued attribute from the original table.

Using this mapping rule, the data would be mapped to two relations:

MALL-STORE

name	store_name

MALL

name	address

and data would look like

MALL

name	address
West Florida Mall	N Davis Hwy, Pensacola, FL
Cordova Mall	9th Avenue, Pensacola, FL
Navy Mall	Navy Blvd, Pensacola, FL
BelAir Mall	10th Avenue, Mobile, AL

And the relation with the multivalued attribute:

MALL-STORE

name	store_name
West Florida Mall	Penny's
West Florida Mall	Sears
West Florida Mall	Dollar Store
West Florida Mall	Rex
Cordova Mall	Dillards
Cordova Mall	Parisian
Cordova Mall	Circuit City
Navy Mall	Belks
Navy Mall	Wards
Navy Mall	Pearl Vision
BelAir Mall	Dillards
BelAir Mall	Sears
BelAir Mall	Penney's

This case study is continued at the end of the next chapter.

5

Beyond the First Entity Diagram

5.1 INTRODUCTION

Now that we have devised a method for drawing, interpreting, and refining one primary entity, we need to move to databases that are more complex. To progress from here, we continue with our primary entity and look for other information that would be associated with (related to) that entity.

The first technique employed in this chapter is methodical: We test our primary entity to see whether our "attributes" ought to be entities themselves. We then look for other pieces of information in our description, add them to (a) an existing entity and examine the existing entity relationship (ER) diagram or (b) create a new entity directly. After creating the new entities, we look to see what kind of relationships exist between the two entities. This chapter develops steps 3 through 5 of the ER design methodology presented in this book. Step 3 examines the attributes of the primary entity, step 4 discusses what to do if another entity is needed, and step 5 discusses developing the relationship between the two entities.

Although the concept of relationships is introduced in this chapter, we do not include any new mapping rules in this chapter since mapping rules can be better understood after the development of structural constraints on relationships, which is discussed in Chapter 6. At the end of this chapter, we continue with the case study that was started in Chapter 4.

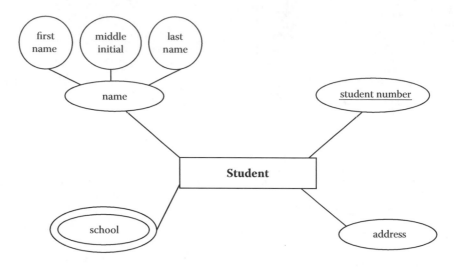

FIGURE 5.1
STUDENT entity with a multivalued attribute.

5.2 EXAMINING AN ENTITY: CHANGING AN ATTRIBUTE TO BE AN ENTITY

Consider Figure 5.1. In this figure, we have a student with the following attributes: name (a composite attribute), student_number (an atomic attribute and key), school (a multivalued attribute), and address (an atomic attribute). Suppose that during our first session with the user, we show the diagram, the English, and the sample data, and the user says, "Wait a minute. I want to record all schools that a student attended, and I want to record not only the name of the school, but also the location (city and state) and school type (community college, university, high school, etc.)."

What the user just told us was that the attribute school should really be an entity. Remember that the definition of an entity was something about which we wanted to record information. Our original thought was that we were recording schools attended, but now we are told that we want to record information about the schools. The first indicator that an attribute should be considered an entity is that we need to store information about the attribute. What we do then is to migrate from Figure 5.1 to Figure 5.2. In Figure 5.2, SCHOOL is now an entity by itself, so we have two separate entities, SCHOOL and STUDENT. We assume school_name to be unique and choose the school_name as the key for the entity SCHOOL.

The next step would be to define a relationship between the two entities.

5.3 DEFINING A RELATIONSHIP FOR OUR NEW ENTITY

Databases are designed to store *related* data. For example, it would ordinarily make no sense to record data about students and foreign currencies or about airline flights and employees at a tennis ball factory listed in the same database. These concepts are not related. In a database, we should be creating a collection of *related* data. Following our method, we clearly have a situation for which an attribute was part of an entity (school was considered "part of" student), but now school has become an entity by itself. What we have to do now is relate the SCHOOL entity to the STUDENT entity.

In Figure 5.2, we have two entities, but they appear as though they are independent. To make the SCHOOL entity and the STUDENT entity function as a database, we have to add something: the relationship that the entity SCHOOL has to the entity STUDENT.

A *relationship* in an ER diagram is a connection between two or more entities or between one entity and itself. The latter kind of relationship, between one entity and itself, is known as a *recursive relationship*, which we discuss in Chapter 8. A **relationship name** is usually a **verb** or **verb phrase** that denotes the connection between entities. Once we have understood how the relationship is denoted, we have a "tool" to draw a database description in the form of an ER diagram.

In the Chen-like model, a relationship is depicted by a diamond on the line that joins the two entities together, as shown in Figure 5.3.

In Figure 5.3, the relationship is depicted as attend. The sense of the relationship is that of a verb connecting two nouns (entities). All relationships are two-way. As we will see, it is necessary to state all relationships from both directions. For example, in the Chen-like model we would informally say, "A STUDENT attended a SCHOOL" or "STUDENTS attend SCHOOLS."

The degree of a relationship refers to the number of entities that participate in the relationship. In Figure 5.3, two entities are participating in the relationship attend, so this is called a binary relationship.

We now have a tool to draw a database description in the form of ER diagrams. In ER diagrams, we record information about *x* and *y* (*x* and *y* are entities) and then express the relationship of *x* to *y*.

Our growing and amended methodology is discussed next.

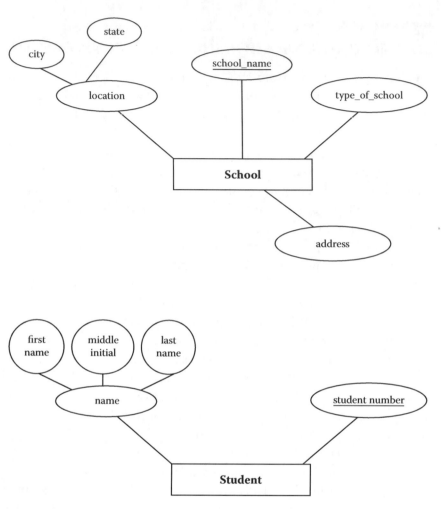

FIGURE 5.2
Two ER diagrams: one of STUDENT and one of SCHOOL.

5.3.1 ER Design Methodology

> *Step 1. Select one primary entity from the database requirements description and show the attributes to be recorded for that entity. Label keys if appropriate and show some sample data.*
>
> *Step 2. Use structured English for entities, attributes, and keys, to describe the database that has been elicited.*
>
> *Step 3. Examine attributes in the primary entity (possibly with user assistance) to find out if information about one of the attributes is to be recorded.*

Step 3a. If information about an attribute is needed, then make the attribute an entity, and then
Step 3b. Define the relationship back to the original entity.
Step 4. Show some sample data.

5.4 A PRELIMINARY GRAMMAR FOR ER DIAGRAMS

In Chapter 4, we outlined a grammar to describe an entity. Now that we have added a relationship to our diagram, we need to embellish our English description of the proposed database. We also want to show the user some sample data to solidify the understanding of the path we are taking. We want to add the following to our list of grammatical expressions:

For each relationship, we add the following comment (in loose English [for now]):

A(n) *Entity1 Relationship Entity2* **(active voice) and a(n)** *Entity2 Relationship Entity1* **(passive voice).**

A discussion of this follows.

5.4.1 The Relationship

A STUDENT attends a SCHOOL, and a SCHOOL is attended by a STUDENT.

The user may be the ultimate judge of the appropriateness of the expression we use, but we will add to this grammar soon. The user may prefer a different tense for the verb and may choose a verb that he or she thinks more appropriately assesses the situation. For example, the user may choose to portray the relationship as "STUDENTs *will matriculate* at SCHOOLs." As an exercise, you will be asked to provide a complete description of the ER diagram in Figure 5.3, with all entities, attributes, keys, and relationships.

5.5 DEFINING A SECOND ENTITY

Having examined the original primary entity for "suspicious" attributes, we may now begin to add more data. Let us presume the user wants to add information about automobiles that students own or drive. Ignoring

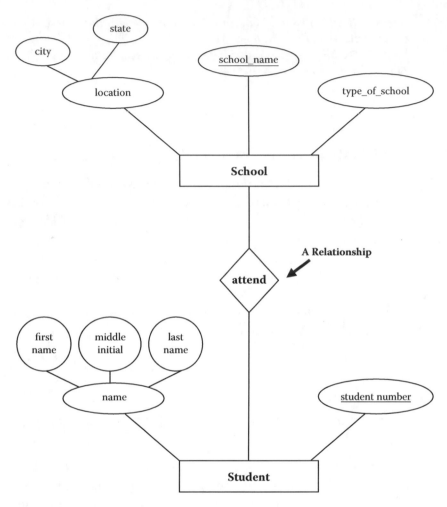

FIGURE 5.3
The STUDENT entity with a relationship to the SCHOOL entity.

the SCHOOL entity for the moment, let us suppose that this time we have developed the following additional description:

We want to record information about students—their name and student numbers. In addition to information about students, we want to record information about their automobiles. We want to record the vehicle identification number, the make of the car, body style, color, and the year of the model. Let us further suppose that we made the decision to choose STUDENT as the primary entity, and we want to add the automobile information.

The automobile is clearly an entity in that it is something about which we want to record information. If we add the automobile into the database, we could have included it in step 1 of our methodology by adding an attribute called automobile, only later to perform step 3 of the methodology and migrate automobile and school to the status of entities. The depiction of automobile as an attribute of the STUDENT entity is shown in Figure 5.4 (in the Chen-like model). (We ignore the SCHOOL entity for the moment.)

If we added the automobile attribute to the STUDENT entity and then recognized that automobile should have been an entity, we would then create the AUTOMOBILE entity and add the relationship to the model. (Note that Figure 5.4 would actually be sufficient if the user did not want to store information about the automobiles themselves.)

Of course, we could have recognized that the attribute automobile was going to be an entity all along and simply recorded it as such in our diagram in the first place. By recognizing AUTOMOBILE as an entity, we would draw the two entities STUDENT and AUTOMOBILE and then look for a relationship between the two. Either way, we would end up with Figure 5.5, with two entities, STUDENT and AUTOMOBILE, and some relationship between the two.

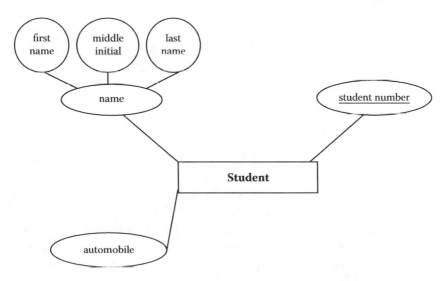

FIGURE 5.4
A STUDENT entity with an attribute called automobile.

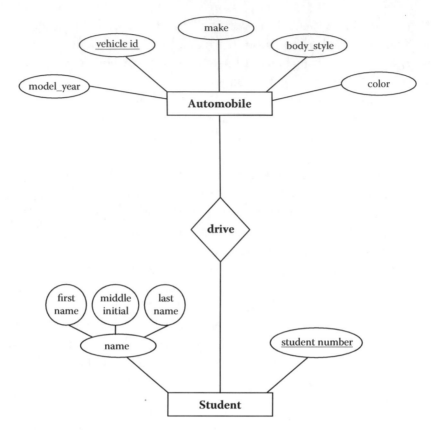

FIGURE 5.5
An ER diagram of the STUDENT-AUTOMOBILE database.

In the Chen-like notation, we now choose some verb to describe the relationship between the two entities (STUDENT and AUTOMOBILE); in this case, we choose **drive** (shown in the diamond in Figure 5.5). Note that later the user may choose to identify the relationship as something else, but with no other information, we *assume* the user means that, "A student **drives** an automobile." Other candidates for a relationship between the STUDENT and AUTOMOBILE entities might be "register," "own," and so on. A relationship between two entities is known as a *binary relationship*.

Relationships in ER diagrams are usually given names that depict how the entities are related. Sometimes, a relationship is difficult to describe (or is unknown); in this case, a two-letter code for the relationship is used. This two-letter relationship is shown in Figure 5.6, in which we have given the relationship the name *SA* to indicate that we understand that

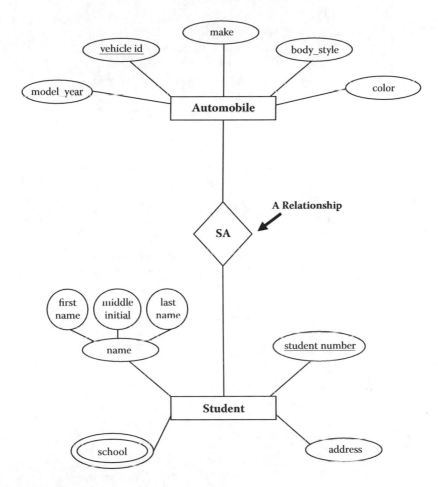

FIGURE 5.6

An ER diagram of the STUDENT-AUTOMOBILE database with an "unknown," "yet-to-be-determined" relationship.

a relationship exists, but we are not clear on exactly what to call it (SA = STUDENT- AUTOMOBILE). Of course, if we were confident of "drive" as the relationship, we would use drive.

The English description of the entities and relationships implies that entities are nouns (N) and relationships are verbs (V). Using the **drive** relationship (as shown in Figure 5.6), Students (N) drive (V) automobiles (N). If the "unknown" relationship is really unknown, we might say "Students (N) are related to (V) automobiles (N)" or "A student (N) is related to (V) an automobile (N)." In the next chapter, we develop this English description as well as the relationship part of the diagram more fully.

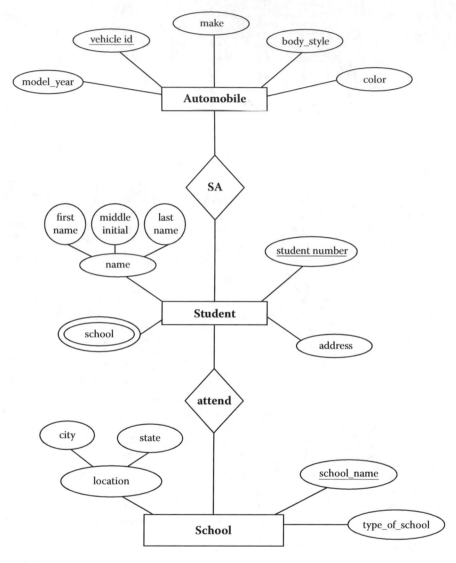

FIGURE 5.7
An ER diagram of the AUTOMOBILE-STUDENT-SCHOOL database.

At this point, we have introduced the STUDENT, AUTOMOBILE, and SCHOOL entities. With all three entities, the STUDENT-AUTOMOBILE-SCHOOL database would look like Figure 5.7.

CHECKPOINT 5.1

1. Can the nature of an entity change over time? Explain.
2. What is a relationship?

3. What are the differences between an entity and a relationship?
4. When would it be preferable to consider an attribute an entity? Why or why not?
5. Does it make sense to have an entity with one attribute?

5.6 DOES A RELATIONSHIP EXIST?

Some situations may unfold for which a relationship might be unclear. For example, consider this user description of a desired database:

Create a database for CUSTOMERS and SUPPLIERS. CUSTOMERS will have a name, address, phone number, and customer number. SUPPLIERS will have a supplier number, name, and address.

In this database, we clearly have two entities: CUSTOMER and SUPPLIER. We want to store information about customers (their name, address, ...) and suppliers (supplier number, name, ...). But, what is the connection between the two?

What we have here is an incomplete, vague user description from which to design our database. The connection for the company that wants the database is that they have both customers and suppliers; however, what they may not realize is that the relationship from CUSTOMER to SUPPLIER is via a COMPANY or a VENDOR, and not a direct relationship. So, what we have so far in this description is two different parts of a company database—one for customers and one for suppliers. If we later have some other entity like "inventory" or "vendor," which is related to customers *and* to suppliers, there may be linking entities and relationships. For now with just two unrelated ideas (customer and supplier), there is no apparent relationship, so the thing to do would be to leave any relationship off the overall diagram until more information is elicited from the user. It may even be that two unrelated databases need to be developed.

5.7 ATTRIBUTE OR RELATIONSHIP?

Sometimes, it may be unclear whether something is an attribute or a relationship. Both attributes and relationships express something about an entity. The attributes of an entity express qualities in terms of properties or characteristics. Relationships express associations with other entities.

Suppose we are constructing a library database. Suppose further that we create another primary entity, BOOK, which has an attribute borrower_ name. In some cases, an attribute construct is likely to be inappropriate for expressing an optional association that really ought to be a relationship between two entities. As a side issue, BORROWER would require the use of a null value for those BOOK entities that were not on loan. In reality, only a fraction of the books in a library is on loan at any given time. Thus, the "borrower" attribute would be null for some of the BOOK entities. This recurrence of many nulls might indicate that the attribute, borrower_ name, could be an attribute of an entity. If a BORROWER entity were created and the association between the entities BOOK and BORROWER was explicitly stated as a relationship, the database designer would likely be closer to putting attributes and entities in their correct places. It is important to understand the distinction between the types of information that can be expressed as attributes and those that should be treated as relationships and entities.

CHECKPOINT 5.2

1. Are relationships between two entities permanent, or can the nature of this relationship change over time?
2. Are attributes of an entity permanent?
3. Does there always exist a relationship between two entities?
4. What is a binary relationship?

Our ER elicitation and design methodology is described next.

5.7.1 ER Design Methodology

Step 1. Select one primary entity from the database requirements description and show attributes to be recorded for that entity. Label keys if appropriate and show some sample data.

Step 2. Use structured English for entities, attributes, and keys to describe the database that has been elicited.

Step 3. Examine attributes in the primary entity (possibly with user assistance) to find out if information about one of the attributes is to be recorded.

Step 3a. If information about an attribute is needed, then make the attribute an entity, and then

Step 3b. Define the relationship back to the original entity.

Step 4. *If another entity is appropriate, draw the second entity with its attributes. Repeat step 2 to see if this entity should be further split into more entities.*
Step 5. *Connect entities with relationships if relationships exist.*
Step 6. *Show some sample data.*

5.8 CHAPTER SUMMARY

Entities, attributes, and relationships were defined in Chapter 4. However, in real life, while trying to design databases, it is often difficult to determine whether something should be an attribute, entity, or relationship. This chapter discussed ways (techniques) to determine whether something should be an entity, attribute, or relationship.

This chapter also introduced the concept of binary relationships. Real-life databases will have more than one entity, so this chapter developed the ER diagram from a one-entity diagram to a two-entity diagram and showed how to determine and depict binary relationships between the two entities using the Chen-like model. Since the concept of relationships was only introduced and structural constraints of relationships have not yet been discussed (Chapter 6), we have not included mapping rules in this chapter.

CHAPTER 5 EXERCISES

Exercise 5.1

Draw an ER diagram (using the Chen-like model) for an entity called HOTEL and include no fewer than five attributes for the entity. Of the five attributes, include at least one composite attribute and one multivalued attribute.

Exercise 5.2

Suppose that we reconsider our STUDENT example, and the only attributes of student are student number and name. Let us suppose that we have another entity called HIGH SCHOOL that is going to be the high school from which the student graduated. For the HIGH SCHOOL entity, we will record the high school name and the location (meaning city and state). Draw the ER diagram using the concise form (as in Figure 4.1c).

What would you name the relationship here? Write out the grammar for the relationship between the two entities.

Exercise 5.3

Suppose that a college had one dormitory with many rooms. The DORMITORY entity, which is actually a "dormitory room" entity since there is only one dorm, has the attributes room number and single/double (meaning that there are private rooms and double rooms). Let us suppose that the STUDENT entity in this case contains the attributes student number, student name, and home telephone number. Draw the ER diagram in the Chen-like model linking the two entities. Name your relationships. Write the grammar for the relationship between the two entities.

Exercise 5.4

If we have two entities, a PLANE and a PILOT, and describe the relationship between the two entities as
   "A PILOT flies a PLANE."
What should the relationship read from the side of the other entity?

Exercise 5.5

Complete the methodology by adding sample data to Figures 5.3, 5.5, and Exercises 5.1, 5.2, 5.3, and 5.4.

BIBLIOGRAPHY

Elmasri, R., and Navathe, S. B, 2007. *Fundamentals of Database Systems*. Reading, MA: Addison-Wesley.

Hoffer, J., Ramesh, V., and Topi, H. 2011. *Modern Database Management*. Upper Saddle River, NJ: Prentice Hall.

CASE STUDY

West Florida Mall (continued)

In Chapter 4, we chose our primary entity, MALL, and used structured English to describe it, its attributes, and keys, and then we mapped MALL to a relational database (with some sample data). In this chapter, we continue to develop this case study by looking at steps 3, 4, and 5 of the ER design methodology.

Step 3 says:

> ***Step 3. Examine attributes in the primary entity (with user assistance) to find out if information about one of the attributes is to be recorded.***

On reexamining the attributes of the primary entity MALL, it appears that we need to store information about the attribute store. So, we look at step 3a, which says

> ***Step 3a. If information about an attribute is needed, then make the attribute an entity, and then proceed to step 3b.***

So, turning the attribute store into an entity, we have the following (repeating Step 2):

The Entity

This database records data about a STORE.

For each STORE in the database, we record a store name (sname), a store number (snum), a store location (sloc), and departments (dept).

The Attributes for STORE

For each STORE, there will be one and only one sname (store name). The value for sname will not be subdivided.

For each STORE, there will be one and only one snum (store number). The value for snum will be unique and will not be subdivided.

For each STORE, we will record a sloc (store location). There will be one sloc recorded for each STORE. The value for sloc will not be subdivided.

For each STORE, we will record dept (departments). There will be more than one dept recorded for each STORE. The value for dept will not be subdivided.

The Keys

For each STORE, we will assume that the snum will be unique.

Note: Once STORE is made into an entity, the attribute store is removed from the entity MALL, as shown in Figure 5.8.

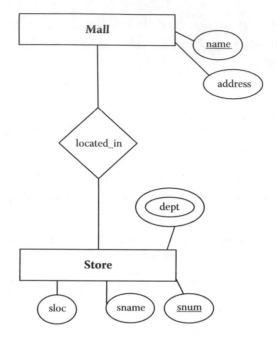

FIGURE 5.8
ER diagram of the mall database so far.

Having defined STORE, we now need to follow step 3b, which says

Step 3b. Define the relationship back to the original entity.

There is a relationship, located_in, between STORE and MALL. This is shown in Figure 5.8.

Next, step 4 says

> **Step 4. If another entity is appropriate, draw the second entity with its attributes. Repeat step 2 to see if this entity should be further split into more entities.**

We select another entity, STORE_MANAGER.
Now, repeating step 2 for STORE_MANAGER:

The Entity

This database records data about a STORE_MANAGER.

For each STORE_MANAGER in the database, we record a store manager name (sm_name), store manager Social Security number (sm_ssn), and store manager salary (sm_salary).

The Attributes for STORE_MANAGER

For each STORE_MANAGER, there will be one and only one sm_name (store manager name). The value for sm_name will not be subdivided.

For each STORE_MANAGER, there will be one and only one sm_ssn (store manager Social Security number). The value for sm_ssn will be unique and will not be subdivided.

For each STORE_MANAGER, we will record a sm_salary (store manager salary). There will be one and only one sm_salary recorded for each STORE_MANAGER. The value for sm_salary will not be subdivided.

The Keys

For each STORE_MANAGER, we will assume that the sm_ssn will be unique.

Having defined STORE_MANAGER, we now follow step 5, which says

Step 5. Connect entities with relationships if relationships exist.

There is a relationship, **manages**, between STORE and STORE_ MANAGER. This is shown in Figure 5.9.

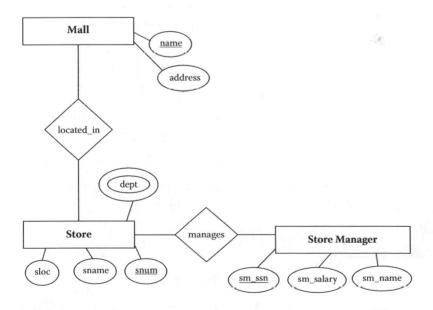

FIGURE 5.9

An ER diagram of West Florida Mall database developing.

Then, we select our next primary entity, OWNER.

Now, repeating step 2 for OWNER:

The Entity

This database records data about a OWNER.

> For each OWNER in the database, we record a store owner name (so_name), store owner Social Security number (so_ssn), store owner office phone (so_off_phone), and store owner address (so_address).

The Attributes for OWNER

> For each OWNER, there will be one and only one so_name (store owner name). The value for so_name will not be subdivided.
>
> For each OWNER, there will be one and only one so_ssn (store owner Social Security number). The value for so_ssn will be unique and will not be subdivided.
>
> For each OWNER, there will be one and only one so_off_phone (store owner office phone). The value for so_off_phone will be unique and will not be subdivided.
>
> For each OWNER, we will record a so_address (store owner address). There will be one and only one so_address recorded for each OWNER. The value for so_address will not be subdivided.

The Keys

> For each OWNER, we will assume that the so_ssn will be unique.

Having defined OWNER, we now follow step 5, which says:

> **Step 5. Connect entities with relationships if relationships exist.**

There is a relationship, owns, between STORE and OWNER. This is shown in Figure 5.10.

MAPPING TO A RELATIONAL DATABASE

Having described the entities, attributes, and keys, the next step would be to map to a relational database. We will also show some data for the entities

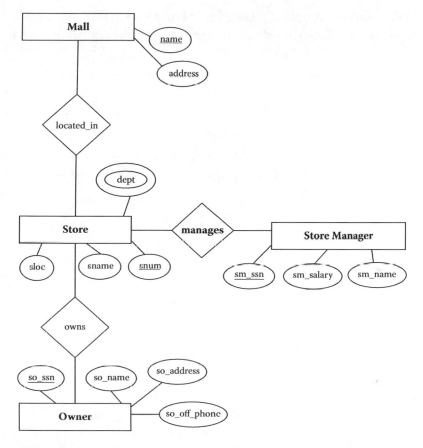

FIGURE 5.10
An ER diagram of West Florida Mall with four entities.

developed in this part of the case study (the mappings of the relationships are shown at the end of Chapter 6).

Relation for the MALL Entity

The relation for the **MALL** entity with some sample data is

MALL

name	address
West Florida Mall	N Davis Hwy, Pensacola, FL
Cordova Mall	9th Avenue, Pensacola, FL
Navy Mall	Navy Blvd, Pensacola, FL
BelAir Mall	10th Avenue, Mobile, AL

Note that we do not need the MALL-Store mapping that was presented in Chapter 4 since Store has changed from a multivalued attribute to an entity.

Relation for the STORE entity

The entity STORE has a multivalued attribute depts, so we again have to use mapping rule 4 to map this entity. First, we will show the relation with the multivalued attribute excised, and then we will show the relation with the multivalued attribute.

Relation with the Multivalued Attribute Excised (with some sample data)

STORE

sloc	sname	snum
Rm 101	Penneys	1
Rm 102	Sears	2
Rm 109	Dollar Store	3
Rm 110	Rex	4

Relation with the Multivalued Attribute (with some sample data)
Relation for the STORE MANAGER Entity (using Mapping Rule 1 and Mapping Rule 2) with some sample data

STORE-dept

snum	depts
1	Tall men's clothing
1	Women's clothing
1	Children's clothing
1	Men's clothing
.	
.	
.	
2	Men's clothing
2	Women's clothing
2	Children's clothing
.	
.	
.	

STORE MANAGER

sm_ssn	sm_name	sm_salary
234-987-0988	Saha	45,900
456-098-0987	Becker	43,989
928-982-9882	Ford	44,000
283-972-0927	Raja	38,988

Relation for the OWNER **Entity (using Mapping Rule 1 and Mapping Rule 2) with some sample data**

OWNER

so_ssn	so_namc	so_off_phone	so_address
879-987-0987	Earp	(850)474-2093	1195 Gulf Breeze Pkwy, Pensacola, FL
826-098-0877	Sardar	(850)474-9873	109 Navy Blvd, Pensacola, FL
928-088-7654	Bagui	(850)474-9382	89 Highland Heights, Tampa, FL
982-876-8766	Bush	(850)474-9283	987 Middle Tree, Mobile, AL

So far, our relational database has developed into (without the data) (note that the primary keys are underlined.)

MALL

name	address

STORE

sloc	sname	snum

STORE-dept

snum	depts

OWNER

so _ ssn	so _ name	so _ off _ phone	so _ address

STORE MANAGER

sm _ ssn	sm _ name	sm _ salary

This case study is continued at the end of the next chapter.

6

Extending Relationships/
Structural Constraints

6.1 INTRODUCTION

In Chapters 4 and 5, we introduced some components of entity relationship (ER) diagrams: entities, attributes, and relationships. It is really insufficient for requirement elicitation to define relationships without also defining what are called ***structural constraints***. Structural constraints are information about how two (or more) entities are related to one another. There are two types of structural constraints: ***cardinality*** and ***participation***.

In this chapter, in addition to the structural constraints of relationships, we want to introduce a grammar to describe what we have drawn. The grammar will help with the requirement elicitation process as we will specify a template for the English that can be imposed on a diagram, which will in turn make us say exactly what the diagram means. This chapter develops steps 6 and 7 of the ER design methodology. Step 6 states the nature of a relationship in English, and step 7 discusses presenting the database (designed so far) to the user.

Mapping rules for relationships are also developed and discussed with examples and sample data. At the end of the chapter, we continue the running case study that we began in Chapter 4 and continued in Chapter 5.

6.2 THE CARDINALITY RATIO OF A RELATIONSHIP

Cardinality is a rough measure of the number of entities (one or more) that will be related to another entity (or entities). For example, there are four ways in which the entities AUTOMOBILE and STUDENT can be

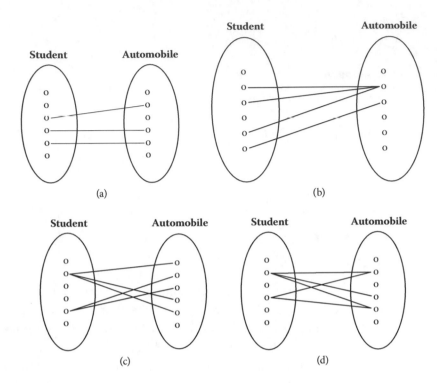

FIGURE 6.1

(a) One-to-one relationship STUDENT:AUTOMOBILE::1:1. (b) Many-to-one relationship STUDENT:AUTOMOBILE::M:1. (c) One-to-many relationship STUDENT:AUTOMOBILE::1:M. (d) Many-to-many relationship STUDENT:AUTOMOBILE::M:N.

"numerically involved" in a relationship: one to one (1:1), many to one (M:1), one to many (1:M), and many to many (M:N). The most common relationships are 1:M and M:N.

6.2.1 One to One (1:1)

In the one-to-one (1:1) type of relationship, one entity is associated with one other entity and vice versa. For example, if in our **drive** relationship (Figure 6.1), we stated that one automobile is driven by one student, and one student drives one automobile, then the student/automobile relationship would be one to one, symbolically:

STUDENT:AUTOMOBILE::1:1

Diagramatically we can represent a 1:1 relationship as shown in Figure 6.1a (Batani, Ceri, and Navathe, 1992).

6.2.2 Many to One (M:1)

If the **SA** (STUDENT:AUTOMOBILE) relationship (shown in Figure 5.6) were many to one, we would be saying that many students are associated with one automobile, and one automobile is associated with many students; that is,

STUDENT:AUTOMOBILE::M:1

We have intentionally used the verb phrase "is associated with" in place of **drive** here because the statement "many students drive one automobile" may be taken in a variety of ways. Also, using a specific verb for a relationship is not always best when the diagram is first drawn unless the analyst is absolutely sure that the verb correctly describes the user's intention. We could have also used the verb phrase "is related to" instead of "is associated with" if we wanted to be uncommitted about the exact verb to use.

We will tighten the language used to describe relationships, but what does a STUDENT:AUTOMOBILE::M:1 relationship imply? It would represent a situation in which perhaps a family owned one car, and that car was driven by multiple people in the family.

Diagrammatically, we can represent an M:1 relationship as shown in Figure 6.1b (Batani, Ceri, Navathe, 1992).

6.2.3 One to Many (1:M)

A one-to-many **SA** (STUDENT:AUTOMOBILE) relationship (shown in Figure 5.6) would imply that one student is associated with many automobiles, and an automobile is associated with one student. Clearly, if we define a relationship as 1:M (or M:1), then we need to be very clear about which entity is 1 and which is M. Here,

STUDENT:AUTOMOBILE::1:M

Diagrammatically, we can represent a 1:M relationship as shown in Figure 6.1c (Batani, Ceri, Navathe, 1992).

6.2.4 Many to Many (M:N)

In many-to-many relationships, many occurrences of one entity are associated with many occurrences of the other entity. Many to many is depicted as M:N as in M of one thing related to N of another thing. Older database texts called this an M:M relationship, but newer books use M:N to indicate that the number of things related is not presumed to be equal (the values of M and N are likely to be different).

If our **SA** relationship were many to many, a student would be associated with many automobiles and an automobile with many students:

STUDENT:AUTOMOBILE::M:N

In this case (if we assumed **SA** = **drive**, as shown in Figure 5.6), multiple students may drive multiple cars (it is hoped that not all drive at the same time), and multiple cars may be driven by multiple students. Or, a student may drive multiple cars, and a car may be driven by multiple students. Picture, for example, a family that has multiple cars, and any one family member may drive any of the cars and any car may be driven by any family member.

Diagrammatically, we can represent an M:N relationship as shown in Figure 6.1d (Batani, Ceri, and Navathe, 1992).

In expressing cardinality, this x:x ratio, where x = 1 or M or N, is called a *cardinality ratio*.

Which way do we depict the actual situation for our students and automobiles? This is an interesting question. The answer is that we are to model reality *as defined by our user*. We listen to the user, make some assumptions, and draw the model. We then pass our model back to the user by using structured English, which the user then approves or corrects.

A trap in ER design is to try to model every situation for every possibility. This cannot be done. The point of creating a database is normally a local situation that will be governed by the systems analysis (software engineering) process. In classical systems analysis, the analyst hears a user, creates a specification, and then presents the result back to the user. Here, the analyst (the database analyst/designer) models the reality that the user experiences—not what every database in the world should look like. If the user disagrees, then the analyst can easily modify the conceptual model, but there has to be a meeting of the minds on what the model is to depict.

In our STUDENT:AUTOMOBILE example, the choice we will make will be that one student is associated with (drives) one automobile. While clearly one can think of exceptions to this case, we are going to adopt a model, and the sense of the model is that we have to choose how we will identify the relationship between the entities as well as the information that we intend to put in the entities themselves. Bear in mind that we are dealing with a conceptual model that could change depending on the reality of the situation; however, we have to choose some sort of model to begin, and the one we are choosing is a one-to-one relationship between students and automobiles.

In the Chen-like model, we will depict the one-to-oneness of this relationship by adding the cardinality numbers to the lines on the ER diagram that connect the relationships and the entities (see Figure 6.2).

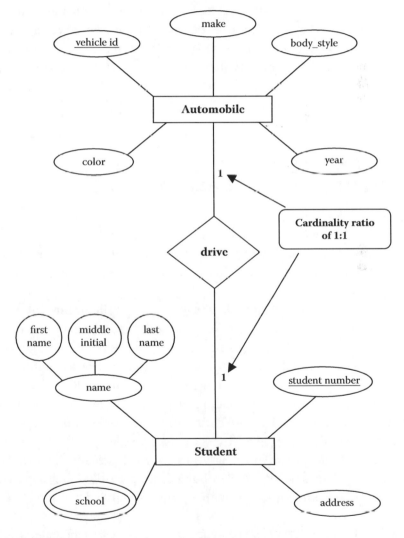

FIGURE 6.2

An ER diagram of a **STUDENT-AUTOMOBILE** database with a relationship named *drive* and cardinality ratios.

In Figure 6.2, we put a "1" on the line between the entity box for the STUDENT and the diamond box for the relationship, and we put another "1" on the line between the diamond relationship and the entity box for the AUTOMOBILE. These 1s loosely mean that a student is related to one automobile, and an automobile is related to one student. We must be quite careful in saying exactly what this relationship means. It does not mean that one student owns one automobile or a student pays insurance for an automobile. In our model, we mean that a student will drive at most one automobile on a college campus. Further, we are saying that an automobile will be driven by one and only one student. Since we are clarifying (refining) the database, we try to settle on the name of the relationship to include the concept that we are modeling—driving—by naming the relationship drive. Again, see Figure 6.2 for the renamed model with 1:1 cardinality.

6.3 PARTICIPATION: FULL/PARTIAL

It is likely that on any campus not all students will drive an automobile. For our model, we could assume that normally all of the automobiles on the campus are associated with a student. (We are for the moment excluding faculty and staff driving by only modeling the student/automobile relationship.)

To show that every automobile is driven by a student, but not every student drives an automobile, we enhance our Chen-like models of ER diagrams by putting a double line between the relationship diamond and the AUTOMOBILE entity to indicate that *every* automobile is driven by a student. Put another way, every automobile in the database participates in the relationship. From the student side, we leave the line between the STUDENT entity and the relationship as a single line to indicate that *not every* student drives an automobile. Some students will not participate in the drive relationship because they do not drive a car on campus. The single/double lines are called *participation constraints* (also known as optionality constraints) and are depicted in Figure 6.3.

The double line indicates *full* participation. Some designers prefer to call this participation *mandatory*. The point is that if part of a relationship is mandatory or full, you cannot have a null value (a missing value) for that

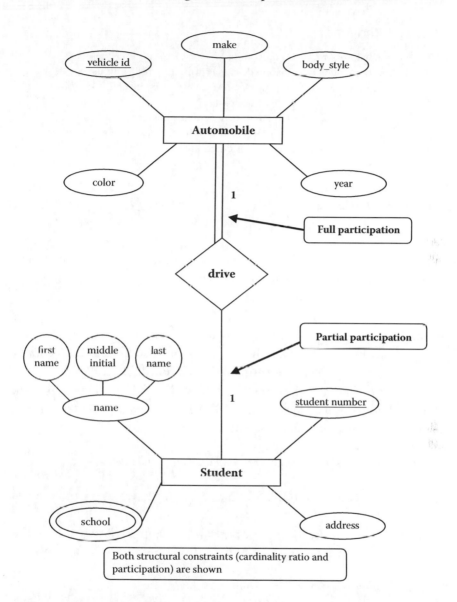

FIGURE 6.3
An ER diagram of the STUDENT-AUTOMOBILE database with the relationship named *drive*, cardinality ratios, and participation.

attribute in relationships. In our case, if an automobile is in the database, it has to be related to some student.

The single line, ***partial*** participation, is also called ***optional***. The sense of partial, optional participation is that there could be students who do not have a relationship to an automobile.

6.4 ENGLISH DESCRIPTIONS

We would now like to tighten the English grammar that describes how a relationship affects entities using our structural constraints and to adopt a standard way of stating the relationship. The standard language should appear on the model, or at least with it. Further, using a standard language approach to describe the ER diagrams allows us not only to close the loop with the user in the systems analysis process, but also to facilitate feedback and "nail down" the exact meaning of the relationship.

In the Chen-like model, the double lines define full participation as in, "Automobiles fully participate in the **drive** relationship." Better yet, the double lines invite us to state the relationship as

*Automobiles **must** be driven by one (and only one) student.*

The *must* part comes from the full (mandatory) participation and the *one* part from the cardinality.

The grammar for describing the partial or optional relationship for the STUDENT entity to the AUTOMOBILE entity, would be

*Students **may** drive one and only one automobile.*

The *may* comes from the single line leaving the STUDENT entity box and the *one and only one* part comes from the cardinality. The point is that when expressing the sense of the ER diagrams, one uses the language that conveys what the relationship really means (i.e., a student **may** drive one automobile, and an automobile **must** be driven by one and only one student). A graphic on how to read an ER diagram is presented in Figure 6.4.

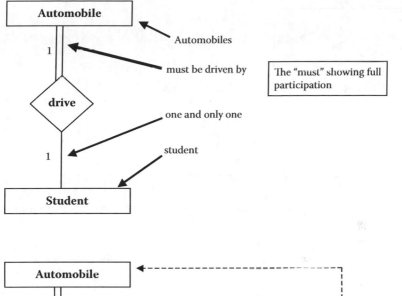

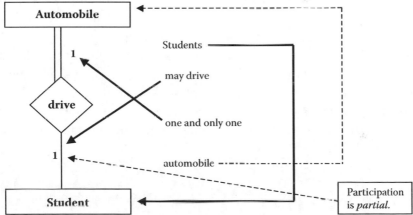

FIGURE 6.4
The STUDENT-AUTOMOBILE database: translating the diagram into English.

6.5 TIGHTER ENGLISH

We strongly recommend that an English sentence accompany each diagram to reinforce the meaning of the figure (refer to Figure 6.4). English is often an ambiguous language. The statement that

*Automobiles **must** be driven by one and only one student.*

actually means

> *Automobiles, which are in the database, **must** be driven by one and only one student.*

The relationship should not be stated loosely, as in

> *A student drives an automobile.*

This could be vaguely interpreted.
Another way to put this is

> *Every automobile **must** be driven by one and only one student. Students **may** drive one and only one automobile.*

To relieve ambiguity in the statement of the relationship, we will take the English statement from the relationship as we have illustrated and define four pattern possibilities for expressing our relationship. All binary relationships must be stated in two ways from both sides. As you will see, we try to stick to the exact pattern match in the following examples, but common sense and reasonable grammar should prevail when the pattern does not quite fit. There is nothing wrong with restating the precise language to make it clearer, but you have to say the same thing.

6.5.1 Pattern 1—x:y::k:1

From the k side, full participation (k = 1 or M): The **x**'s, which are recorded in the database, ***must*** be related to one and only one **y**. No **x** is related to more than one **y**.

Example 6.1   Student:Advisor::M:1, Full Participation

*Students **must** be advised by one advisor.*

or,

> *Students, which are recorded in the database, **must** be advised by one and only one advisor. No student is advised by more than one advisor.*

The phrase "which are recorded in the database" has proven to be helpful because some database designers tend to generalize beyond the problem at hand. For example, one could reasonably argue that there might be a case where thus-and-so are true/not true, but the point is, "Will that case ever be encountered in this particular database?" The negative statement is often helpful to solidify the meaning of the relationship.

6.5.2 Pattern 2—x:y::k:1

From the k side, partial participation (k = 1 or M): x, but not necessarily all **x** (which are recorded in the database) *may* be related to one and only one **y**. Some **x**'s are not related to a **y**. The **x**'s *may* not be related to more than one **y**.

Example 6.2   Student:Fraternity::M:1

Some students join a fraternity.
which becomes

Students, but not necessarily all students (which are recorded in the database), may join a fraternity. Some students may not join a fraternity. Students may not join more than one fraternity.

6.5.3 Pattern 3—x:y::k:M

From the k side, full participation (k = 1 or M): The **x**'s, which are recorded in the database, *must* be related to many (one or more) **y**'s. Sometimes, it is helpful to include a phrase like: "No **x** is related to a non-**y**" or "Non-**x** are not related to a **y**." The negative will depend on the sense of the statement.

Example 6.3   Automobile:Student::M:N

Automobiles are driven by (registered to) many students.

which means

Automobiles, which are recorded in our database, must be driven by many (one or more) students.

There are several ideas implied here. First, we are only talking about vehicles registered at this school. Second, in this database, only student cars are registered in this database. Third, if an automobile from this database is driven, it has to be registered and driven by a student (at least one). Fourth, the "one or more" comes from the cardinality constraint. Fifth, there is a strong temptation to say something about the **y**, the M side back to the **x**, but this should be avoided as this is covered elsewhere in another pattern and because we discourage inferring other relationships from the one covered. For example, one might try to say here that all students drive cars or all students are related to a vehicle … neither statement is true.

6.5.4 Pattern 4—x:y::k:M

From the k side, partial participation (k = 1 or M): x, but not necessarily all **x** (which are recorded in the database), *may* be related to many (zero or more) **y**'s. Some **x** may not be related to a **y**.

Example 6.4   Course:Book::k:M

*Some courses **may** require (use) many books.*

which restated becomes

*Courses, but not necessarily all courses (which are recorded in the database), **may** use many (zero or more) textbooks. Some courses **may** not require textbooks.*

Note that due to partial participation (the single lines), the phrase "zero or more" is used for cardinality. If a relationship is modeled with the patterns we have used and then the English sounds incorrect, it may be that the wrong model has been chosen. Generally, the grammatical expression will be most useful in (a) restating the designed database to a "naïve user" and (b) checking the meaning on the designed database among the designers. The complete version of the English may eventually prove tiresome to a database designer, but one should never lose track of the fact that a statement like "x are related to one y" can be interpreted in several ways unless it is nailed down with constraints stated in an unambiguous way. Furthermore, a negation statement may be useful to elicit requirement definitions, although at times the negation is so cumbersome it may be omitted. What we are saying is to add the negative or other noncontradictory grammar if it makes sense and helps with requirement elicitation. The danger in adding sentences is that we may end up with contradictory or confusing remarks.

6.5.5 Summary of the Patterns and Relationships

6.5.5.1 Pattern 1

The relationship is

x:y::1(full):1

and is diagramatically shown by Figure 6.5.

6.5.5.2 Pattern 1

The relationship is

x:y::M(full):1

and is diagramatically shown by Figure 6.6.

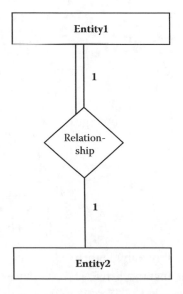

FIGURE 6.5
Chen model of 1(full):1 relationship: pattern 1.

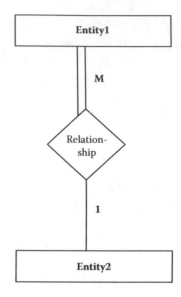

FIGURE 6.6
Chen model of M(full):1 relationship: pattern 1.

This pattern implies that an instance of **ENTITY1** must participate in a relationship with **ENTITY2** and can only exist for one (and only one) of **ENTITY2**.

6.5.5.3 *Pattern 2*

The relationship is

x:y::1(partial):1

and is diagramatically shown by Figure 6.7.

6.5.5.4 *Pattern 2*

The relationship is

x:y::M(partial):1

and is diagramatically shown by Figure 6.8.

In this pattern, some instances in **ENTITY1** may exist without a relationship to **ENTITY2**, but when **ENTITY1** is related to **ENTITY2**, it can only be related to one and only one of **ENTITY2**.

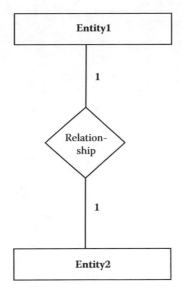

FIGURE 6.7
Chen model of 1(partial):1 relationship: pattern 2.

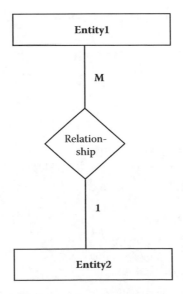

FIGURE 6.8
Chen model of M(partial):1 relationship: pattern 2.

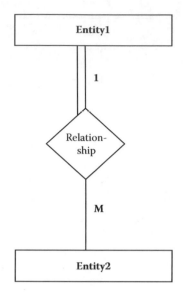

FIGURE 6.9
Chen model of 1(full):M relationship: pattern 3.

6.5.5.5 Pattern 3

The relationship is

x:y::1(full):M

and is diagramatically shown by Figure 6.9.

6.5.5.6 Pattern 3

The relationship is

x:y::M(full):N

and is diagramatically shown by Figure 6.10.

This pattern implies that an instance of **ENTITY1** must participate in a relationship with **ENTITY2** and can exist for more than one of **ENTITY2**.

6.5.5.7 Pattern 4

The relationship is

x:y::1(partial):M

and is diagramatically shown by Figure 6.11.

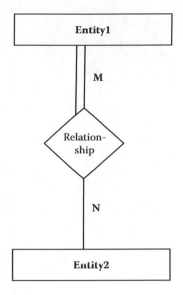

FIGURE 6.10
Chen model of M(full):N relationship: pattern 3.

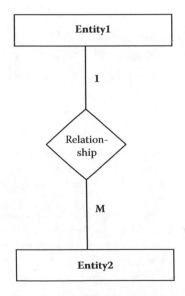

FIGURE 6.11
Chen model of 1(partial):M relationship: pattern 4.

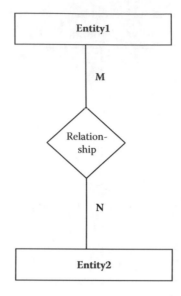

FIGURE 6.12
Chen model of M(partial):N relationship: pattern 4.

6.5.5.8 *Pattern 4*

The relationship is

x:y::M(partial):N

and is diagramatically shown by Figure 6.12.

In this pattern, some instances in **ENTITY1** may exist without a relationship to **ENTITY2**, but when **ENTITY1** is related to **ENTITY2**, it can be related to more than one of **ENTITY2**.

CHECKPOINT 6.2

1. Sketch an ER diagram that shows the participation ratios (full/partial) and cardinalities for the following:
   a. Students must be advised by one advisor, and an advisor can advise many students.
   b. Students, but not necessarily all students, may join a fraternity. Some students may not join a fraternity. Students may not join more than one fraternity. A fraternity may have many students (in its membership).

Our refined methodology may now be restated with the relationship information added.

6.5.6 ER Design Methodology

Step 1. Select one primary entity from the database requirements description and show attributes to be recorded for that entity. Label keys, if appropriate, and show some sample data.

Step 2. Use structured English for entities, attributes, and keys to describe the database that has been elicited.

Step 3. Examine attributes in the primary entity (possibly with user assistance) to find out if information about one of the attributes is to be recorded.

Step 3a. If information about an attribute is needed, then make the attribute an entity, and then

Step 3b. Define the relationship back to the original entity.

Step 4. If another entity is appropriate, draw the second entity with its attributes. Repeat step 2 to see if this entity should be further split into more entities.

Step 5. Connect entities with relationships if relationships exist.

Step 6. State the exact nature of the relationships in structured English from all sides; for example, if a relationship is A:B::1:M, then there is a relationship from A(1) to B(M) and from B(M) back to A(1).

Step 7. Present the "as designed" database to the user complete with the English for entities, attributes, keys, and relationships. Refine the diagram as necessary.

Step 8. Show some sample data.

6.6 SOME EXAMPLES OF OTHER RELATIONSHIPS

In this section, we consider three other examples of relationships—two 1:M relationships and an M:N relationship—in more detail to practice and further clarify the process we have presented. As stated, the 1:M and M:N relationships are common in a database.

6.6.1 An Example of the One-to-Many Relationship (1:M)

Relationships that are 1:M or M:1 are really relative views of the same problem. When specifying 1:M or M:1, we need to be especially careful to specify which entity is 1 and which is M. The designation is really which view is more natural for the database designer. As an example of a 1-to-M

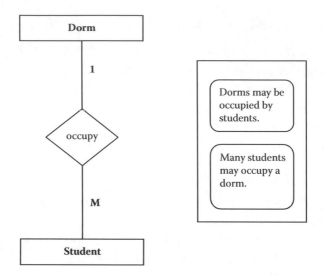

FIGURE 6.13
An ER diagram (without attributes) of a 1:M relationship.

relationship, consider dorm rooms and students. One dorm room may have many students living in it, and many students can live in one dorm room. So, the relationship between dorm room and students would be considered a one-to-many (1:M::DORM:STUDENT) situation and would be depicted as in Figure 6.13 (without attributes). We will let the term DORM mean dorm room.

In Figure 6.13 (the Chen-like model), the name that we chose for the DORM-STUDENT relationship was occupy.

Note that not all dorms have students living in them; hence, the participation of dorms in the relationship is partial. Informally,

*Dorms **may** be occupied by many students.*

Furthermore, all students may not live in dorms, so the relationship of STUDENT to DORM is also partial:

*Students **may** occupy a dorm room.*

Now, let us restate the relationships in the short and long English forms.

The first statement, "Dorms may be occupied by many students," fits **pattern 4,** x:y::1(partial):M.

6.6.1.1 Pattern 4—1:M, from the 1 Side, Partial Participation

"Some **x** are related to many **y**."

Therefore, the more precise statement is

x, but not necessarily all **x**, (which are recorded in the database) ***may*** be related to many (zero or more) **y**'s. Some **x** are not related to a **y** …

or

*Dorms, but not necessarily all dorms, (which are recorded in the database) **may** be occupied by many (zero or more) students.*

For the inverse relation:

*Students **may** occupy a dorm room.*

This fits **pattern 2**, M(partial):1.

6.6.1.2 Pattern 2—M(Partial):1, from M Side, Optional Participation

"Some **x** are related to one **y**."

Therefore, the long "translation" of the statement is

x, but not necessarily all **x** (which are recorded in the database), ***may*** be related to one and only one **y**. Some **x** ***may*** not be related to **y**. (No **x** is related to more than one **y**.) […] indicates optional clarification.

This **x** and **y** notation resolves into **x** = students, **y** = dorms, and hence

*Students, but not necessarily all students (which are recorded in the database), **may** occupy one and only one dorm. Some students **may** not occupy a dorm room. No student occupies more than one dorm.*

Or, stated another way:

*A student **may** occupy a (one and only one) dorm and a dorm **may** be occupied by many students.*

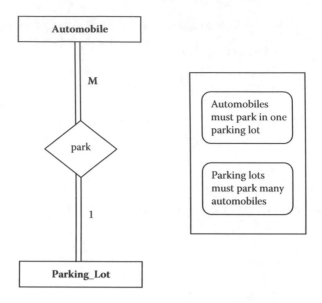

FIGURE 6.14
An ER diagram (without attributes) of an M:1 relationship.

6.6.2 An Example of the Many-to-One Relationship (M:1)

For another database, let us assume that a school that we are modeling has student parking lots. Let us further assume that every student is assigned to park his or her car in some (one) specific parking lot. We then have an entity called PARKING_LOT that will have parking locations described by some descriptive notation such as East Lot 7, North Lot 28, and so on. In this case, if we viewed many automobiles as assigned to one parking lot and a parking lot as containing many automobiles, we could depict this relationship as a many-to-one, M:1::AUTOMOBILE:PARKING_LOT. This diagram is shown in Figure 6.14 (again without attributes).

We have depicted participation of the relationship between automobile and parking lot as full in both instances—meaning that all automobiles have one parking lot, and all parking lots are assigned to students' automobiles.

The grammatical expressions of this relationship are discussed next.

6.6.2.1 Pattern 1—M:1, from the M Side, Full Participation

The **x**, which are recorded in the database, ***must*** be related to one and only one **y**. No **x** are related to more than one **y**.

x = automobile, **y** = parking lot, relationship = park

*Automobiles, which are recorded in the database, **must** be parked in one and only one parking lot. No automobiles may be parked in more than one parking lot. An automobile **must** park in only one parking lot.*

The inverse is discussed next.

6.6.2.2 Pattern 3—1:M, from the 1 Side, Full Participation

The **x**, which are recorded in the database, **must** be related to many (one or more) **y**'s. ("No **x** is related to a non-**y**" or "Non-**x** are not related to a **y**." [The negative will depend on the sense of the statement].)

*Parking lots, which are recorded in the database, **must** park many (one or more) automobiles.*

The negative in this case seems misleading, so we will omit it. The point is that recorded parking lots must have students parking there.

Or, stated another way:

*An automobile **must** be parked in a (one and only one) parking lot, and a parking lot **must** have at least one automobile parked in it (and can have many automobiles parked in it).*

6.6.3 An Example of the Many-to-Many Relationship (M:N)

The classic example of the M:N relationship we will study here is students taking courses. At the outset, we know that students take (enroll in) many courses, and that any course is populated by many students. The basic diagram for the STUDENT-COURSE relationship is that shown in Figure 6.15.

We have chosen the word enroll to depict the relationship. The participation of students in enroll is depicted as full (mandatory); course enrollment is depicted as partial. This choice was arbitrary as both could be full or partial, depending on user needs and desires. Look carefully at the exact grammatical expressions and note the impact of choosing full in one case and partial in the other.

The grammatical expressions of this relationship are discussed next.

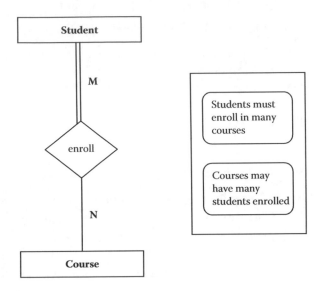

FIGURE 6.15
An ER diagram (without attributes) of an M:N relationship.

6.6.3.1 Pattern 3—M:N, from the M Side, Full Participation

The **x**, which are recorded in the database, must be related to many (one or more) **y**. ("No **x** is related to a non-**y**" or "Non-**x** are not related to a **y**" or "No **x** is not related to a **y**." [The negative will depend on the sense of the statement].)

> **x** = students, **y** = courses, relationship = enroll
>
> *Students, which are recorded in the database, **must** be enrolled in many (one or more) courses.*

The inverse is explained next.

6.6.3.2 Pattern 4—N:M, from the N Side, Partial Participation

The **x**, but not necessarily all **x** (which are recorded in the database), *may* be related to many (one or more) **y**. Some **x** may not be related to **y**.

> **x** = course, **y** = student, relationship = enroll
>
> *Courses, but not necessarily all courses (which are recorded in the database), **may** enroll many (one or more) students. Some courses **may** not enroll students.*

Or, stated another way:

> A student **must** enroll in one or more courses, and a course **may** have one or more students enrolled in it.

This "course partiality" likely reflects courses that are in the database but are not currently enrolling students. It could mean potential courses or courses that are no longer offered. Of course, if the course is in the database only if students are enrolled, then the participation constraint becomes full, and the sense of the entity relationship changes.

Also, this database tells us that while we can have courses without students, we only store information about active students. Obviously, we could make the student connection partial and hence store all students—even inactive ones. We chose to represent the relationships in this manner to make the point that the participation constraint is supposed to depict reality—the reality of what the user might want to store data about.

Note that all the examples in this chapter deal with only two entities, that is, they are binary relationships. The example in the following section is also another example of a binary relationship.

CHECKPOINT 6.3

1. Give an example of a 1(full):1 relationship? Does such a relationship always have to be mandatory? Explain with examples.
2. Give an example of a 1(partial):1 relationship? Does such a relationship always have to be optional? Explain with examples.
3. Give an example of a M(full):N relationship? Would such a relationship always be optional or mandatory? Explain with examples.
4. Give an example of a M(partial):N relationship? Would such a relationship always be optional or mandatory? Explain with examples.

6.7 ONE FINAL EXAMPLE

As a final example to conclude the chapter, we present one more problem and then our methodology.* Consider a model for a simplified airport where PASSENGERS and FLIGHTS are to be recorded. Suppose that

---

* Modeled after Elmasri and Navathe (2007).

the attributes of PASSENGER are name, luggage_pieces, and frequent_flier_no. Suppose the attributes for FLIGHT are flight_no, destination, arrive_time, and depart_time. Draw the ER diagram.

Note: We are leaving out many attributes that we could consider. Assume that this is all of the information that we choose to record.

The solution is given next.

6.7.1 ER Design Methodology

> **Step 1. Select one primary entity from the database requirements description and show attributes to be recorded for that entity. Label keys if appropriate and show some sample data.**

Suppose we choose PASSENGER as our primary entity. PASSENGER has the following attributes: frequent_ flier_no, name [first, middle, last], luggage_pieces.

We draw this much of the diagram, choosing frequent_flier_no as a key and noting the composite attribute name. This diagram is shown in Figure 6.16.

> **Step 2. Use structured English for entities, attributes, and keys, to describe the database which has been elicited.**

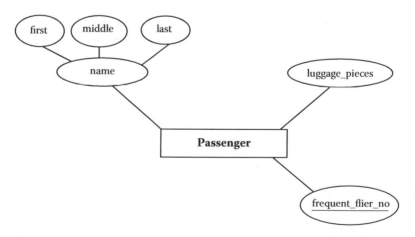

FIGURE 6.16
The PASSENGER entity diagram.

6.7.1.1 The Entity

This database records data about PASSENGERS. For each passenger, we record frequent_flier_no, name [first, middle, last], pieces_of_luggage.

6.7.1.1.1 The Attributes

For atomic attributes, att(j):

> For each PASSENGER, there will be one and only one frequent_flier_no. The value for frequent_flier_no will not be subdivided.
> For each PASSENGER, there will be one and only one recording of luggage_pieces. The value for luggage_pieces will not be subdivided.

For composite attributes, att(j):

> For each PASSENGER, we will record their name, which is composed of first, middle, and last. First, middle, and last are the component parts of name.

6.7.1.1.2 The Keys

> For each PASSENGER, we will have the following primary key: frequent_flier_no.

Note that we have chosen frequent_flier_no as a primary key for PASSENGER. If this were not true, some other means of unique identification would be necessary. Here, this is all the information we are given.

> **Step 3. Examine attributes in the primary entity (possibly with user assistance) to find out if information about one of the attributes is to be recorded.**

No further information is suggested.

> **Step 4. If another entity is appropriate, draw the second entity with its attributes. Repeat step 2 to see if this entity should be further split into more entities.**

The other entity in this problem is FLIGHT, with attributes flight_no, destination, depart_time, arrive_ time.

Again, we use structured English as in the following.

6.7.1.2 The Entity

This database records data about Flights. For each FLIGHT, we record flight_no, destination, depart_time, and arrive_time.

6.7.1.2.1 The Attributes

For atomic attributes, att(j):

> For each FLIGHT, there will be one and only one flight_no. The value for flight_no will not be subdivided.
> For each FLIGHT, there will be one and only one recording of destination. The value for destination will not be subdivided.
> For each FLIGHT, there will be one and only one recording of depart_time. The value for depart_time will not be subdivided.
> For each FLIGHT, there will be one and only one recording of arrive_time. The value for arrive_time will not be subdivided.

6.7.1.2.2 The Keys

For the key(s): One candidate key (strong entity):

> For each FLIGHT, we will have the following primary key: flight_no.

We are assuming flight_no is unique.

Step 5. Connect entities with relationships if relationships exist.

What relationship is there between flights and passengers?

All passengers will fly on one flight. All flights will have multiple passengers. The diagram for this problem is illustrated in Figure 6.17 and Figure 6.18.

Note that we have again made a choice: We will depict one flight per passenger in this database. The specifications do not tell us whether this should be 1 or M, so we chose 1. We also chose full participation on both sides. It would seem illogical to record data about passengers who did not fly on a flight and flights for which there were no passengers. But again, if the database called for storing information about potential passengers who might not book a specific flight or flights that did not involve passengers, then we would have to change the conceptual design. Figure 6.17 is good for displaying just the entities and the attributes. Figure 6.18 uses the

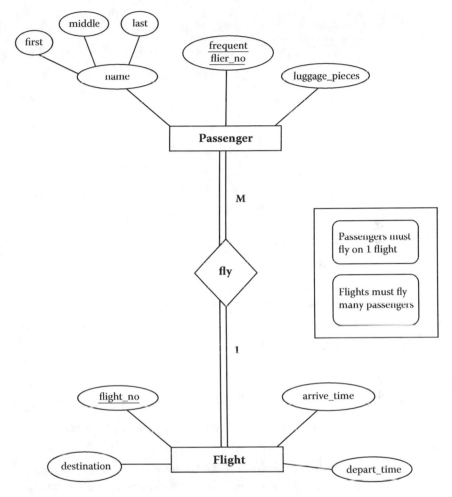

FIGURE 6.17
ER diagram for PASSENGER-FLIGHT database.

concise form of describing attributes and includes some of the preceding steps and some sample data. For conceptualizing, Figure 6.17 may be used and later converted into Figure 6.18 style for documentation. Either figure requires an accompaniment of structured English (step 6).

As designers, we make a choice and then present our choice to the user. If the user decided to store information about all flights and all passengers over some period of time, that would be a different database (an M:N relationship and perhaps partial participations for nonpassenger flights and nonflying passengers). The point is that this is eventually a user's choice,

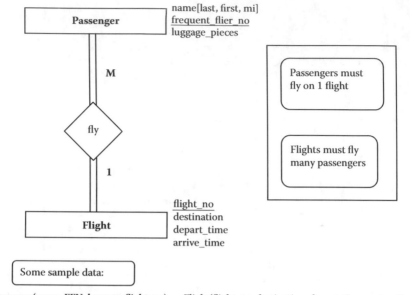

FIGURE 6.18
Sample problem. Alternate presentation of attributes with explanation and sample data.

and at this point we are trying to generate a model to present to the user to validate.

> **Step 6. State the exact nature of the relationships in structured English from all sides, such as, if a relationship is A:B::1:M, then there is a relationship from A(1) to B(M) and from B(M) back to A(1).**

6.7.2 Pattern 1—M:1, from the M Side, Full Participation

The **x**, which are recorded in the database, ***must*** be related to one and only one **y**. No **x** are related to more than one **y**.

x = passenger, **y** = flight, relationship = fly

*Passengers, which are recorded in the database, **must** fly on one and only one flight. No passenger flies on more than one flight.*

6.7.3 Pattern 3—1:M, from the 1 Side, Full Participation

The **x**, which are recorded in the database, must be related to many (one or more) **y**'s.

x = flight, **y** = passenger, relationship = fly

> *Flights, which are recorded in the database, **must** fly many (one or more) passengers.*

Or, stated another way:

> *A passenger **must** fly on a flight, and a flight **must** have at least one (and can have many) passengers on it.*

Attribute descriptions follow previous patterns and are left to the exercises.

> **Step 7. Present the "as designed" database to the user complete with the English for entities, attributes, keys, and relationships. Refine the diagram as necessary.**
> **Step 8. Show some sample data.**

See Figure 6.18.

6.8 MAPPING RELATIONSHIPS TO A RELATIONAL DATABASE

In this section, we continue with the mapping rules that we began at the end of Chapter 4. In Chapter 4, we learned how to map entities, entities with composite attributes, and entities with multivalued attributes. In this chapter, having covered structural constraints of relationships, we learn how to map relationships.

6.8.1 Mapping Binary M:N Relationships

For mapping binary M:N relationships, we present mapping rule 5.

> *Mapping rule 5—Mapping binary M:N relationships.* **For each M:N relationship, create a new table (relation) with the primary keys of each of the two entities (owner entities) that are being related in the M:N relationship. The primary key of this new table will be the concatenated keys of the owner entities. Include any attributes that the M:N relationship may have in this new table.**

For example, refer to Figure 6.15. If the STUDENT and COURSE tables have the following data:

STUDENT

name. first	name.last	name.mi	student_number	address
Richard	Earp	W	589	222 2nd St
Boris	Backer		909	333 Dreistrasse
Helga	Hogan	H	384	88 Half Moon Ave
Arpan	Bagui	K	876	33 Bloom Ave
Hema	Malini		505	100 Livingstone

COURSE

cname	c_number	credit_hrs
Database	COP4710	4
Visual Basic	CGS3464	3
Elements of Stats	STA3023	3
Indian History	HIST2022	4

Before performing mapping rule 5, one must first ensure that the primary keys of the entities involved have been established. If c_number and student_number are the primary keys of COURSE and STUDENT, respectively, then to map the M:N relationship, we create a relation called ENROLL as follows:

ENROLL

c_number	student_number
COP4710	589
CGS3464	589
CGS3464	909
STA3023	589
HIST2022	384
STA3023	505
STA3023	876
HIST2022	876
HIST2022	505

Both c_number and student_number together are the primary key of the relation, ENROLL.

The relational mapping for Figure 6.15 would be as follows:

STUDENT(name.first, name.last, name.mi, <u>student_number</u>, address)
COURSE(cname, <u>c_number</u>, credit_hrs)
ENROLL(<u>c_number, student_number</u>)

What often happens in M:N relationships is that data arises that fits better with the relationship than with either entity. Relationship attributes are covered in Chapter 8, but should a relationship attribute arise, it will be mapped with the primary keys.

6.8.2 Mapping Binary 1:1 Relationships

To map binary 1:1 relationships, include the primary key of EntityA into EntityB as the foreign key. The question is, which is EntityA and which is EntityB? This question is answered in the mapping rules presented in this section.

> *Mapping rule 6—Mapping binary 1:1 relationships when one side of the relationship has full participation and the other has partial participation.* **When one of the sides of the relationship has full participation and the other has partial participation, then store the primary key of the side with the partial participation constraint on the side with the full participation constraint as a foreign key. Include any attributes on the relationship on the same side to which the key was added.** (We cover attributes of relationships in Chapter 8 and then embellish the mapping rules accordingly.)

For example, refer to Figure 6.3. It says:

> *An automobile, recorded in the database,* **must** *be driven by one and only one student.*

And

> *A student* **may** *drive one and only one automobile.*

Here, the full participation is on the AUTOMOBILE side since "An automobile '**must**' be driven by a student."

So, we take the primary key from the partial participation constraint side STUDENT and include it in the AUTOMOBILE table. The primary key of STUDENT is student_number, so this will be included in the

AUTOMOBILE relation as the foreign key. A relational database realization of the ER diagram in Figure 6.3 will look like

> AUTOMOBILE(vehicle_id,   make,   body_style,   color,   year, student_number)
> STUDENT(name.first, name.last, name.mi, student_number, address)

And with some data, it would look like this:

AUTOMOBILE

vehicle_id	make	body_style	color	year	student_number
A39583	Ford	Compact	Blue	1999	589
B83974	Chevy	Compact	Red	1989	909
E98722	Mazda	Van	Green	2002	876
F77665	Ford	Compact	White	1998	384

STUDENT

name.first	name.last	name.mi	student_number	address
Richard	Earp	W	589	222 2nd St
Boris	Backer		909	333 Dreistrasse
Helga	Hogan	H	384	88 Half Moon Ave
Arpan	Bagui	K	876	33 Bloom Ave
Hema	Malini		505	100 Livingstone

Since STUDENT has a multivalued attribute school, we need to map the multivalued attribute to its own table (as per mapping rule 4, mapping multivalued attributes):

Name-School

student_number	school
589	St. Helens
589	Mountain
589	Volcano
909	Manatee U
909	Everglades High
384	PCA
384	Pensacola High
876	UWF
505	Cuttington
505	UT

In this case, if the relationship had any attributes, they would be included in the AUTOMOBILE relation since that is where the key went.

> ***Mapping rule 7—Mapping binary 1:1 relationships when both sides have partial participation constraints.***

When both sides have partial participation constraints in binary 1:1 relationships, the relationships can be mapped in one of two ways. For the first option:

> ***Mapping rule 7A. Select either one of the relations to store the key of the other*** (and live with some null values).

Again, refer to Figure 6.2. The participation constraints are partial from both sides (and let us assume for the time being that there is no school attribute). Then, Figure 6.2 would read:

> *An automobile may be driven by one and only one student.*

And

> *A student may drive one and only one automobile.*

A relational realization could be the following: Take the vehicle_id (primary key of AUTOMOBILE) and store it in STUDENT as follows:

AUTOMOBILE(vehicle_id, make, body_style, color, year)
STUDENT(name.first,   name.last,   name.mi,   student_number, address, vehicle_id)

And with some sample data:

AUTOMOBILE

vehicle_id	make	body_style	color	year
A39583	Ford	Compact	Blue	1999
B83974	Chevy	Compact	Red	1989
E98722	Mazda	Van	Green	2002
F77665	Ford	Compact	White	1998
G99999	Chevy	Van	Grey	1989

STUDENT

name. first	name. last	name. mi	student_ number	address	vehicle_ id
Richard	Earp	W	589	222 2nd St.	A39583
Boris	Backer		909	333 Dreistrasse	B83974
Helga	Hogan	H	384	88 Half Moon Ave.	F77665
Arpan	Bagui	K	876	33 Bloom Ave	E98722
Hema	Malini		505	100 Livingstone	

In the STUDENT relation, vehicle_id is a foreign key.

For the second option:

> *Mapping rule 7B.* **Depending on the semantics of the situation, you can create a new relation to house the relationship that would contain the key of the two related entities** (as is done in mapping rule 5). In this case, if there were any null values, these would be left out of the linking table.

We illustrate the mapping of Figure 6.2 using this rule. The relational realization would be

AUTOMOBILE(vehicle_id, make, body_style, color, year)
STUDENT(name.first, name.last, name.mi, student_number, address)
STUDENT-AUTOMOBILE(vehicle_id, student_number)

And with some data,

Student-Automobile

vehicle_id	student_number
A39583	589
B83974	909
E98722	876
F77665	384

In this case, the two relations, STUDENT and AUTOMOBILE, would remain as

STUDENT

name.first	name.last	name.mi	student_number	address
Richard	Earp	W	589	222 2nd St
Boris	Backer		909	333 Dreistrasse
Helga	Hogan	H	384	88 Half Moon Ave
Arpan	Bagui	K	876	33 Bloom Ave
Hema	Malini		505	100 Livingstone

AUTOMOBILE

vehicle_id	make	body_style	color	year
A39583	Ford	Compact	Blue	1999
B83974	Chevy	Compact	Red	1989
E98722	Mazda	Van	Green	2002
F77665	Ford	Compact	White	1998
G99999	Chevy	Van	Grey	1989

Mapping rule 8—Mapping binary 1:1 relationships when both sides have full participation constraints. **Use the semantics of the relationship to select which of the relations should contain the key of the other. If this choice is unclear, then use mapping rule 7B.**

Now, assuming full participation on both sides of Figure 6.2, the two tables STUDENT and AUTOMOBILE could be

STUDENT(name.first, name.last, name.mi, <u>student_number</u>, address)
AUTOMOBILE(<u>vehicle_id</u>, make, body_style, color, year, student_number)

And with some sample data,

STUDENT

name.first	name.last	name.mi	student_number	address
Richard	Earp	W	589	222 2nd St
Boris	Backer		909	333 Dreistrasse
Helga	Hogan	H	384	88 Half Moon Ave
Arpan	Bagui	K	876	33 Bloom Ave
Hema	Malini		505	100 Livingstone

AUTOMOBILE

vehicle_id	make	body_style	color	year	student_number
A39583	Ford	Compact	Blue	1999	589
B83974	Chevy	Compact	Red	1989	909
E98722	Mazda	Van	Green	2002	876
F77665	Ford	Compact	White	1998	384
G99999	Chevy	Van	Grey	1989	505

In this case, student_number was included in AUTOMOBILE, making student_number a foreign key in AUTOMOBILE. We could have also taken the primary key, vehicle_id, from AUTOMOBILE and included that in the STUDENT table. But, it would be inappropriate to include foreign keys in both tables as that would be introducing redundancy into the database.

6.8.3 Mapping Binary 1:N Relationships

Next, we develop mapping rules to map binary 1:N relationships. These mappings will depend on what kind of participation constraint the N side of the relationship has.

> *Mapping rule 9—Mapping binary 1:N relationships when the N side has full participation.* **Include the key of the entity on the 1 side of the relationship as a foreign key on the N side.**

For example, in Figure 6.13 if we assume full participation on the student side, we will have

Dorm rooms may have zero or more students.

and

Students must live in only and only one dorm room.

The "1 side" is DORM; the "N side" is STUDENT. So, a reference to DORM (dname, the key of DORM) is included in STUDENT.

And, if we had the following sample data,

STUDENT

name.first	name.last	name.mi	student_number	dname
Richard	Earp	W	589	A
Boris	Backer		909	C
Helga	Hogan	H	384	A
Arpan	Bagui	K	876	A
Hema	Malini		505	B

DORM

dname	supervisor
A	Saunders
B	Backer
C	Hogan
D	Eisenhower

The relational mapping would be

STUDENT(name.first, name.last, name.mi, <u>student_number</u>, dname)
DORM(<u>dname</u>, supervisor)

Mapping rule 10—Mapping binary 1:N relationships when the N side has partial participation. **This situation would be handled just like a binary M:N relationship with a separate table for the relationship. The key of the new relation would consist of a concatenation of the keys of the related entities. Include any attributes that were on the relationship on this new table.**

CHECKPOINT 6.4

1. State the mapping rule(s) that would be used to map Figure 6.14. Map Figure 6.14 to a relational database and show some sample data.
2. State the mapping rule(s) that would be used to map Figure 6.17. Map Figure 6.17 to a relational database and show some sample data.

6.9 CHAPTER SUMMARY

This chapter discussed the cardinality and participation ratios in ER diagrams. Several examples and diagrams of binary relationships with structural constraints (developed in the Chen-like model) were discussed.

Tighter English grammar was presented for each of the diagrams, and steps 7 and 8 of the ER design methodology were defined. The final section of the chapter discussed mapping relationships. As our model becomes more complex, we will revisit the mapping rules to accommodate this complexity in further chapters.

CHAPTER 6 EXERCISES

Exercise 6.1

Let us suppose that we reconsider our student example in Exercise 5.2 in which the only attributes of student are student number and name. Let us suppose that we have another entity called "high school," which is going to be the high school from which the student graduated. For the high school entity, we will record the high school name and the location (meaning city and state). Draw the ER diagram using the Chen-like model. Follow the methodology and include all English descriptions of your diagrams. Map the ER diagram to a relational database.

Exercise 6.2

Suppose that a college had one dormitory with many rooms. The dormitory entity, which is actually a "dormitory room" entity since there is only one dorm, has the attributes room number and single/double (meaning that there are private rooms and double rooms). Let us suppose that the student entity in this case contains the attributes student number, student name, and home telephone number. Draw the ER diagram using the Chen-like model. Follow the methodology and include all English descriptions of your diagram. Map the ER diagram to a relational database.

Exercise 6.3

Consider a student database with students and campus organizations. Students will have the attributes of student number and student name. Organizations will have the attributes organization name and organization type. Draw the ER diagram using the Chen-like model. Follow the methodology and include all English descriptions of your diagram. Map the ER diagram to a relational database and include some sample data.

Exercise 6.4

Consider a student and advisor database. Students have a student number and student name. Advisors have names, office numbers, and advise in some major. The major that the advisor advises in is designated by a major code (e.g., Chemistry, CHEM; Biology, BIOL; Computer Science, COMPSC; ...). Draw the ER diagram using the Chen-like model. Follow the methodology and include all English descriptions of your diagram. Map the ER diagram to a relational database and include some sample data.

Exercise 6.5

You want to record the following data in a database: restaurant name and location, employee names and IDs, capacity of restaurant (smoking and nonsmoking), hours of operation (assume same hours every day), employee salaries and titles. An employee can work for only one restaurant. Draw the ER diagram using the Chen-like model. Follow the methodology and include all English descriptions of your diagram. Map the ER diagram to a relational database and include some sample data.

Exercise 6.6

Record the following data in a database: business name, owner, location(s), telephone numbers, delivery truck number, truck capacity, usual route description (e.g., North, West, Central, Lake, ...). Draw the ER diagram using the Chen-like model. Follow the methodology and include all English descriptions of your diagram.

Exercise 6.7

Refer to Figure 6.19. What are the English language statements you can make about the figure?

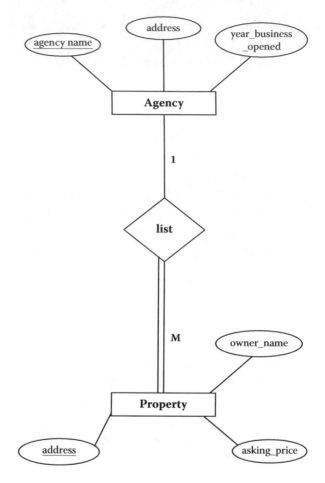

FIGURE 6.19
Exercise 7.

Exercise 6.8

Refer to Figure 6.18. Complete the diagram by adding a precise English description of each attribute. Map Figure 6.18 to a relational database.

Exercise 6.9

What is the cardinality of the following:

a. Each student must own a car and can own only one car. A car may be owned by only one student.

b. Each student may drive a car and can drive more than one car. A car can be driven by one student and can only be driven by one student.

c. Each student may rent many cars and cars may be rented by many students.

Which of these cardinality rules are optional? Which rules are mandatory? Show these relationships diagrammatically.

BIBLIOGRAPHY

Batani, C., Ceri, S., and Navathe, S. B. 1992. *Conceptual Database Design*. Redwood City, CA: Benjamin Cummings.

Earp, R., and Bagui, S. 2001. Extending relationships in the entity relationship diagram. *Data Base Management Journal*, 22–10–42:1–14.

Elmasri, R., and Navathe, S. B. 2007. *Fundamentals of Database Systems*. Reading, MA: Addison-Wesley.

Kroenke, D. M. 2010. *Database Processing*. Upper Saddle River, NJ: Prentice Hall.

McFadden, F. R., and Hoffer, J. A. 2007. *Modern Database Management*. Upper Saddle River, NJ: Pearson Education.

Ramakrishnan, R., and Gehrke, J. 2003. *Database Management Systems*. New York: McGraw Hill.

CASE STUDY

West Florida Mall (continued)

In the last couple of chapters, we selected our primary entities (as per the specifications from the user so far) and defined the relationships between the primary entities. In this chapter, we proceed with the ER diagram for this case study by looking at steps 6 and 7 of the ER design methodology, and we map the ER diagram to a relational database (with some sample data) as we proceed.

Step 6 develops the structural constraints of binary relationships by stating

> *Step 6. State the exact nature of the relationships in structured English from all sides, for example, when a relationship is A:B::1:M, there is a relationship from A(1) to B(M) and from B(M) back to A(1).*

Refer to Figure 6.20.

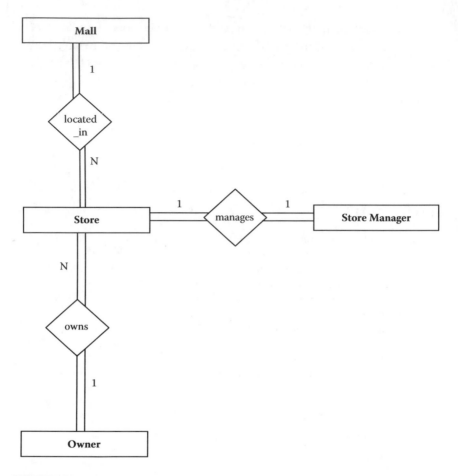

FIGURE 6.20
ER diagram of West Florida Mall with four entities and structural constraints.

First, for the relationship located_in:

From **MALL** to **STORE**, this fits pattern 3, **1(full):N**:
A mall must have at least one store and can have many stores.

Or,
Malls, which are recorded in the database, must have many (one or more) stores located in them.

From **STORE** to **MALL**, this fits pattern 1, **M(full):1**:
Many stores (one or more) must be in one mall.

Or,
Stores, which are recorded in the database, must be in one mall.

The MALL entity is mapped as mapped in Chapter 5:

MALL

name	address
West Florida Mall	N Davis Hwy, Pensacola, FL
Cordova Mall	9th Avenue, Pensacola, FL
Navy Mall	Navy Blvd, Pensacola, FL
BelAir Mall	10th Avenue, Mobile, AL

Next, we have to map the relationship between the MALL entity and the STORE entity. This is a binary 1:N relationship; hence, we use mapping rule 9, which states:

> **Include the key of the entity on the 1 side of the relationship to the N side as a foreign key.**

So, the key from the 1 side, the MALL side, will be included in the N side, STORE side, as the foreign key. We show this next with some sample data:

STORE

sloc	sname	snum	mall_name
Rm 101	Penneys	1	West Florida Mall
Rm 102	Sears	2	West Florida Mall
Rm 109	Dollar Store	3	West Florida Mall
Rm 110	Rex	4	West Florida Mall

Due to the multivalued attribute depts in STORE, we will keep the relation with the multivalued attribute (as developed in Chapter 5). It is shown next with some sample data:

STORE-dept

snum	depts
1	Tall men's clothing
1	Women's clothing
1	Children's clothing
1	Men's clothing
.	
.	
.	

Then, for the relationship **owns**:

From OWNER to STORE, this fits pattern 3, **1(full):M**:
Owners, which are recorded in the database, must own one or more stores.

Or,
One owner must own at least one store and may own many stores.

From STORE to OWNER, this fits pattern 1, **M(full):1**:
Stores, which are recorded in the database, must have one and only one owner.

Or,
Many stores can have one owner.

For the relationship **owns**, from OWNER to STORE, a **1:N** relationship:

Again, using mapping rule 9, we will take the key from the 1 side, so_ssn, and include this as the foreign key in the N side, STORE. STORE, with some sample data, is now:

STORE

sloc	sname	snum	mall_name	so_ssn
Rm 101	Penneys	1	West Florida Mall	879-987-0987
Rm 102	Sears	2	West Florida Mall	928-088-7654
Rm 109	Dollar Store	3	West Florida Mall	826-098-0877
Rm 110	Rex	4	West Florida Mall	982-876-8766

And, the relation for the OWNER entity remains as developed in Chapter 5. With some sample data, it is:

OWNER

so_ssn	so_name	so_off_phone	so_address
879-987-0987	Earp	(850)474-2093	1195 Gulf Breeze Pkwy, Pensacola, FL
826-098-0877	Sardar	(850)474-9873	109 Navy Blvd, Pensacola, FL
928-088-7654	Bagui	(850)474-9382	89 Highland Heights, Tampa, FL
982-876-8766	Bush	(850)474-9283	987 Middle Tree, Mobile, AL

For the relationship **manages**:

From STORE to STORE MANAGER, this fits pattern 1, **1(full):1**:
Stores, which are recorded in the database, must have one store manager.

Or,
Stores must have one store manager and can only have one and only one store manager.

From STORE MANAGER to STORE, this also fits pattern 1, **1(full):1**:
Store managers, which are recorded in the database, must manage one and only one store.

Or,
Store managers must manage at least one store and can manage only one store.

The relationship between STORE and STORE MANAGER is a binary 1:1 relationship; hence, using mapping rule 8, the relation STORE would develop into (we are taking the key from STORE MANAGER and including it in STORE as the foreign key) what is shown next with some sample data:

STORE

sloc	sname	snum	mall_name	so_ssn	sm_ssn
Rm 101	Penneys	1	West Florida Mall	879-987-0987	283-972-0927
Rm 102	Sears	2	West Florida Mall	928-088-7654	456-098-0987
Rm 109	Dollar Store	3	West Florida Mall	826-098-0877	234-987-0988
Rm 110	Rex	4	West Florida Mall	982-876-8766	928-982-9882

The relation for the STORE MANAGER entity remains as developed in Chapter 5. We show this with some sample data:

STORE MANAGER

sm_ssn	sm_name	sm_salary
234-987-0988	Saha	45,900
456-098-0987	Becker	43,989
928-982-9882	Ford	44,000
283-972-0927	Raja	38,988

Our next step is step 7, which is

> **Step 7. Present the "as designed" database to the user complete with the English for entities, attributes, keys, and relationships. Refine the diagram as necessary.**

In summary, our relational database has so far been mapped to (without the data) (*note* that the primary keys are underlined):

MALL

<u>name</u>	address

STORE

sloc	sname	<u>snum</u>	mall_name	so_ssn	sm_ssn

STORE-dept

<u>snum</u>	<u>depts</u>

OWNER

<u>so_ssn</u>	so_name	so_off_phone	so_address

STORE MANAGER

<u>sm_ssn</u>	sm_name	sm_salary

We continue the development of this case study at the end of the next chapter.

7

The Weak Entity

7.1 INTRODUCTION

Chapters 4 and 5 introduced the concepts of the entity, the attribute, and the relationship. Chapter 6 dealt with structural constraints, that is, how two entities are related to one another. In this chapter, we discuss the concept of the "weak" entity, which is used in the Chen-like model. Weak entities may not have a key attribute of their own as they are dependent on a strong or regular entity for their existence. Strong entities always have a primary key. The weak entity has some restrictions on its use and generates some interesting diagrams. This chapter revisits and redefines steps 3 and 4 of the entity relationship (ER) design methodology to include the concept of the weak entity. Grammar and mapping rules for the weak entity are also developed.

7.2 STRONG AND WEAK ENTITIES

As we mentioned in Chapter 4, there are situations for which finding a key for an entity is difficult. So far, we have concentrated on examples with strong (regular) entities—entities with easily identifiable keys. Strong entities almost always have a unique identifier that is a subset of all the attributes; however, a unique identifier may be an attribute or a group of attributes. For example, a student number, an automobile vehicle identification number (VIN), a driver's license number, and so on may be unique identifiers of strong entities.

A weak entity is one that clearly will be an entity but will depend on another entity for its existence. As we mentioned, a weak entity will not necessarily have a unique identifier. A classic example of this kind

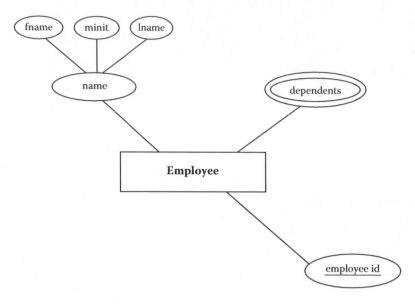

FIGURE 7.1
EMPLOYEE entity showing dependents as a multivalued attribute.

of entity is a DEPENDENT as related to an EMPLOYEE entity. If one were constructing a database about employees and their dependents, an instance of a dependent would depend entirely on some instance of an employee or else the dependent would not be kept in the database. The EMPLOYEE entity is called the *owner* entity or *identifying* entity for the weak entity DEPENDENT.

How can a weak entity come about in our diagrams? In the creation of a database, we might have a dependent name shown as a multivalued attribute as in Figure 7.1. An example of data for a diagram like Figure 7.1 would be as follows:

EMPLOYEE

fname	minit	lname	emp ID	dependents
John	J	Jones	0001	John, Jr; Fred; Sally
Sam	S	Smith	0004	Brenda; Richard
Adam	A	Adams	0007	John; Quincy; Maude .
Santosh	C	Saha	0009	Ranu; Pradeep; Mala

Suppose that in our conversations with the user, we discover that more information is supposed to be gathered about the dependents themselves.

Following our methodology, this is an acknowledgment that the dependents should be entities—that is, they fit the criteria for "entity," which is that we would be recording information about "something" (the dependent). Hence, we would be describing an entity called DEPENDENT. If we make DEPENDENT an entity, we would embellish the diagram in Figure 7.1 to that of Figure 7.2.

Figure 7.2 poses a problem: The DEPENDENT entity is dependent on the EMPLOYEE for its being. Also, it has no clear unique identifier. This

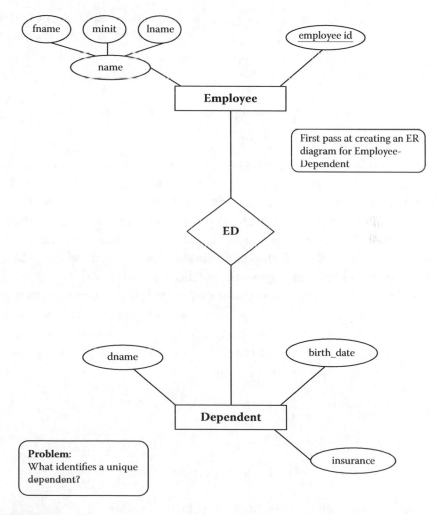

FIGURE 7.2
The EMPLOYEE-DEPENDENT ER diagram, first pass.

dependence on EMPLOYEE makes DEPENDENT a weak entity. As is often the case with weak entities, name, birth_date, and insurance are not candidate keys by themselves. None of these attributes would have unique values. There is no single attribute candidate key.

In the Chen-like model, for weak entities, we enclose the entity in a double box and the corresponding relationship to the owner in a double diamond. Refer to Figure 7.3. The weak entity in Figure 7.3, the DEPENDENT, is said to be *identified by* the entity EMPLOYEE. The EMPLOYEE is called the *identifying entity* or *owner entity* for the weak entity DEPENDENT.

Attributes are handled the same way for weak entities as for strong entities (except that there may be no primary keys for weak entities). We have included some attributes in Figure 7.3 so that the figure depicts the following (in loose grammar):

> *A dependent **must** be related to **one** employee, and an employee **may** have **many** dependents.*

The DEPENDENT entity has the attributes dname, birth_date and insurance.

In dealing with weak entities, it is appropriate to consider how each instance of the entity would be identified. Since the owner of the weak entity, DEPENDENT, is the strong entity EMPLOYEE, the identification process would involve the employee key plus some information from the weak entity DEPENDENT. The attribute dname is a likely candidate as an identifier for DEPENDENT and will be called a *partial key*.

In Figure 7.3, we underlined dname with dashes. The attribute dname is a *partial key* as it identifies dependents, but not uniquely. This assumes that all dependents have unique names. We did not "name" the relationship and left it as ED for EMPLOYEE-DEPENDENT. Suitable names for the relationship might be "have" as in

> *Employees may **have** many dependents.*

or "dependent on" as in

> *Employees may **have** many dependents **dependent on** them.*

We could also have used "related to" as in

> *Employees are related to many dependents.*

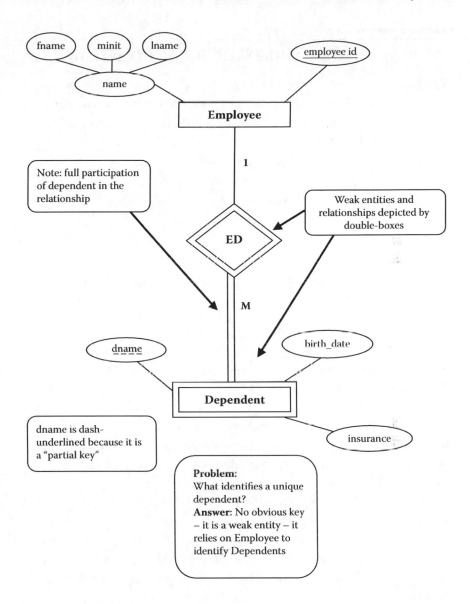

FIGURE 7.3
The EMPLOYEE-DEPENDENT ER diagram.

Each of these verb phrases seems to have a redundancy (dependent on) or perhaps misleading (related to) air about them. So, probably the best thing to do is to leave the relationship unnamed (ED). If the user chooses to use a relationship verb characterization, then the analyst can rename the relationship.

7.3 WEAK ENTITIES AND STRUCTURAL CONSTRAINTS

Weak entities always have full or mandatory participation from the weak side toward the owner. If the weak entity did not have total participation, then we would have a data item in the database that was not uniquely identified and was not tied to a strong entity. In our EMPLOYEE-DEPENDENT example, this would be like keeping track of a dependent not related in any way to an employee. The cardinality of the relationship between the weak and strong entity will usually be 1:M, but not necessarily so.

7.4 WEAK ENTITIES AND THE IDENTIFYING OWNER

There are situations for which a weak entity may be connected to an owner entity while other relationships exist apart from the "owner" relationship. For example, consider Figure 7.4. In this figure, we show two relationships—owns and drives—connecting the two entities EMPLOYEE and AUTOMOBILE. Here, the AUTOMOBILE entity is considered a weak entity; that is, if there is no employee, then there will be no automobile (the automobile has to have an employee to exist in the database). Further, the automobile is identified by the owner; note the double diamond on the owns relationship and the full participation of the AUTOMOBILE entity in the owns relationship.

In Figure 7.4, we also have a drives relationship. The automobile is driven by employees other than the owner. All automobiles are driven by some employee; hence, the participation is full. But, the driver-employee may not necessarily be the actual owner. To identify AUTOMOBILE, we are saying that we need the owns relationship, but other nonowner drivers may exist.

According to Figure 7.4, one employee may own many automobiles. To answer the question of which automobiles an employee owns, in addition to the employee's ID, we need to know the make, model, and color of the automobiles. The make, model, and color of the AUTOMOBILE entity are partial keys (dotted underlined in Figure 7.4).

One final point about the AUTOMOBILE-EMPLOYEE situation: It could be that the vin of the AUTOMOBILE could be recorded. Vins are unique; hence, the weak entity AUTOMOBILE could have a primary key. In this

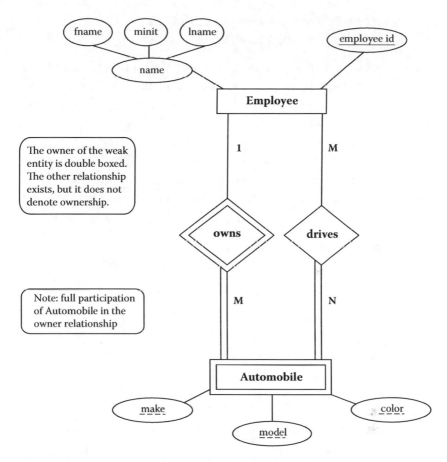

FIGURE 7.4
A weak entity with two relationships.

case, although AUTOMOBILE would have a primary key, it would still be weak because it would not be in the database without the owner or driver employee. Having a primary key does not necessarily make an entity "strong."

CHECKPOINT 7.1

1. How would you identify a strong entity?
2. How would you identify a weak entity?
3. What kind of a relationship line (single or double) would be leading up to the weak entity in a Chen-like diagram?
4. What kind of relationship does a weak entity have in a Chen-like model?
5. What is a partial key?

7.4.1 Another Example of a Weak Entity and the Identifying Owner

As another example of a weak entity in an ER diagram and the identifying owner, consider Figure 7.5. In Figure 7.5, we have two strong entities: PERSON and VET. There is one weak entity, PET. Figure 7.5 illustrates that the PERSON owns the PET, but the VET treats the PET. In the diagram, PERSON is the identifying or controlling entity for PET; hence, the relationship owns has a double diamond to PERSON. Here, owns is a weak relationship. PET is a weak entity in relation to PERSON.

The relationship treats does not have a double diamond because VET is not the owner of PET. Here, treats is not a weak relationship, and PET is not a weak entity in relation to VET.

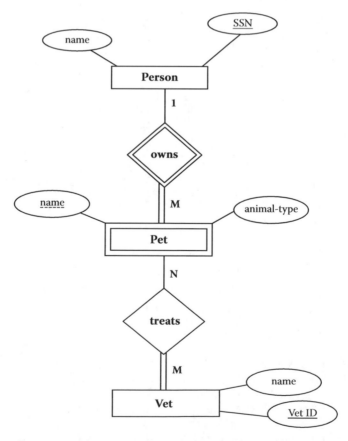

FIGURE 7.5
The PERSON-PET-VET ER diagram.

7.5 WEAK ENTITIES CONNECTED TO OTHER WEAK ENTITIES

We would like to make a final point regarding weak entities. Just because an entity is weak does not preclude it from being an owner of another weak entity. For example, consider Figure 7.6. In this figure, the EMPLOYEE-DEPENDENT relationship has been enhanced to include hobbies of the dependents. (Never mind why one would want to keep this information, but let us suppose that they do anyway.)

DEPENDENT is a weak entity. The entity HOBBY is also weak. Hobbies might be identified by their type (stamp collecting, baseball, tying knots,

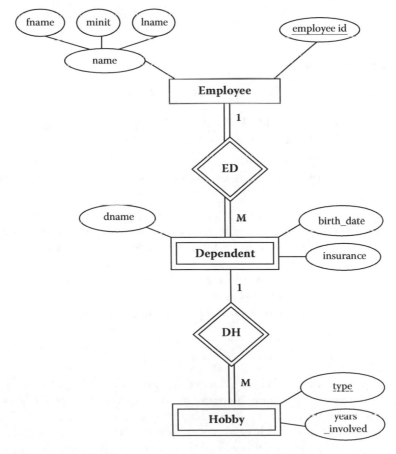

FIGURE 7.6
The EMPLOYEE-DEPENDENT-HOBBY ER diagram.

observing trains, etc.). The type attribute of HOBBY is a partial key for HOBBY.

The entity DEPENDENT is the owner of the weak entity HOBBY, and the entity EMPLOYEE is the owner of the weak entity DEPENDENT.

The reason that this situation is brought up here is to show that it can exist. In further discussion, when we map this situation, we treat this special situation carefully.

> **CHECKPOINT 7.2**
>   1. Can a weak entity be dependent on another weak entity?
>   2. Can a weak entity have a relationship that is not "weak" with the identifying entity?
>   3. Can a weak entity be related to more than one entity (strong or weak)?

7.6 REVISITING THE METHODOLOGY

The inclusion of a weak entity in an ER diagram causes us to revisit our methodology and make some adjustments. We might discover the weak entity in one of two places: one would be as we illustrated with the evolution of the multivalued attribute, the "dependent"; this would occur in steps 3a and 3b:

> *Step 3. Examine attributes in the primary entity (possibly with user assistance) to find out if information about one of the attributes is to be recorded.*
> *Step 3a. If information about an attribute is needed, then make the attribute an entity, and then*
> *Step 3b. Define the relationship back to the original entity.*

So, we add

> *Step 3c. If the new entity depends entirely on another entity for its existence, then draw the entity as weak (double boxed) and show the connection to the identifying entity as a double diamond. The participation of the weak entity in the relationship is full. Dash underline the partial key identifier(s) in the weak entity.*

The second place that a weak entity might appear would be as part of step 4 when new entities are considered:

> **Step 4. If another entity is appropriate, draw the second entity with its attributes. Repeat step 2 to see if any attributes should be further split into more entities.**

So, we add

> **Step 4a. If the additional entity or entities do not have candidate keys, then draw them as weak entities (as explained in step 3c) and show the connection to an identifying entity. The participation of the weak entity in the relationship is full or mandatory. Dash underline the partial key identifier(s) in the weak entity.**

Again, note that a weak entity cannot exist without an identifying entity, so if the weak entity is "discovered" independent of an identifying entity, the relationship connection should be made immediately.

7.7 WEAK ENTITY GRAMMAR

Previously, we covered some grammar associated with weak entities, but now we want to revise and enhance the idea when we have no primary key for the weak entity. It is possible for a weak entity to have a primary key; therefore, it might appear in item (b), so we add part (c) to the grammar for the keys, given next.

7.7.1 The Keys

For the key(s):

(a) More than one candidate key (strong entity): One key is chosen as the primary key ... (covered previously).
(b) One candidate key (strong or weak entity): The primary key is the candidate key. For each weak entity, it is assumed that no weak entity will be recorded without a corresponding owner (strong) entity.

For each weak entity that has a primary key, we also must record the primary key of the owner entity.

(c) No candidate keys (weak entity):

For each *(weak) entity*, we do not assume that any attribute will be unique enough to identify individual entities.
In this case, the DEPENDENT entity would be depicted as

> For each DEPENDENT entity, we do not assume that any attribute will be unique enough to identify individual entities.

We now enhance this description to include the identifying entity:

> Since the **weak** entity does not have a candidate key, each **weak entity** will be identified by key(s) belonging to its **strong** entity. For each DEPENDENT, entities will be identified by the concatenation of its partial key and the owner primary key: (DEPENDENT. DNAME+EMPLOYEE.EMPLOYEE_ID).

In this case, the DEPENDENT entity is identified by the EMPLOYEE entity, and this second statement becomes:

> Since the DEPENDENT entity does not have a candidate key, each DEPENDENT entity will be identified by key(s) belonging to the EMPLOYEE entity plus dname in the DEPENDENT entity.

7.8 MAPPING WEAK ENTITIES TO A RELATIONAL DATABASE

In this section, we develop the mapping rules for mapping weak entities to a relational database.

Mapping Rule 11—Mapping weak entities. **Develop a new table (relation) for each weak entity. As is the case with the strong entity, include any atomic attributes from the weak entity in the table. If there is a composite attribute, include only the atomic parts of** the composite attribute and be sure to qualify the atomic parts in order not to lose information. To relate the weak entity to its owner, include the primary key of the owner entity in the weak relation. The primary key of the weak relation will be the partial key of the weak entity concatenated to the primary key of the owner entity.

If a weak entity owns other weak entities, then the weak entity that is connected to the strong entity must be mapped first. The key of the weak owner entity has to be defined before the "weaker" entity (the one furthest from the strong entity) can be mapped.

For example, refer to Figure 7.3. The EMPLOYEE relation and DEPENDENT relation would be mapped as

EMPLOYEE(fname, minit, lname, employee_id)
DEPENDENT(employee_id, dname, insurance, birth_date)

And with data:

EMPLOYEE

fname	lname	minit	employee_id
Richard	Earp	W	589
Boris	Backer		909
Helga	Hogan	H	384
Arpan	Bagui	K	876
Hema	Malini		505

DEPENDENT

dname	birth_date	insurance	employee_id
Beryl	1/1/94	Vista	589
Kaityln	2/25/07	Vista	909
David	3/4/05	BlueCross	589
Fred	3/7/08	BlueCross	589
Chloe	5/6/08	SE	384

Here, employee_id is the primary key of EMPLOYEE. The employee id from the owner relation EMPLOYEE is included in the weak relation DEPENDENT. The employee_id now becomes part of the primary key of DEPENDENT. Since dname is the partial key of the DEPENDENT relation, the primary key of the DEPENDENT relation now finally becomes dname and employee_id together.

Now, refer to Figure 7.6. Here, the DEPENDENT entity is dependent on the EMPLOYEE entity, and the HOBBY entity is dependent on the DEPENDENT entity. The EMPLOYEE relation and DEPENDENT relation would be mapped as shown, and then the HOBBY relation would be mapped as

HOBBY(dname, employee_id, type, years_involved)

And, with some sample data:

HOBBY

dname	employee_id	type	years_involved
Beryl	589	swimming	3
Kaitlyn	909	reading	5
David	589	hiking	1
Fred	589	fishing	2
Chloe	384	singing	4

The partial key of HOBBY was type. The primary key of the HOBBY relation now becomes dname, employee_id, and type all together.

> **CHECKPOINT 7.3**
> 1. What are the rules for mapping weak entities? Map Figure 7.5 and show some sample data.
> 2. When mapping weak entities, what becomes their new primary key?
> 3. How would you map multivalued attributes in a weak entity? Discuss.

7.9 CHAPTER SUMMARY

This chapter discussed and developed the concept of the weak entity. The grammar for the weak entity was enhanced, along with the ER design methodology. The mapping rules for mapping the weak entity were also developed. This concept of the weak entity is available in the Chen-like model but is treated differently in other ER models.

CHAPTER 7 EXERCISES

Exercise 7.1

Construct an ER diagram (in the Chen-like model) for a database that is to contain employee name, employee number, employee address, skill(s). An employee may have more than one skill. Then, enhance the diagram to include level of skill, date skill certified (if certified), date began using the skill. Are there any weak entities in this database? Map this ER diagram to a relational database.

Exercise 7.2

Construct an ER diagram (in the Chen-like model) for sports and players. Attributes of sport are sport name, type of sport, timed or untimed. Attributes of players are name, person ID, date of birth. Players may play multiple sports. Which entity/entities would you consider weak? Write out the grammar for the ER diagram. Map this ER diagram to a relational database.

Exercise 7.3

How are weak entities generally identified?

Exercise 7.4

What mapping rules would be used to map Figure 7.4? Map Figure 7.4 to a relational database and show some sample data.

BIBLIOGRAPHY

Chen, P. P. 1976. The entity relationship model—toward a unified view of data. *ACM Transactions on Database Systems*, 1(1).

Connolly, E., and Begg, C. 2009. *Database Systems, a Practical Approach to Design, Implementation, and Management.* Reading, MA: Addison-Wesley.

Elmasri, R., and Navathe, S. B. 2007. *Fundamentals of Database Systems.* Reading, MA: Addison-Wesley.

Ramakrishnan, R., and Gehrke, J. 2003. *Database Management Systems.* New York: McGraw Hill.

CASE STUDY

West Florida Mall (continued)

In the previous chapters, we selected our primary entities, defined the attributes and relationships for this case study, and mapped it to a relational database (with some sample data). In Chapter 6, we also determined the structural constraints of the relationships and adjusted some of the mappings accordingly. Then, on reviewing step 7, which says

> *Step 7. Present the "as designed" database to the user complete with the English for entities, attributes, keys, and relationships. Refine the diagram as necessary.*

Suppose we obtained some additional input from the user:

A store must have one or more departments. A department will not exist without a store. For each department we will store the department name, department number, and department manager. Each department has at least one employee working for it.

We have to record information about the employees in the store. For each employee in a store, we will have to keep an employee's name, Social Security number, and the department where the employee works. Employees must work in one and only one department.

In Chapter 5, we determined that departments was a multivalued attribute of STORE (that is, one store had many departments). But, on reviewing these additional (given here) specifications, we can now see that DEPARTMENT needs to be an entity on its own since we have to record information about a DEPARTMENT. Also, we can see that we have to record information about another new entity, EMPLOYEE. So, these current specifications add two new entities, DEPARTMENT and EMPLOYEE.

CASE STUDY

First, we select an entity, DEPARTMENT.

Now, repeating step 2 for DEPARTMENT:

The Entity

This database records data about a DEPARTMENT.

For each DEPARTMENT in the database, we record a department name (dname) and department number (dnum).

The Attributes for DEPARTMENT

For each DEPARTMENT there will be one and only one dname. The value for dname will not be subdivided.
For each DEPARTMENT, there will be one and only one dnum. The value for dnum will not be subdivided.

The Keys

For each DEPARTMENT, we do not assume that any attribute will be unique enough to identify individual entities without the accompanying reference to STORE, the owner entity.

Note that the language leads you to think of DEPARTMENT as a weak entity.
Next, we select our next entity, EMPLOYEE.
Now, repeating step 2 for EMPLOYEE:

The Entity

This database records data about an EMPLOYEE.

For each EMPLOYEE in the database, we record an employee name (ename) and employee Social Security number (essn).

The Attributes for EMPLOYEE

For each EMPLOYEE, there will be one and only one ename. The value for ename will not be subdivided.
For each EMPLOYEE, there will be one and only one essn. The value for essn will not be subdivided.

The Keys

For each EMPLOYEE, we will assume that the essn will be unique (so EMPLOYEE will be a strong entity).

These entities have been added to the diagram in Figure 7.7.

Using step 6 to determine the structural constraints of relationships, we get:

First, for the relationship, **dept_of**:
From STORE to DEPARTMENT, this fits pattern 3, **1(full):N**:

Stores, which are recorded in the database, must have many (one or more) departments.

From DEPARTMENT to STORE, this fits pattern 1, **M(full):1**:

Many departments (one or more) must be in one store.

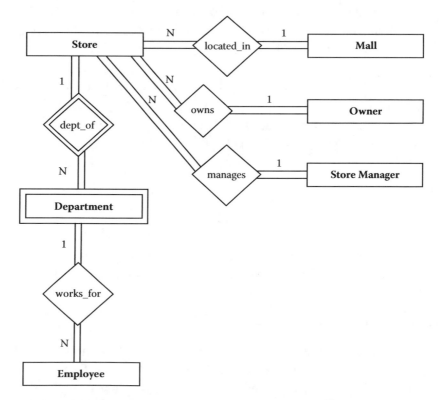

FIGURE 7.7
ER diagram of West Florida Mall developed so far.

To map this relationship

The relationship between STORE and DEPARTMENT is a strong/weak relationship, so using mapping rule 11, we will take the key from the owner, snum, and include this as part of the key on the weak side, DEPARTMENT, so the DEPARTMENT relation becomes DEPARTMENT(dname, dnum, snum)

And, with some data:

DEPARTMENT

dname	dnum	snum
Tall Men's Clothing	501	1
Men's Clothing	502	1
Women's Clothing	503	1
Children's Clothing	504	1
Men's Clothing	601	2
.		
.		
.		

The STORE relation will be the same as it was in Chapter 6, but we will not need the relation Store_depts. (In Chapter 6, departments was still a multivalued attribute of STORE, so we had the STORE and Store_depts relations.) From the specifications at the beginning of the case study in this chapter, it is apparent that DEPARTMENT is an entity on its own, so the Store_depts relation is replaced by the DEPARTMENT relation.

Then, for the relationship **works_for**:
From EMPLOYEE to DEPARTMENT, this fits pattern 1, **1(full):1**:

Employees, which are recorded in the database, must work for one and only one department.

From DEPARTMENT to EMPLOYEE, this fits pattern 3, **1(full):N**:
Departments, which are recorded in the database, must have one or more employees working for it.

To map this relationship:

From EMPLOYEE to DEPARTMENT, the relationship is 1:1, and since both sides have full participation, using mapping rule 8 we may select which side may store the key of the other. But, since the relationship between DEPARTMENT and EMPLOYEE is a binary 1(full):N relationship, using mapping rule 9, we will take the key from the 1 side (DEPARTMENT side), dnum and snum, and include this concatenated key as the foreign key in the N side (EMPLOYEE side), so the relation EMPLOYEE becomes
EMPLOYEE(ename, essn, dnum, snum)

And, with some sample data:

EMPLOYEE

ename	essn	dnum	snum
Kaitlyn	987-754-9865	501	1
Fred	276-263-9182	502	1
Katie	982-928-2726	503	1
Seema	837-937-9373	501	1
Raju	988-876-3434	601	2

.
.
.

   In summary, our relational database has so far been mapped to (without the data)

MALL

name	address

STORE

sloc	sname	snum	mall_name	so_owner	sm_ssn

OWNER

so_ssn	so_name	so_off_phone	so_address

STORE MANAGER

sm_ssn	sm_name	salary

DEPARTMENT

dname	dnum	snum

EMPLOYEE

ename	essn	dnum	snum

We continue the development of this case study at the end of the next chapter.

8

Further Extensions for ER Diagrams with Binary Relationships

8.1 INTRODUCTION

Having developed the basic entity relationship (ER) model in Chapters 4 through 7, this chapter deals with some extensions to the basic model. In this chapter, we introduce a new concept—attributes of relationships; we present several examples. We then revisit step 6 of the ER design methodology to include attributes of relationships. Next, the chapter looks at how more entities and relationships are added to the ER model and how attributes and relationships evolve into entities, all the while refining our ER design methodology. Relationships may develop into entities, creating an intersection entity. The grammar and structured English for the intersection entity are also presented. Then, this chapter introduces the concept of recursive relationships.

Also, in previous chapters we mostly looked at cases in which two entities had a (one) relationship between them. In this chapter, we present additional scenarios of how two entities can have more than one relationship between them. Step 5 of the ER design methodology is also redefined to include more than one relationship between two entities. This chapter discusses derived and redundant relationships, and the ER design methodology is again refined; step 6b is included to deal with these structures. Finally, in this chapter we include an optional section that looks at an alternative ER notation for specifying structural constraints on relationships.

8.2 ATTRIBUTES OF RELATIONSHIPS

In Chapter 6, we considered the M:N relationship STUDENT-COURSE. The STUDENT-COURSE relationship is M:N because students take many courses and courses are taken by many students. Now, consider adding the attribute grade to the ER diagram. If we tried to put grade with the STUDENT entity, we would have a multivalued attribute that had to somehow be related to the COURSE entity to make sense. Similarly, if we tried to put the grade attribute with the COURSE entity, the COURSE entity would have to be related to the STUDENT entity. The correct place for the grade attribute in the diagram would be on the relationship enroll because grade requires both a STUDENT and a COURSE to make sense. See Figure 8.1 for the placement of the grade attribute in an M:N, full:full participation model.

A few other attributes have been added to Figure 8.1 to show the relative position of the attributes. Again, since grade is necessarily identified by both STUDENT and COURSE, it cannot reside with either entity by itself. An attribute like grade is called a *relationship attribute* or *intersection attribute*.

An intersection attribute may arise first as a multivalued attribute on some entity during the design process only later to be questioned; that is, "Why is this attribute here when it requires another entity to identify it?" When it is recognized that the attribute has to be identified by more than one entity, the attribute is moved to the relationship between the two (or more) entities that identify it.

Relationship attributes may occur with an ER diagram containing any cardinality, but one will most often find relationship attributes in the binary, M:N situation. We now need to revisit our methodology to add a guideline for the attributes of a relationship:

> *Step 6. State the exact nature of the relationships in structured English from all sides, for example, if a relationship is A:B::1:M, then there is a relationship from A to B, 1 to Many, and from B back to A, Many to 1.*

And, we add:

> *Step 6a. Examine the list of attributes and determine whether any of them need to be identified by two (or more) entities. If so, place the attribute on the appropriate relationship that joins the two entities.*

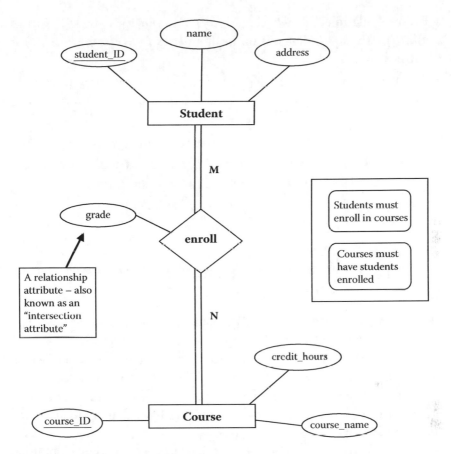

FIGURE 8.1
M:N relationship showing a relationship attribute.

Note that step 6a may also help in deciding which entities need to be related. If it had not been recognized up to this point that a relationship was needed, then the discovery of a relationship attribute would be a clear signal that such a relationship would be in order.

The grammar to describe the attribute of a relationship is discussed next.

8.2.1 The Attributes

For atomic attributes, *att(j)*: ...   (same as in previous chapters)
For composite attributes, att(j): ...   (same as in previous chapters)
For multivalued attributes, att(j): ...   (same as in previous chapters)
For attributes of relationships att(j):

For the relationship between *Entity1 and Entity2*, we will record a(n) *att(j)*. The *att(j)* depends on both entities *Entity1 and Entity2* for identification.

Example 8.1

For the relationship between the STUDENT entity and the COURSE entity, we will record a grade attribute. The grade attribute depends on both STUDENT and COURSE entities for identification.

8.3 RELATIONSHIPS DEVELOPING INTO ENTITIES: THE M:N RELATIONSHIP REVISITED

We previously defined the M:N relationship and noted in the beginning of the chapter that often an attribute appears that should be associated with the relationship and not with one entity. The example was grade, which would clearly not fit with either the STUDENT or the COURSE entity. In a sense, it appears that the relationship has itself taken on an entity quality. This observation is true since we have information (an attribute) that clearly belongs to the relationship.

There are two options in depicting this relationship attribute situation. One option is to leave the attribute where it is, as we have shown it, on the relationship. If the number of attributes is small (one or two), then the sense of the diagram is still intact, and the grammar representing the diagram will be understandable to the user.

The other option for relationship attributes would be to make the relationship an entity and tie both of the "identifying entities" to it. This option is shown in Figure 8.2. In this figure, the middle entity, STUDENT+COURSE, is depicted as weak because STUDENT+COURSE depends entirely on the STUDENT *and* COURSE entities. Note that the participations are always full between the new, weak "intersection entity" and the relationship that joins it to the strong owners. Why? This is because the weak entity *must* have a corresponding strong entity or it would not be there. The participation on the strong relationship side (between STUDENT and Rel1 [short for relationship 1] or between COURSE and Rel2 [again, short for

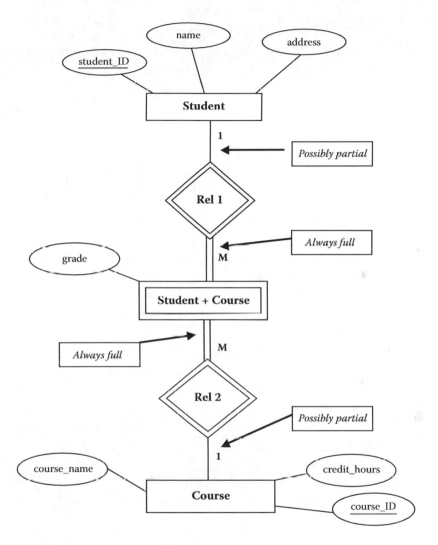

FIGURE 8.2
M:N relationship that has been replaced with by 1:M relationships.

relationship 2]) can be partial or full depending on whether it was partial or full originally. What would a partial COURSE-Rel 2 connection mean? It would indicate that classes existed in the database that were not offered and hence had no students in them.

Now that we have a STUDENT+COURSE entity (an intersecting entity), our grammatical description of this intersecting entity would be as discussed next.

8.3.1 The Entity

This database records data about STUDENT-COURSE combinations: STUDENT+COURSE. For each STUDENT+COURSE in the database, we record a grade.

8.3.1.1 The Attributes

For each STUDENT+COURSE combination, there will be one and only one grade. The value for grade will not be subdivided.

8.3.1.2 The Keys

(d) Intersecting entity: The key of the intersection entity will consist of the concatenation of the foreign keys of the owner entities.

In the STUDENT-COURSE example, the intersection entity will contain a student_ID and a course_ID—both foreign keys; hence, the key of this entity will be student_ID+course_ID (the plus sign here means concatenation). Both attributes are necessary to identify a unique row in the database.

The last statement is very close (and for a user, it is hoped indistinguishable) from the key statements found in the "attribute on a relationship" grammar given:

For the relationship between STUDENT *and* COURSE, we will record a grade. The grade depends on both entities STUDENT *and* COURSE for identification.

8.4 MORE ENTITIES AND RELATIONSHIPS

In the handling of a database, we have to model the information presented. We will likely have situations that call for more than two entities and more than one binary relationship. Again, a binary relationship is a relationship between two entities. (In Chapter 9, we look at ternary and higher relationship combinations.) This section deals with situations for which the information about the database indicates that we have to expand our diagrams with more entities, but all the connections will be binary.

8.4.1 More than Two Entities

Let us again reconsider the STUDENT-COURSE ER diagram (Figure 8.1). If this database were oriented toward a college, the courses would have instructors, and the instructors would be related to the courses. We may add INSTRUCTOR to our database per our methodology steps 4 and 5, which say:

> *Step 4. If another entity is appropriate, draw the second entity with its attributes. Repeat step 2 to see if this entity should be further split into more entities.*
> *Step 5. Connect entities with relationships (one or more) if relationships exist.*

If we added instructors to Figure 8.1, we arrive at Figure 8.3 (attributes other than the primary keys are intentionally left off to unclutter the diagram). The relationship between INSTRUCTOR and COURSE is teach; instructors teach many courses, a course is taught by an instructor (loosely speaking). The participation would be determined by the situation, but we will choose one for our example. Stated more precisely, we would say it in the way that follows.

8.4.1.1 Pattern 4—x:y::1:M, from the 1 Side, Partial Participation

Short: An instructor may teach many courses.

which actually means

> *Long: An instructor, but not necessarily all instructors (which are recorded in the database), may teach many (one or more) courses. Some instructors may not teach courses.*

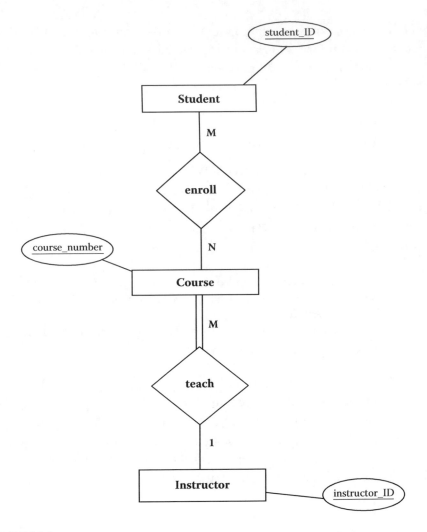

FIGURE 8.3
An ER diagram (with only primary keys) showing a STUDENT/COURSE/INSTRUCTOR database.

8.4.1.2 Pattern 1—x:y::M:1, from the M Side, Full Participation

Short: *Courses must be taught by instructors.*

which actually means:

Long: *Courses, which are recorded in the database, must be taught by one and only one instructor. No course is taught by more than one instructor.*

In this diagram (Figure 8.3), the INSTRUCTOR entity is related to the COURSE entity. There could be a relationship between the INSTRUCTOR and STUDENT entities, but the relationships in Figure 8.3 are assumed to be the only ones that exist. One could argue that the other possible relationships are advisor, mentor, counselor, coach, … , but remember that we are modeling only what exists and not what might be. We assume that the diagram represents the information given and only the information given.

8.4.2 Adding More Attributes that Evolve into Entities

Now, consider adding "building" to each of the entities. Students live in buildings (dorms), courses are taught in buildings (classrooms and labs), and instructors have offices in buildings. "Building" may be added as an attribute of each of the three entities and not considered as an entity unto itself. Why is it not an entity? At this stage, we have not expressed the desire to record information about buildings. If buildings (dorm rooms, classrooms, office rooms) were considered as attribute items for appropriate entities, then we would have the ER diagram as in Figure 8.4.

Now that we have added buildings to our database (Figure 8.4), suppose we evolve yet again to where we now decide that we want to record more information about buildings, or put another way, we want to make BUILDING an entity. We would then have to connect other entities to BUILDING with appropriate relationships. Such a design is depicted in Figure 8.5 (only key attributes are shown). Whether we begin with the idea of BUILDING as an entity or evolve to it by starting with STUDENTS, COURSES, and INSTRUCTORS, we need to constantly ask the question, "Is this item in the ER diagram one that we want to record information about or not? Should this be an entity?" In Figure 8.5, we have depicted BUILDING as an entity with only key attributes. In the evolution of our database, we will add attributes to entities once the frame-like diagram is clear. For an embellished ER diagram with more attributes and cardinalities, see Figure 8.6.

CHECKPOINT 8.1
1. In Figure 8.6, why is BUILDING an entity and not an attribute of another entity?
2. Why is the room_number attribute attached to the lives in relationship rather than the STUDENT entity?

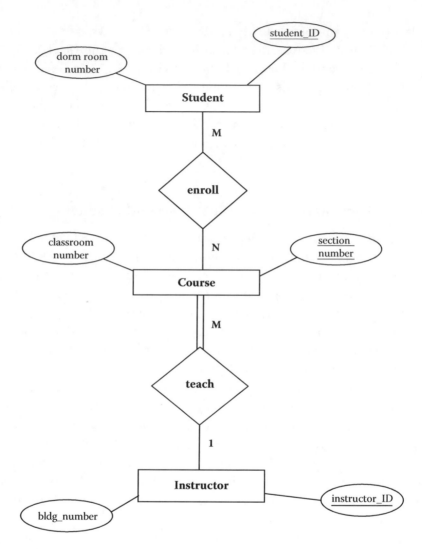

FIGURE 8.4
An ER diagram (with only primary keys) showing a STUDENT/COURSE/INSTRUCTOR database with building attributes.

3. What will make you decide whether an attribute should be connected to ENTITYA or ENTITYB or on the relationship connecting ENTITYA and ENTITYB?

4. Why are all the lines leaving BUILDING (on Figure 8.6) single lines (partial participation)?

5. According Figure 8.6, does a student have to enroll in a course?

6. According to Figure 8.6, how many courses can an instructor teach?

7. According to Figure 8.6, does an instructor have to teach a course?

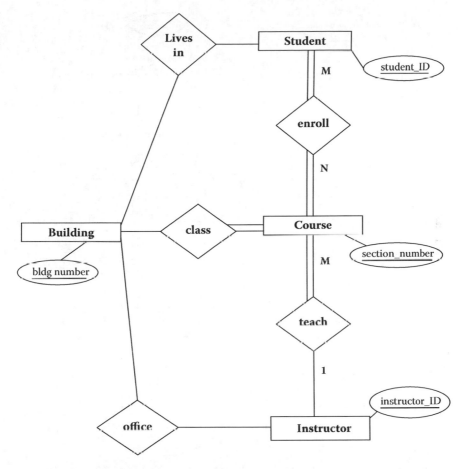

FIGURE 8.5
ER diagram (with only primary keys) showing a STUDENT/COURSE/INSTRUCTOR/ BUILDING database.

8. According to Figure 8.6, does a course have to be taught by an instructor?
9. According to Figure 8.6, a course can be taught by how many instructors?

8.5 MORE EVOLUTION OF THE DATABASE

Let us reconsider the ER diagram in Figure 8.6. As the diagram is analyzed, the user may ask: "Why is a room_number attribute not included in the class relationship?" Why is there not an office number for the office

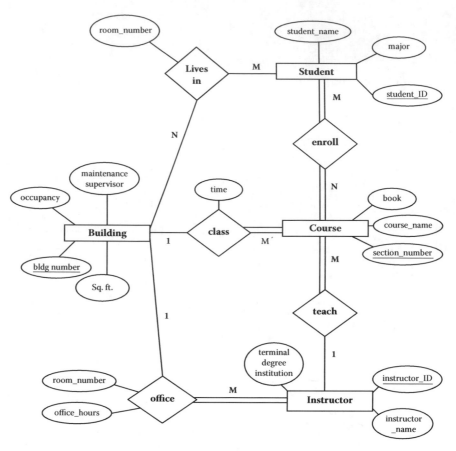

FIGURE 8.6
ER diagram showing a STUDENT/COURSE/INSTRUCTOR/BUILDING database.

relationship? There may be several reasons for the omission: (a) This information was not mentioned in the analysis stage; (b) the data is not necessary (that is, there may be only one classroom per building, or office numbers may not be recorded for advisors); (c) it was an oversight, and the data should be added. Suppose now it is decided that room_number is important for all of the relationships or entities. Suppose that we want to identify the room_number associated with instructors and buildings, courses and buildings, and students and buildings. We might "evolve" the diagram to that of Figure 8.7.

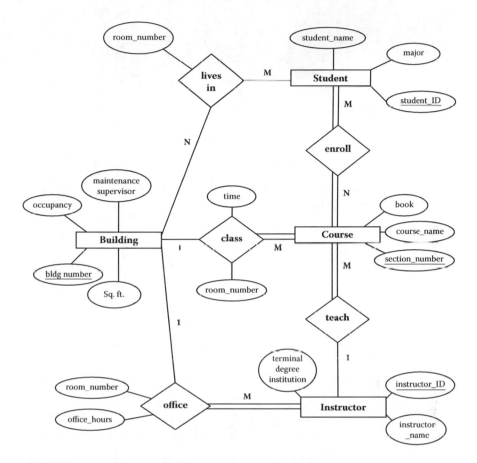

FIGURE 8.7

ER diagram showing a STUDENT/COURSE/INSTRUCTOR/BUILDING database with room_number added to the relationships where needed.

In Figure 8.7, we have room number as a relationship attribute. In this case, we have also added information attached to BUILDING: bldg_number, occupancy, maintenance supervisor, and sq. ft.

8.6 ATTRIBUTES THAT EVOLVE INTO ENTITIES

In this section, we illustrate one more time the idea that we have to model "what is" and not necessarily "what might be." Also, we again see how an attribute might become an entity. Suppose in the design process, you

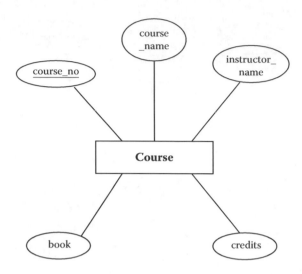

FIGURE 8.8
COURSE entity with attributes.

are given some data by a user and told to design a database. Suppose the following data is presented:

Here, you have a course name, a course number, credit hours, an instructor, and a book identified by its authors. The beginning ER diagram *might* look like Figure 8.8, regarding an ER diagram of the COURSE entity in a database. Why "*might* look like … "? The answer lies in eliciting correct requirements from our user.

If all of the information that was ever to be recorded about this data was mentioned, then this single-entity ER diagram would describe the database. However, one could realistically argue that things that we have described as attributes could themselves be entities. Both the instructor and the book would be candidates for being diagrammed as entities if the envisioned database called for it. Now, suppose we expand the database to include information about instructors. If this were the case, we might want to go beyond recording the instructor_name and include such attributes as the instructor's department, date_hired, the school where the instructor received the terminal degree. With the additional information about the INSTRUCTOR, the ER diagram would have two entities and would look like Figure 8.9.

In Figure 8.9, we have depicted the INSTRUCTOR entity as weak because of the dependence on COURSE. Also, it is presumed that instructor names

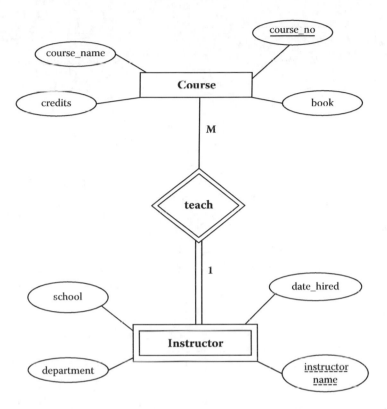

FIGURE 8.9
ER diagram of the COURSE-INSTRUCTOR database with INSTRUCTOR as a weak entity.

may not be unique. If the instructor were identified uniquely with an attribute like instructor Social Security number, and if instructors could exist independent of course, then the entity could become strong and would look like Figure 8.10. The point of this section is to bring out the idea that an entity is not an entity just because one might want to record information "someday." There would have to be some *planned intent* to include the data that would be identified by the entity. Further, the definition of weak or strong entity would depend on the identifying information that was to be provided.

Finally, if no information about instructors were ever planned, then the first ER diagram (Figure 8.8) could well describe the database. We will leave as an exercise the extension of Figure 8.10 to include BOOK as an entity.

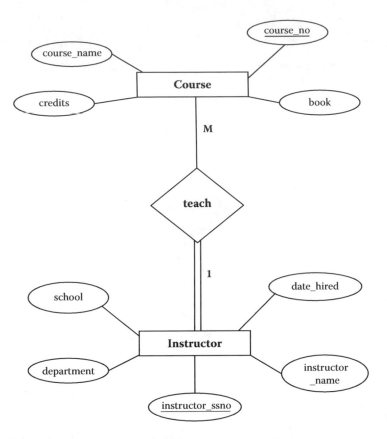

FIGURE 8.10
ER diagram of the COURSE-INSTRUCTOR database with INSTRUCTOR as a strong entity.

8.7 RECURSIVE RELATIONSHIPS

In a recursive relationship, the same entity participates more than once in different roles. Recursive relationships are also sometimes called **unary** relationships.

Consider a human resources department in a company. Personnel are likely to have an employee number, a name, and so on. In addition to existing as an entity for all employees of an organization, there are relationships between individuals of the entity set, personnel. The most obvious relationship is that of employee-supervisor. How would we depict the employee-supervisor relationship when we have only one entity? The answer is shown in Figure 8.11.

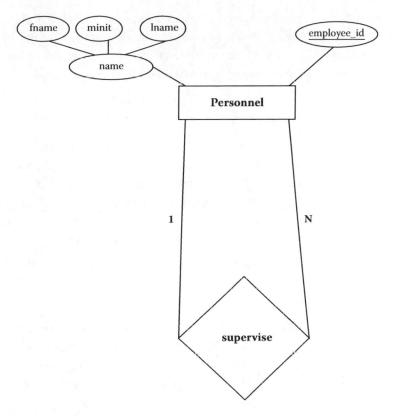

FIGURE 8.11
A classic recursive relationship: EMPLOYEE-SUPERVISOR.

Figure 8.11 shows the **PERSONNEL** entity with some set of attributes. Then, the relationship of supervise is added and connected to **PERSONNEL** on both ends. The cardinality of the relationship is 1:N with some employee's supervisor supervising many other employees and employees having one supervisor. We use partial participation from the supervisor side as not all personnel are supervisors—an employee may supervise many other employees. The participation of supervised employee is also partial. Although most employees are supervised by one supervisor, some employee will be at the top of the hierarchy with no supervisor. In recursive relationships, we often represent a hierarchy. All hierarchies have a top spot with no "supervision" (as far as the database is concerned). All hierarchies are always partial-partial.

So, when a relationship between individuals arises within the same entity set, it would be improper to have two entities since most of the information in the entities is basically the same. If we created two entities, then we would have redundancy in the database. Using the example given, if we used two different entities rather than a recursive relationship, then an employee would be recorded in two different places.

8.7.1 Recursive Relationships and Structural Constraints

Recursive relationships can only have partial participation, but the cardinality can be one to one, one to many, and many to many. Full participation in a recursive relationship would mean that every instance of an entity participates in a relationship with itself, which would not make sense.

Next, we look at some examples of cardinalities as interpreted in recursive relationships using our human resources database example:

8.7.1.1 One-to-One Recursive Relationship (Partial Participation on Both Sides)

Figure 8.12 presents an example of an entity, PERSONNEL, that is related to itself through a married_to relationship. This means that a person in this database may be married to one other person in this same database. In this example, we have a relationship that is not a hierarchy.

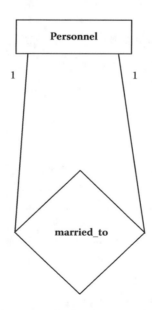

FIGURE 8.12
One-to-one recursive relationship (partial participation on both sides).

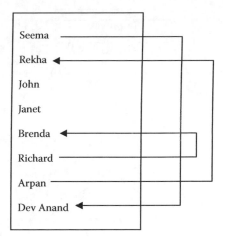

FIGURE 8.13
Instances of one-to-one recursive relationship (partial participation on both sides).

Some instances of this relationship are shown in Figure 8.13. From Figure 8.13, we can see that Seema is married to Dev Anand, Arpan is married to Rekha, and so on.

8.7.1.2 One-to-Many Recursive Relationship (Partial Participation on Both Sides)

The one-to-many recursive relationship (partial participation on both sides) is the most common recursive relationship cardinality. An example of this relationship may be if one employee may supervise many other employees (as shown in Figure 8.14). As we mentioned, this is a hierarchical relationship and is always partial-partial.

Instances of this relationship are shown in Figure 8.15. From Figure 8.15, we can see that Tom Smith supervises Sudip Bagui and Tim Vaney, Rishi Kapoor supervises Mala Saha and Korak Gupta, Korak Gupta supervises Roop Mukerjee, and so on.

8.7.1.3 Many-to-Many Recursive Relationship (Partial on Both Sides)

In the example of the many-to-many recursive relationship (partial on both sides), we could say that courses may be prerequisites to zero or more other courses. This relationship is depicted in Figure 8.16. The sense of prerequisite here is not hierarchical, but more like a situation for which there are many courses that are interrelated.

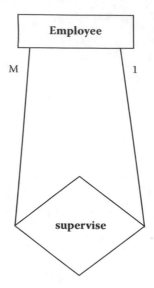

FIGURE 8.14
One-to-many recursive relationship (partial participation on both sides).

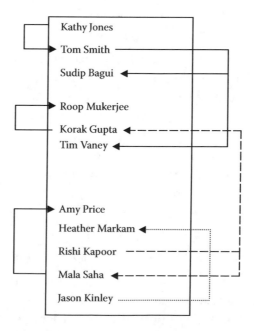

FIGURE 8.15
Instances of one-to-many recursive relationship (partial participation on both sides).

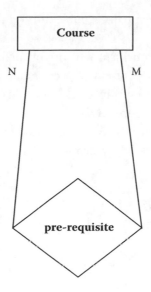

FIGURE 8.16

Many-to-many recursive relationship (partial participation on both sides).

8.8 MULTIPLE RELATIONSHIPS

So far, we have mostly discussed two entities with one relationship. This section discusses how two entities can have more than one binary relationship.

Consider a diagram that has two entities: STUDENT and FACULTY. Suppose we have no other entities in the database. Suppose further that the STUDENT entity has the following attributes: name, student_ no, birthdate, and high_school from which the student graduated. The FACULTY entity could have the following attributes: name, ssno (Social Security number), department, office_number. In developing the diagram, we find two distinct verbs to describe the connection between STUDENT and FACULTY. STUDENTs are *instructed by* FACULTY, and FACULTY *advise* STUDENTs. There are two distinct relationships that we need to add to our diagram: instruct and advise. Each distinct relationship is given its own "diamond." The ER diagram for this is shown in Figure 8.17a.

In this diagram, all relationships are arbitrarily shown as partial; that is, there will be some faculty who do not advise students, and some students who are not instructed by faculty. In constructing ER diagrams, one has to include however many distinct relationships exist. It would be incorrect to try to make a relationship do "double duty" and stand for two different relationship ideas.

In this example, an embellishment might include intersection data for the instruct relationship (a grade in a course, for example). Intersection data for the advise relationship could be date_assigned, last_meeting, and so on, as shown in Figure 8.17b.

The placing of relationships in the ER diagram is covered in our ER design methodology in step 5, which we redefine here:

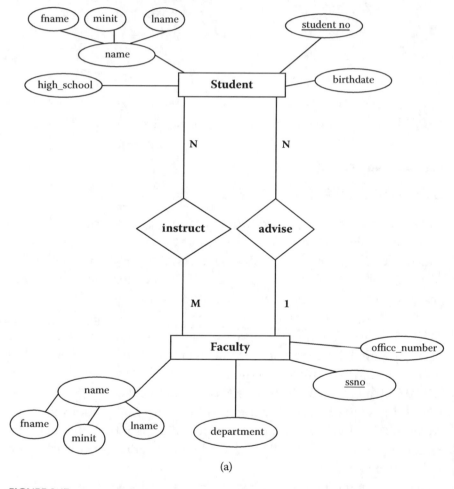

(a)

FIGURE 8.17
(a) ER diagram with two entities and two relationships.

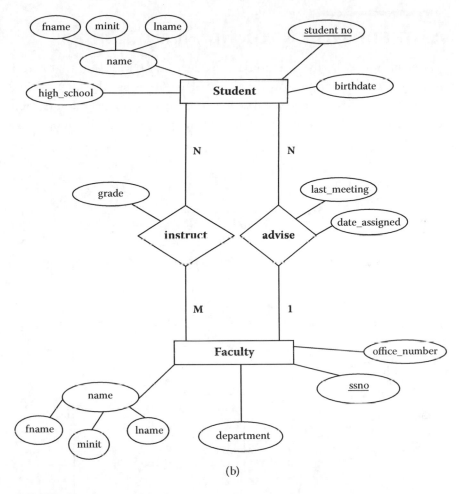

FIGURE 8.17
(b) ER diagram with two entities and two relationships and some intersection attributes.

The original Step 5 was

> **Step 5. Connect entities with relationships as they are elicited.**

We may add to this guideline that if multiple relationships are present, they are added to the diagram; however, this is likely redundant, so we will simply append the phrase (one or more):

> **Step 5. Connect entities with relationships (one or more) as relationships are elicited.**

8.9 THE DERIVED OR REDUNDANT RELATIONSHIP

Many authors describe a redundant or derived relationship that could arise in a relationship "loop" like that of Figure 8.18. The loop notion comes from the pictorial idea that the lines form a closed graph (which is actually more like a rectangle, but we are going to call it a loop). The

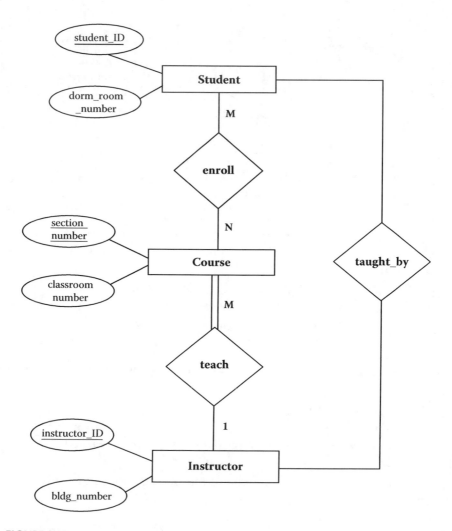

FIGURE 8.18

ER diagram showing a STUDENT/COURSE/INSTRUCTOR database with a "redundant" relationship.

idea of redundancy is that since students take courses and each course is taught by an instructor, you do not need a taught_by relationship because you can get that information without the extra relationship. If such a relationship exists, then it should be excised, but there are caveats.

First, one has to be sure that the redundant relationship is truly redundant. If the added relation were advised_by instead of taught_by, then the relationship should stay because it has a completely different sense than taught_by.

Second, if the relationship loop is present it may mean that only one of the two redundant relationships should be kept, and the semantics should point to which one. In Figure 8.18, the INSTRUCTOR is more likely related to a COURSE than to a STUDENT. So, the better choice of which relationship to keep would be the original one, teach. It is conceivable that a designer might have included the taught_by relationship first, only later to include the teach relationship. Then, by examining the diagram for loops, one could deduce that the taught_by was redundant.

Third, one or both of the relationships may have an intersection attribute that would suggest which relationship (or both) should be kept. In Figure 8.19, we included the time attribute, which was put with the teach relationship as an instructor teaches a course at a particular time.

The idea of derived or redundant relationships causes us to suggest one more step in our methodology:

> **Step 6b. Examine the diagram for loops that might indicate redundant relationships. If a relationship is truly redundant, excise the redundant relationship.**

CHECKPOINT 8.2
1. What is a recursive relationship?
2. What would you look for if you are trying to see if a relationship is recursive?
3. What kinds of structural constraints can recursive relationships have?
4. Can recursive relationships have full participation? Why or why not?
5. How is the recursive relationship denoted diagrammatically in the Chen-like ER model?
6. Can the same two entities have more than one relationship?
7. How would you determine if a relationship is redundant?

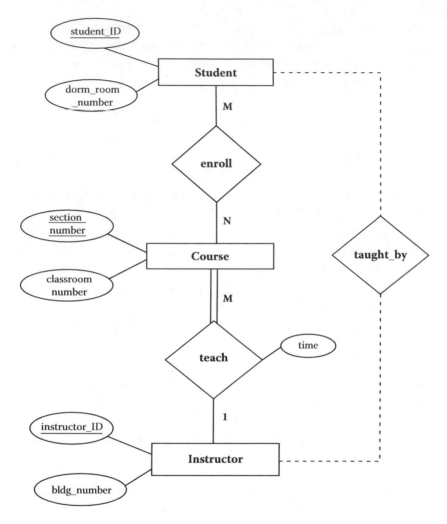

FIGURE 8.19
ER diagram showing a STUDENT/COURSE/INSTRUCTOR database with a "redundant" relationship and a time attribute.

8.10 OPTIONAL: AN ALTERNATIVE ER NOTATION FOR SPECIFYING STRUCTURAL CONSTRAINTS ON RELATIONSHIPS

We call Section 8.10 an optional section because it adds information to the ER diagram; however, the information added is not necessary to map the diagram to a functional database. Some may find this section usefully descriptive; others may find it unwarranted.

So far, we have discussed cardinality ratios in terms of their upper bounds (the maximum cardinality), shown by the M or N in the ER diagrams (shown in this and previous chapters). You will recall (from Chapter 6) that cardinality is a rough measure of the number of entity instances in one entity set that can be related to instances in another entity set.

In this section, we describe an alternative ER notation for specifying structural constraints on relationships. This notation will associate a pair of numbers (*min, max*) with each structural constraint of a relationship. This *min* and *max* may provide more information about the entities and how they are related.

The *min* is the minimum number of instances in one entity set that can be related to an instance of another entity. The *min* can be between zero and the maximum. If the *min* is zero, it implies that every instance of an entity does not have to participate in the relationship. If *min* is zero it implies partial participation. If the *min* is greater than zero, it implies full participation. We now present an ER diagram with (*min, max*) ratios.

First, let us start with the recursive relationship shown in Figure 8.20.

The (*min, max*) of (0, 1) means that each person in the PERSONNEL entity may or may not be married (shown by the zero for the *min*) and can only be married to at most one other person (shown by the *max*).

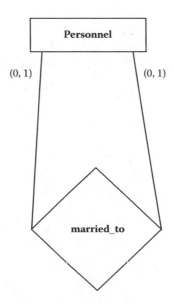

FIGURE 8.20
Recursive relationship with (*min, max*) ratios.

Next, look at Figure 8.21. From this figure, we can say that a student may not be advised by any faculty member and may be advised by up to two faculty members (shown by the minimum of zero and maximum of two). A faculty member may advise between 0 and 30 students. A faculty member may instruct between 0 and 40 students. And, a student must be instructed by one faculty member and can be instructed by up to two faculty members in this database. With the *min/max* notation, it is optional (albeit redundant) to keep the single-/double-line participation constraint. Since the single-/double-line notation is so common, we suggest keeping it.

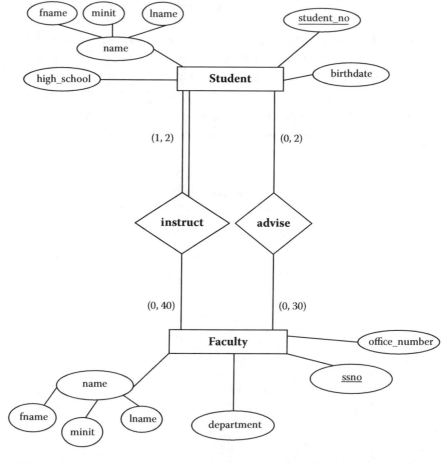

FIGURE 8.21
ER diagram showing an alternative ER notation for specifying structural constraints.

CHECKPOINT 8.3 (OPTIONAL)

1. What lower bound of cardinality does full participation imply?
2. What does a *min/max* ratio of (1, 1) between two entities imply?
3. What kind of participation ratio (full participation or partial participation) does a *min/max* ratio of (0, 1) imply?

8.11 REVIEW OF THE METHODOLOGY

To review, our methodology for designing ER diagrams has now evolved to:

8.11.1 ER Design Methodology

Step 1. Select one primary entity from the database requirements description and show attributes to be recorded for that entity. Label keys if appropriate and show some sample data.

Step 2. Use structured English for entities, attributes, and keys to describe the database that has been elicited.

Step 3. Examine attributes in the existing (primary) entities (possibly with user assistance) to find out if information about one of the entities is to be recorded.

(We change "primary" to "existing" because we redo step 3 as we add new entities.)

Step 3a. If information about an attribute is needed, then make the attribute an entity, and then

Step 3b. Define the relationship back to the original entity.

Step 4. If another entity is appropriate, draw the second entity with its attributes. Repeat steps 2 and 3 to see if this entity should be further split into more entities.

Step 5. Connect entities with relationships (one or more) if relationships exist.

Step 6. State the exact nature of the relationships in structured English from all sides, for example, if a relationship is A:B::1:M, then there is a relationship from A(1) to B(M) and from B(M) back to A(1).

Step 6a. Examine the list of attributes and determine whether any of them need to be identified by two (or more) entities. If so, place the attribute on an appropriate relationship that joins the two entities.

> **Step 6b. Examine the diagram for loops that might indicate redundant relationships. If a relationship is truly redundant, excise the redundant relationship.**
> **Step 7. Show some sample data.**
> **Step 8. Present the "as designed" database to the user complete with the English for entities, attributes, keys, and relationships. Refine the diagram as necessary.**

The grammar to describe our entities, attributes, and keys has evolved as discussed next.

8.11.2 The Entity

This database records data about ENTITY. For each ENTITY in the database, we record *att(1), att(2), att(3), ... att(n)*.

8.11.2.1 The Attributes

For atomic attributes, *att(j)*:
>   For each ENTITY, there will be one and only one *att(j)*. The value for *att(j)* will not be subdivided.

For composite attributes, *att(j)*:
>   For each ENTITY, we will record *att(j)*, which is composed of *x, y, z, ... (x, y, z)* are the component parts of *att(j)*.

For multivalued attributes, *att(j)*:
>   For each ENTITY, we will record *att(j)*'s. There may be more than one *att(j)* recorded for each ENTITY.

For attributes of relationships, *att(j)*:

For the relationship between ENTITY1 and ENTITY2, we will record a(n) *att(j)*. The *att(j)* depends on both entities ENTITY1 and ENTITY2 for identification.

8.11.2.2 The Keys

For the key(s):

(a) More than one candidate key (strong entity):
>   For each ENTITY, we will have the following candidate keys: *att(j), att(k), ...* (where *j, k* are candidate key attributes).

(b) One candidate key (strong entity):
>   For each ENTITY, we will have the following primary key: *att(j)*

(c) No candidate keys (perhaps a weak entity):
    For each ENTITY, we do not assume that any attribute will be
    unique enough to identify individual entities.

(d) No candidate keys (perhaps an intersecting entity):
    For each ENTITY, we do not assume that any attribute will be
    unique enough to identify individual entities.

8.12 MAPPING RULES FOR RECURSIVE RELATIONSHIPS

Recursive relationships are really binary 1:1, 1:N, or M:N relationships. We
discussed the mapping rules for these types of relationships in Chapter 6.

In Chapter 6, the mapping rule was discussed for two entities. If there is
only one entity (as in a recursive relationship) rather than two entities, the
rules basically stay the same, but the single entity is viewed as two entities, ENTITY_A and ENTITY_B. The primary key is rerecorded in the same
table with a different connotation or role. Two types of mapping rules can
be developed to map recursive entities.

> *Mapping Rule 12—Mapping 1:N recursive relationships.* **Re-include
> the primary key of the table with the recursive relationship in the
> same table, giving it some other role name.**

For example, Figure 8.11 will be mapped to

PERSONNEL(fname, lname, minit, <u>employee_id</u>, super_id)

The employee_id is the primary key of the PERSONNEL relation. The
super_id is also an employee_id, but its role and its connotation are different. Here is some sample data:

PERSONNEL

fname	lname	minit	employee_id	super_id
Richard	Earp	W	8945	9090
Boris	Yelsen		9090	null
Helga	Hogan	H	3841	9090
Sudip	Bagui	K	8767	9090
Tina	Tanner		5050	8945

Mapping Rule 13—Mapping M:N recursive relationships. **Create a separate table for the relationship (as in mapping rule 5).**

As an example, assume that Figure 8.11 was an M:N relationship. Then Figure 8.11 would map to the above relation (**PERSONNEL**) and a new linking relationship-entity:

PERSONNEL_SUPERVISOR(employee_id, super_id)

And with some sample data:

PERSONNEL_SUPERVISOR

employee_id	super_id
8945	9090
9090	null
3841	9090
8767	9090
5050	8945

CHECKPOINT 8.4
1. Map the recursive relationship shown in Figure 8.14 to a relational database and show some sample data.
2. If Figure 8.14 was an M:N relationship, how would you map this recursive relationship to a relational database? Show the mapping with some sample data.

8.13 CHAPTER SUMMARY

This chapter looked at different aspects of binary relationships in ER diagrams and refined several steps in the ER design methodology. The refining of the ER design methodology means a continuous assessment and reassessment of the ER diagram that is drawn after discussion with the users. The idea that relationships could have attributes, how attributes evolve into entities, recursive relationships, and derived and redundant relationships was discussed with examples and diagrams. The ER design methodology steps were refined to include all of this information into the new and evolving methodology. Toward the end of the chapter, an alternative

ER notation for specifying structural constraints on relationships was presented. On completing this chapter, the reader or database creator should be able to efficiently design a database with binary relationships. The next chapter deals with ternary and other higher-order relationships.

CHAPTER 8 EXERCISES

In each of the exercises that follow, the admonition to "construct an ER diagram" implies not only the diagram but also the structured grammatical description of the diagram.

Exercise 8.1

Define and state in precise terms the cardinality and participation in Figure 8.6, the student/course/instructor/building database. Discuss the structural constraints of Figure 8.6. What are the participations, what are the cardinalities, and under which circumstances would the ones depicted be correct or incorrect?

Exercise 8.2

Consider the following data and construct an ER diagram; use structured grammar to rationalize your constraints. The following are the data: horse name, race, owner, odds at post, post position, date of race, order of finish, year to date earnings, owner name and address.

Exercise 8.3

In the chapter, we described a database that had two entities, COURSE and INSTRUCTOR (refer to Figure 8.10). Book was left as an attribute of COURSE. Extend the database to include BOOK as an entity. Attributes of BOOK might include book title, author, price, edition, publisher.

Exercise 8.4

Refer to Figure 8.7. Change Figure 8.7 to include the following information: One building can have a maximum of 99 students living in it. A student has to enroll in at least one class and can enroll in a maximum of five classes. A class has to enroll at least 5 students and can enroll a maximum of 35 students. An instructor may or may not teach a class and can teach up to three classes. A course has to have one instructor teaching it, and only one instructor can teach a particular course. An instructor may or may not have an office and can have up to two offices. A building may or may not have an office and can have up to 15 offices. A course has to be offered in one classroom and can only be offered in one classroom.

BIBLIOGRAPHY

Earp, R., and Bagui, S. 2000. Binary relationships in entity relationships in entity relationship (ER) diagrams. *Data Base Management Journal,* 22:10–43.

Elmasri, R., and Navathe, S. B. 2007. *Fundamentals of Database Systems.* Reading, MA: Addison-Wesley.

Sanders, L. 1995. *Data Modeling.* Danvers, MA: Boyd & Fraser.

Teorey, T. J., Nadeau, T., and Lightstone, S. S. 2005. *Database Modeling and Design: Logical Design.* Morgan Kaufman, San Francisco, CA.

CASE STUDY

West Florida Mall (continued)

So far in our case study, we have developed the major entities and relationships and mapped these to a relational database (with some sample data). Then, on reviewing step 7, which says

> *Step 7. Present the "as designed" database to the user complete with the English for entities, attributes, keys, and relationships. Refine the diagram as necessary.*

Suppose we got some additional input from the user:

An employee can also be a department manager, and a department manager can manage at most one department. We have to store information on the department manager: the name, Social Security number, which store he or she is working for, which department he or she is working for. A department manager supervises at least one employee and may manage several employees.

On reviewing these additional specifications, we can see that we have a recursive relationship developing since an employee can be a department manager supervising other employees.

So, using mapping rule 12, we will reinclude the primary key of the EMPLOYEE entity in itself, giving us the following EMPLOYEE relation:

EMPLOYEE(ename, essn, dnum, snum, dm_ssn)

And, with some sample data:

EMPLOYEE

ename	essn	dnum	snum	dm_ssn
Kaitlyn	987-754-9865	501	1	276-263-9182
Fred	276-263-9182	502	1	null
Katie	982-928-2726	503	1	987-754-9865
Seema	837-937-9373	501	1	276-263-9182

.
.
.

This recursive relationship is also shown in Figure 8.22.

So, in summary our relational database has now developed to (without the data)

MALL

name	address

STORE

sloc	sname	snum	mall_name	so_ssn	sm_ssn

OWNER

so_ssn	so_name	so_off_phone	so_address

STORE MANAGER

sm_ssn	sm_name	salary

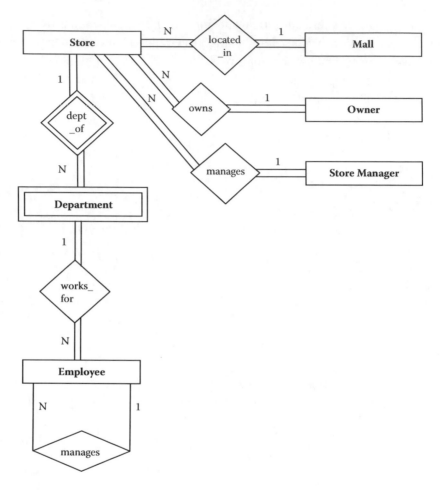

FIGURE 8.22
ER diagram of West Florida Mall developed so far.

DEPARTMENT

dname	dnum	snum

EMPLOYEE

ename	essn	snum	dm_ssn	dnum

We continue the development of this case study at the end of the next chapter.

9

Ternary and Higher-Order ER Diagrams

9.1 INTRODUCTION

All relationships that we have dealt with so far in previous chapters have been binary relationships. Although binary relationships seem natural to most of us, in reality it is sometimes necessary to connect three or more entities. If a relationship connects three entities, it is called a *ternary* or *3-ary* relationship. If a relationship connects more than three entities (*n* entities), it is called an *n*-ary relationship, where *n* equals the number of entities that participate in the relationship. The *n*-ary relationships ($n \geq 3$) are also referred to as *higher-order* relationships.

In this chapter, we consider relationships that connect three or more entities. First we look at ternary (3-ary) relationships. Ternary relationships arise for three main reasons: (a) if we have intersection attributes that require three different entities to identify the attribute; (b) if we have a relationship of a relationship; and (c) by reverse engineering. Since we discuss reverse engineering in Chapter 11, we do not discuss the development of ternary relationships from reverse engineering in this chapter.

In this chapter, we first discuss how intersection attributes create ternary relationships, and then we look at structural constraints. Next, we discuss how ternary and other *n*-ary relationships do not preclude binary relationships with the same entities and how some ternary diagrams may be resolved into binary relationships. The development of ternary relationships from relationships of relationships is also introduced. Step 6 of the entity relationship (ER) design methodology is redefined in this chapter to include ternary and other higher-order relationships.

9.2 BINARY OR TERNARY RELATIONSHIP?

Ternary relationships are required when binary relationships are not sufficient to accurately describe the semantics of an association among three entities. In this section, we explain the difference between a binary and a ternary relationship with the help of an example and show how an intersection attribute necessitates a ternary relationship.

Where binary relationships exist between entities, these relationships have structural constraints (cardinality and participation). Further, we found that attributes of relationships were also possible. In particular, we found that the M:N relationship often spawned an attribute that we called an intersection attribute (recall the STUDENT/CLASS M:N relationship and the intersection attribute grade as shown in Figure 8.1). In the binary relationship case, we made the point that an attribute like grade would infer that an M:N binary relationship must exist. Whether one determined the M:N relationship first or found the "orphaned" attribute first—the end result would be an M:N relationship with an intersection attribute.

Cases exist in database design when a relationship between more than two entities is needed. The usual case would be to find one of these orphaned attributes that necessitated the *n*-ary relationship. Consider this example:

You have a database for a company that contains the entities PRODUCT, SUPPLIER, and CUSTOMER. The usual relationships might be PRODUCT/SUPPLIER; the company buys products from a supplier—a normal, binary relationship. The intersection attribute for PRODUCT/SUPPLIER is wholesale_price (as shown in Figure 9.1a). Now, consider the CUSTOMER entity and that the customer buys products. If all customers buy products irrespective of supplier, then you have a simple, binary relationship between CUSTOMER and PRODUCT. For the CUSTOMER/PRODUCT relationship, the intersection attribute is retail_price (as shown in Figure 9.1b).

Some sample data for Figure 9.1a would be:

productID	supplierID	wholesale_price
Beans	Acme Bean Co	1.49
Beans	Baker Bean Co	1.57
Carrots	Joe's Carrots	0.89

Some sample data for Figure 9.1b would be:

customerID	productID	retail_price
Jones	Beans	2.67
Smith	Beans	2.67
Jones	Carrots	1.57

Now consider a different scenario. Suppose the customer buys products, but the price depends not only on the product but also on the supplier. Suppose you needed a **customerID**, a **productID**, and a **supplierID** to identify a price. You then have an attribute that depends on three entities; hence, you have a relationship between three entities (a ternary relationship) that will have an intersection attribute, **price**. This situation is depicted in Figure 9.2.

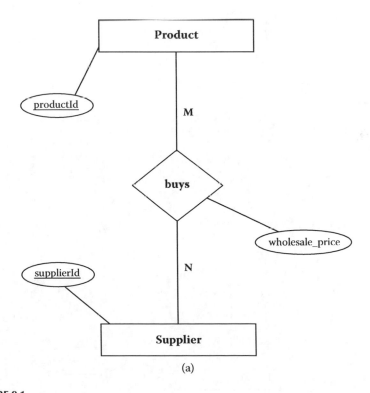

(a)

FIGURE 9.1
(a) Binary relationship between PRODUCT and SUPPLIER and an intersection attribute, WHOLESALE_PRICE.

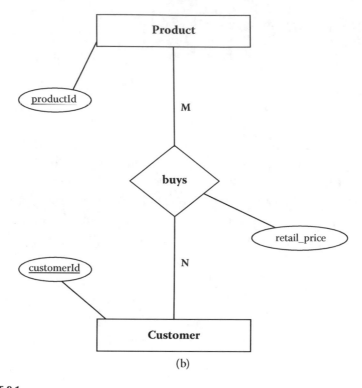

FIGURE 9.1

(b) Binary relationship between PRODUCT and CUSTOMER and an intersection attribute, RETAIL_PRICE.

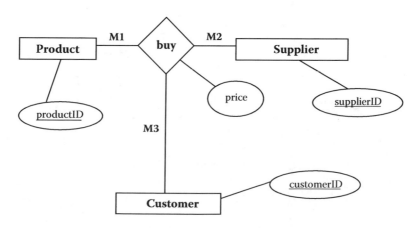

FIGURE 9.2

ER diagram (with only primary keys) showing a three-way relationship.

Figure 9.2 represents the entities PRODUCT, SUPPLIER, and CUSTOMER and a relationship, buy, among all three entities, shown by a single relationship diamond attached to all three entities.

Some sample data for Figure 9.2 would be:

customerID	productID	supplierID	price
Jones	Beans	Acme	2.65
Jones	Beans	Baker	2.77
Jones	Carrots	Joe's	1.57

This ternary case is more realistic as customers generally pay different prices for the same product by different manufacturers or suppliers. For different suppliers, one may also assume different prices for a product at different points in time. Also, for customers, one may assume that some items are bought on sale, some not. Another intersection attribute (in Figure 9.2) could be date, which could be the date of the sale of a product to a customer by a supplier.

In the case of higher-order relationships, they are most often found by finding an attribute that necessitates the existence of the n-ary relationship. Next, we look at the structural constraints of ternary relationships.

9.3 STRUCTURAL CONSTRAINTS FOR TERNARY RELATIONSHIPS

Ternary relationships can have the following types of structural constraints: one to one to one (1:1:1), one to one to many (1:1:M), one to many to many (1:M:M), and many to many to many (M:M:M or M:M:N), with full or partial participation on each one of the sides. The following presents an example of the M:M:M relationship with partial participation on all sides.

9.3.1 Many to Many to Many (M:M:M)

Figure 9.3 shows an example of a M:M:N relationship using the three entities PRODUCT, SUPPLIER, and CUSTOMER, all with partial participation. This figure shows that many customers may buy many products from many suppliers, at different prices.

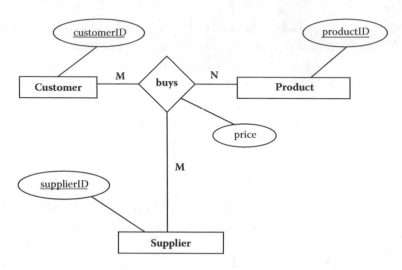

FIGURE 9.3

ER diagram showing a ternary many-to-many-to-many relationship (partial participation on all sides).

Instances of this relationship can be illustrated as shown in Figure 9.4:

CHECKPOINT 9.1

1. What is a ternary relationship?
2. What is an *n*-ary relationship?
3. What are higher-order relationships?
4. Using the three entities presented (**PRODUCT**, **SUPPLIER**, and **CUSTOMER**), draw an ER diagram that depicts the following: A customer must buy one and only one product from a supplier at a particular price on a particular date.
5. Using the three entities presented (**PRODUCT**, **SUPPLIER**, and **CUSTOMER**), draw an ER diagram that depicts the following: A supplier must supply many products to many customers at different prices on different dates.
6. Think of some more intersection attributes for the **PRODUCT**, **SUPPLIER**, and **CUSTOMER** ternary example presented in Figure 9.3.
7. What situations might create each of the following structural constraints?
   a. **PRODUCT:SUPPLIER:CUSTOMER::1:1:1**, partial participation on all sides
   b. **PRODUCT:SUPPLIER:CUSTOMER::1:M:M**, partial participation on all sides
   c. **PRODUCT:SUPPLIER:CUSTOMER::1:1:1**, full participation on all sides

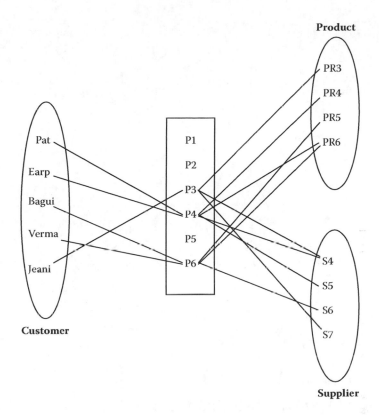

FIGURE 9.4

Instances of a ternary many-to-many-to-many relationship for CUSTOMER:PRODUCT:SUPPLIER.

9.4 AN EXAMPLE OF AN *N*-ARY RELATIONSHIP

An *n*-ary relationship describes the association among *n* entities. For our ternary example, we said that the price was dependent on a PRODUCT, SUPPLIER, and CUSTOMER. If we have a situation for which the price is dependent on a PRODUCT, SUPPLIER, CUSTOMER, as well as STATE, then price is dependent on four entities; hence, it is an *n*-ary (in this case, a 4-ary) relationship. In an *n*-ary (or, in this case, 4-ary) relationship, a single relationship diamond connects the *n* (4) entities, as shown in Figure 9.5. Here, also, the intersection attribute is price. (More nonintersection attributes on the entities would be expected but were not included in the diagram.)

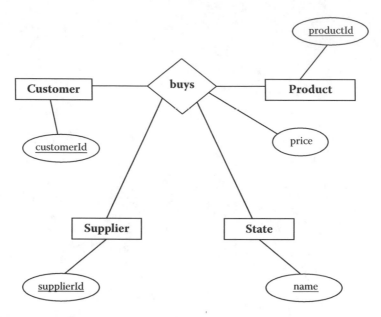

FIGURE 9.5
ER diagram showing *n*-ary relationship.

9.5 *N*-ARY RELATIONSHIPS DO NOT PRECLUDE BINARY RELATIONSHIPS

Just because there is a ternary relationship does not mean that binary relationships among the entities may not exist. Using a similar example of CUSTOMERS, VENDORS, and PRODUCTS, suppose retail vendors and suppliers of products have a special relationship that does not involve customers, such as wholesaling with an entirely different price structure. This binary relationship may be shown separately from, and in addition to, a ternary relationship. See Figure 9.6 for a basic version of this two-way (binary) relationship and three-way (ternary) relationship ER diagram in the same database.

Figure 9.6 tells us that we have a binary relationship between PRODUCT and VENDOR, with all PRODUCTs and VENDORs participating. Both the VENDOR and the CUSTOMER buy the PRODUCT, but in the VENDOR-PRODUCT binary relationship, the action is wholesale buying; hence, the relationship is labeled buy_wholesale and does not involve the customer. We changed the ternary relationship to read buy_retail to distinguish the two relationships.

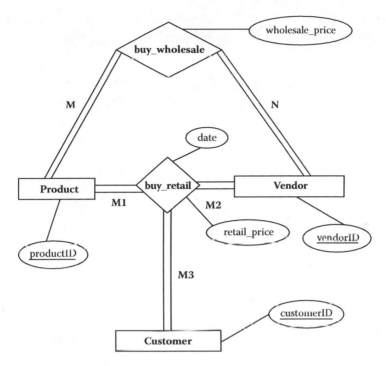

FIGURE 9.6
ER diagram (with only primary keys) showing a three-way and a two-way relationship.

9.6 METHODOLOGY AND GRAMMAR FOR THE *N*-ARY RELATIONSHIP

We need to revisit step 6 in the ER design methodology to cover the possibility of the *n*-ary relationship. The old version was:

> *Step 6. State the exact nature of the relationships in structured English from all sides, for example, if a relationship is A:B::1:M, then there is a relationship from A to B, 1 to Many, and from B back to A, Many to 1.*

We add the following sentence to step 6:

> *For ternary and higher-order (n-ary) relationships, state the relationship in structured English, being careful to mention all entities for the n-ary relationship. State the structural constraints as they exist.*

The grammar for the *n*-ary relationship must involve all of the entities linked to it. Therefore, a suitable *informal* sentence would go something like this:

ENTITY1 *Relationship* **(from/to/by)** ENTITY2 **(and) (from/to/by)** ENTITY3. It is understood that *attribute* will necessitate naming all *n* entities to identify it.

Here, if we choose some combination for Entity1, … Entity*n*, this process resolves into

Entity1:CUSTOMER
Relationship: buy
Relationship attribute: retail_price

Entity2: PRODUCT
Entity3: VENDOR
CUSTOMERS buy PRODUCTS from VENDORS. It is understood that retail_price will necessitate referencing all three entities to identify it.

With a binary relationship, we have to state two relationships. One would think that with ternary relationships, we would be bound to state three. Since the relationship attribute has already been stated, let us look at the other possibilities:

Suppose

Entity1: PRODUCT
Entity2: CUSTOMER
Entity3: VENDOR
PRODUCTS are bought by CUSTOMERS from VENDORS.

In the informal version of the statement from the diagram, little information is gained by repetition. It is suggested that other combinations be tried; however, in the *informal* statement, it seems likely that one statement, inferred from the semantics of the situation, would suffice to informally declare the nature of the relationship.

9.6.1 A More Exact Grammar

A more exact grammar for the *n*-ary relationship would be an extension of that developed for the binary relationship. Unlike the informal case, in a more formal grammatical presentation, it would be necessary to make three statements for a ternary relationship, one starting with each entity. In the binary relationship, M:N full participation case, we used the description of the relationship given next.

9.6.1.1 Pattern 3—M:N, from the M Side, Full Participation

Short: x must be related to many y.

which actually means

Long: x, which are recorded in the database, must be related to many (one or more) y. No x is related to a non-y (or) Non-x are not related to a y. (The negative will depend on the sense of the statement.)

We could generalize the structural constraint patterns to the pattern given next.

9.6.1.2 Pattern 3—k:M, from the k Side, Full Participation (k = 1 or M)

Short: Same as in Section 9.6.1.1.
Long: Same as in Section 9.6.1.1.

For the *n*-ary relationship, we extend the notation of the generalized statement using the Boolean operator "and" as shown next.

9.6.1.3 Pattern 5 (n-ary)—x:y:z::a:b:c, from the a Side, Full/Partial Participation

Short: x must/may be related to many y and many z.

The "must" comes from full participation; "may" comes from a partial one. The *a* cardinality will not matter. The *b* and *c* force us to say "one" or "many" in the statement. So, for example, for *x* as full:

Long: x, which are recorded in the database, must be related to
$b = m$ *[many (one or more)] y*
$b = 1$ *one and only one y*

and (or other appropriate linking word [from, by, to, ...])
 c = m [many (one or more)] z
 c = 1 one and only one z

No x is related to more than one z.
No x is related to more than one y.

Example 9.1

For CUSTOMERS:PRODUCTS:VENDORS::M1:M2:M3, full participation all around:

Short: CUSTOMERS *must buy many* PRODUCTS *from many* VENDORS.

Long: CUSTOMERS, *which are recorded in the database, must buy many (one or more)* PRODUCTS *from many (one or more)* VENDORS.

Other grammatical expressions are derived similarly.

Products, which are recorded in the database, must be bought by many (one or more) customers from many (one or more) vendors.
Vendors, which are recorded in the database, must sell many (one or more) products to many (one or more) customers.

A negative could be: *No customer (in this database) buys products from nonvendors.*

As with the binary cases, the negative statements would be optional, if they make sense.

9.6.2 Grammar in a Partial Participation, Ternary Relationship with an M:1:M Relationship

Let us consider Figure 9.7. In this figure, we are trying to represent a database about a graduation ceremony that has some students and some faculty attending. Roughly, we are trying to say that some STUDENTS attend a given GRADUATION with some FACULTY; some FACULTY attend a GRADUATION with some STUDENTS, and all GRADUATIONs are attended by some STUDENTS and some FACULTY. The intersection attribute is derived_attendance.

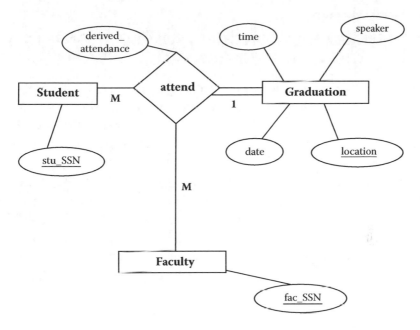

FIGURE 9.7
ER diagram (with only primary keys) showing three-way relationship with partial participations and a 1-relationship.

Here, we have partial participation on the M cardinality relationships and a 1-relationship with full participation. Using the grammar presented, we have this outcome:

STUDENT:GRADUATION:FACULTY::M:1:M
Short: *Students may attend one graduation with many faculty.*
Long: *Students, which are recorded in the database, may attend (b = 1)*
   one and only one graduation
with
   (c = m) [many (one or more)] faculty.
No student attends more than one graduation [with many faculty].

We put the [with many faculty] in square brackets because it is not really needed to make sense of the diagram.
Similarly:

> *Faculty, which are recorded in the database, may attend one graduation with*
> *many students. Some faculty do not attend graduation [with many students].*
> *Graduations must be attended by some students and some faculty. No grad-*
> *uation takes place without some students and some faculty.*

9.7 TERNARY RELATIONSHIPS FROM RELATIONSHIP-RELATIONSHIP SITUATIONS

Another scenario for which ternary relationships become necessary is if we have a scenario developing that results in a relationship of a relationship. Chen-like ER diagrams do not allow relationships of relationships; therefore, to represent this situation correctly we need to develop a ternary relationship.

For example, let us start with two entities, BOOK_PUBLISHER and MANUSCRIPT. We can initially relate the two entities as shown in Figure 9.8a. A BOOK_PUBLISHER may review many MANUSCRIPTS.

At a later stage, if some MANUSCRIPT results in a BOOK after being reviewed, this calls for a relationship of a relationship, as shown in Figure 9.8b. This relationship of a relationship becomes necessary here

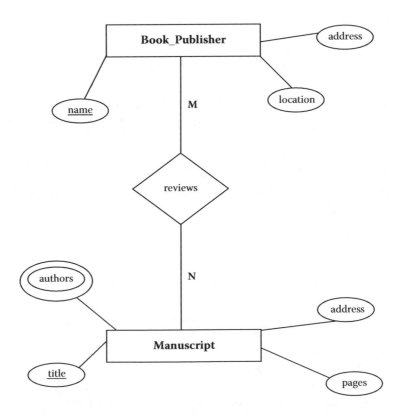

FIGURE 9.8

(a) A binary relationship between BOOK_PUBLISHER and MANUSCRIPT.

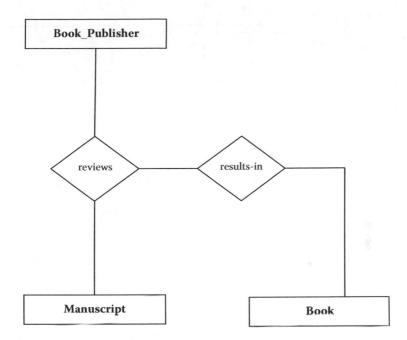

FIGURE 9.8
(b) A relationship of a relationship.

because the BOOK_PUBLISHER, reviews, and MANUSCRIPT *taken together* results-in a BOOK, as shown in Figure 9.8c.

In Figure 9.8c, the BOOK_PUBLISHER, the reviews relationship, and MANUSCRIPT *taken together* are like creating a higher-level aggregate class composed of BOOK_PUBLISHER, review, and MANUSCRIPT. This aggregate class (of the two entities and a relationship) then needs to be related to BOOK, as shown in Figure 9.8c.

To represent this situation correctly in the ER model schema presented in this book, since we cannot show a relationship of a relationship to represent this situation, we need to create a weak entity REVIEW and relate it to BOOK_PUBLISHER, MANUSCRIPT, and BOOK as shown in Figure 9.8d. The relationship BMR connects BOOK_PUBLISHER, MANUSCRIPT, and REVIEW. This review may result in a BOOK (as shown in Figure 9.8d).

In Figure 9.8d, we give priority to the weak REVIEW entity because without a review, there is no book; the manuscript and the publisher must both contribute to the review. If we tried to connect the book to the manuscript without the publisher, we would not depict the real situation.

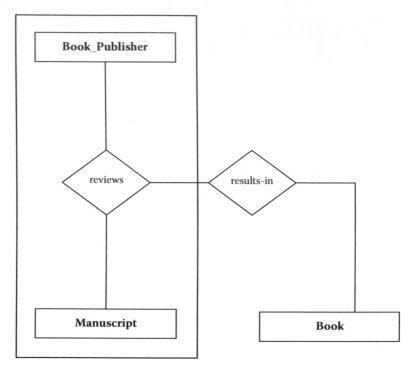

FIGURE 9.8

(c) A relationship of a relationship with a higher level aggregate class composed of BOOK-PUBLISHER, REVIEWS and MANUSCRIPT.

9.8 *N*-ARY RELATIONSHIPS THAT MAY BE RESOLVED INTO BINARY RELATIONSHIPS

Just because three entities are related does not necessarily imply a ternary relationship. In this section, we show how some ternary relationships can be resolved into binary relationships, and then we give another example of how a ternary relationship cannot be resolved into binary relationships (a real ternary relationship).

Just as the binary M:N relationship may be decomposed into two 1:M relationships, so may many *n*-ary relationships be decomposed. First, note the decomposition of the M:N into two 1:M relationships in Figure 9.9. The idea is to make the relationship an entity and hence form two simpler binary relationships.

Next, let us look again at Figure 9.7. If we decompose Figure 9.7 into three binary relationships, we have Figure 9.10. In Figure 9.10, the

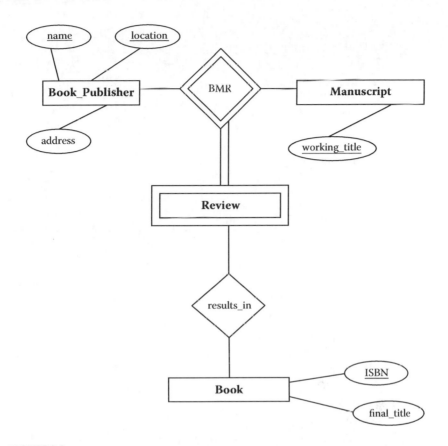

FIGURE 9.8
(d) A relationship of a relationship resolved into a ternary relationship.

new entity **ATTENDANCE** is weak and depends on the three entities **FACULTY**, **STUDENT** and **GRADUATION** for its existence. The sense of **ATTENDANCE** would be a roll of attendees for a **GRADUATION** ceremony event.

There are situations, however, for which a relationship inherently associates more than two entities. Let us take Figure 9.2 as an example. Here, if we had another attribute like an **order** that a customer places to a supplier for a product, this attribute would require all three entities—**CUSTOMER**, **PRODUCT**, and **SUPPLIER**—at the same time. An **order** would specify that a supplier would supply some quantity of a product to a customer. This relationship cannot adequately be captured by binary relationships. With binary relationships, we could only say that a customer placed an order for a product, or a supplier received an order for a product.

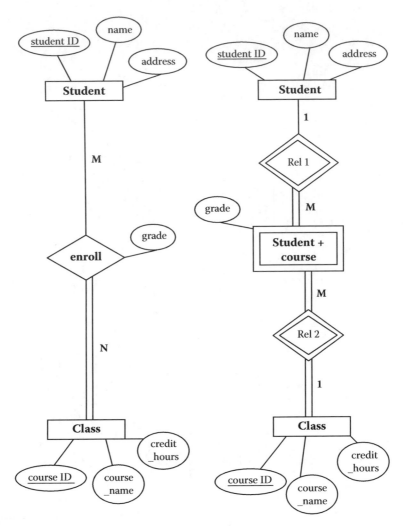

FIGURE 9.9
ER diagram of an M:N relationship replaced with two 1:M relationships.

The fact that a customer places an order for a product does not imply that the customer, C, is getting the product, P, from a supplier, S, unless all three entities are related.

CHECKPOINT 9.2
1. Can all ternary relationships be expressed in the form of binary relationships? Explain.
2. Come up with some attributes and entities of a relationship that you think could be a ternary relationship. Can this relationship be expressed in the form of a binary relationship?

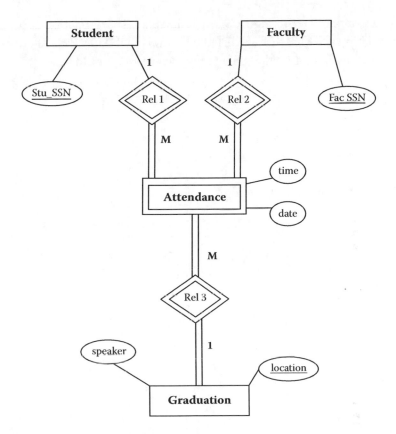

FIGURE 9.10
ER diagram (with only primary keys) showing a three-way relationship "decomposed" into three binary relationships.

9.9 MAPPING *N*-ARY RELATIONSHIPS TO A RELATIONAL DATABASE

In this section, we develop mapping rules to map *n-ary* relationships to a relational database.

> *Mapping Rule 14—Mapping* n-*ary relationships.* **For each *n*-ary relationship, create a new relation. In the new relation, include the keys of the connected entities and any attributes of the relationship. Make the keys of the connected entities the concatenated primary key of the new relation.**

For example, refer to Figure 9.2; you have a ternary relationship called buy relating PRODUCT, SUPPLIER, and CUSTOMER. There is an intersection attribute, price. The mapped relations would be:

> BUY(price, <u>productID, supplierID, customerID</u>)
> PRODUCT(<u>productID</u>, ...)
> SUPPLIER(<u>supplierID</u>, ...)
> CUSTOMER(<u>customerID</u>, ...)

And, some sample data would be:

BUY

price	productID	supplierID	customerID
$87.10	TAG1	F1	PENS
$83.98	TAG2	G25	MOB
$95.25	TAG3	G20	DEL
$99.10	TAG4	F4	GULF

PRODUCT

productID	...
TAG1	
TAG2	
TAG3	
...	

SUPPLIER

supplierID	...
F1	
G25	
G20	
...	

CUSTOMER

customerID	...
PENS	
MOB	
DEL	
...	

CHECKPOINT 9.3
1. Could Figure 9.5 be described in the form of binary relationships? Discuss.
2. What mapping rules would you follow to map Figure 9.5?
3. Map Figure 9.5 to a relational database and show some sample data.

9.10 REVIEW OF THE METHODOLOGY

Our ER design methodology has now finally evolved to the presentation that follows.

9.10.1 ER Design Methodology

Step 1. Select one primary entity from the database requirements description and show the attributes to be recorded for that entity. Label keys if appropriate and show some sample data.

Step 2. Use structured English for entities, attributes, and keys to describe the database that has been elicited.

Step 3. Examine attributes in the existing entities (possibly with user assistance) to find out if information about one of the entities is to be recorded.

(We change *primary* to *existing* because we redo step 3 as we add new entities.)

Step 3a. If information about an attribute is needed, then make the attribute an entity, and then

Step 3b. Define the relationship back to the original entity.

Step 4. If another entity is appropriate, draw the second entity with its attributes. Repeat steps 2 and 3 to see if this entity should be further split into more entities.

Step 5. Connect entities with relationships (one or more) if relationships exist.

Step 6. State the exact nature of the relationships in structured English from all sides, for example, if a relationship is A:B::1:M, then there is a relationship from A(1) to B(M) and from B(M) back to A(1).

For ternary and higher-order (n-ary) relationships, state the relationship in structured English being careful to mention all entities for the n-ary relationship. State the structural constraints as they exist.

Step 6a. Examine the list of attributes and determine whether any of them need to be identified by two (or more) entities. If so, place the attribute on an appropriate relationship that joins the two entities.

Step 6b. Examine the diagram for loops that might indicate redundant relationships. If a relationship is truly redundant, excise the redundant relationship.

Step 7. Show some sample data.

Step 8. Present the "as designed" database to the user complete with the English for entities, attributes, keys, and relationships. Refine the diagram as necessary.

9.11 CHAPTER SUMMARY

Binary relationships are the most commonly occurring kind of relationships. Some ER diagram notations do not have expressions for ternary or other higher-order relationships; that is, everything is expressed in terms of a binary relationship. In this chapter, we showed how the need for ternary relationships comes about from unique situations. For example, intersection attributes arise that need all three entities taken together for their identification. Ternary relationships can also be developed through reverse engineering, and this is discussed in Chapter 11. Also in this chapter, we discussed the structural constraints of ternary relationships and their grammar in detail and showed how some ternary or *n*-ary relationships may be resolved into binary relationships. The final section of this chapter discussed mapping rules for *n-ary* relationships.

CHAPTER 9 EXERCISES

Exercise 9.1

In Chapter 8, we described a database that had two entities, COURSE and INSTRUCTOR. "Book" was left as an attribute of COURSE. Extend the database to include book as an entity. Attributes of book might include book title, author, price, edition, and publisher. Explore the relationships that might exist here: use "in" or "by," "write," "teach," and so on. Draw an ER diagram with at least two relationships, one of them ternary. What would be some attributes of the relationships?

Exercise 9.2

Construct an ER diagram for a broker, a security, and a buyer. Include in the diagram the price of the security, the commission paid, the broker name and address, the buyer name and address, and the security exchange, symbol, and price. Include in the diagram the number of shares of the security held by a buyer (you may choose to include this by broker or not).

Exercise 9.3

Using three entities—INSTRUCTOR, CLASS, and ROOM—draw an ER diagram that depicts the following: Each CLASS in a ROOM has one INSTRUCTOR, but each INSTRUCTOR in a room may have many CLASSes, and each INSTRUCTOR of a CLASS may be in many ROOMs.

BIBLIOGRAPHY

Elmasri, R., and Navathe, S. B. 2007. *Fundamentals of Database Systems*, 5th ed. Reading, MA: Addison-Wesley.

Teorey, T. J., Nadeau, T., and Lightstone, S. S. 2005. *Database Modeling and Design: Logical Design*. San Francisco, CA: Morgan Kaufman.

Teorey, T. J., Yang, D., and Fry, J. P. 1986. A logical design methodology for relational databases using the extended entity-relationship model. *ACM Computing Surveys*, 18(2):197–222.

10

The Enhanced Entity
Relationship (EER) Model

10.1 INTRODUCTION

In the first several chapters of this book, we presented the entity relationship (ER) diagram as a conceptual database tool. The approach we took in developing an ER diagram was to assume that we were to model reality for a user. Although we worked on the basics of the ER diagram, there are situations for which the basic model fails to completely describe the reality of the data to be stored. With the increase in the types of database applications, the basic concepts of ER modeling (as originally developed by Chen) were not sufficient to represent the requirements of more complex applications like generalizations and specializations (class hierarchies). An ER model that supports these additional semantic concepts is called the *enhanced entity relationship* (EER) model (Elmasri and Navathe, 2007). In this chapter, we discuss generalizations and specializations in the EER model and develop a methodology and grammar for this extension. We also discuss shared subclasses and categories or union types. We present a methodology to map the EER diagram to a relational database.

10.2 WHAT IS A GENERALIZATION OR SPECIALIZATION?

The EER model includes all the concepts of the original ER model and additional concepts of generalizations/specializations (class hierarchies). Generalizations and specializations are associated with the idea of superclasses, subclasses, and attribute inheritance. As an example of a class hierarchy, suppose we have this entity for a store that sells sports equipment:

CUSTOMER(customer_number, name, address)

Now, suppose the database evolves to a situation for which we want to keep information that is pertinent to specific sports for some customers:

GOLF(customer_number, handicap, preferred_clubmake)
BASEBALL(customer_number, position, preferred_batsize)

The GOLF and BASEBALL entities are subclasses (specializations) within the CUSTOMER (a generalization). This example illustrates a hierarchy in which CUSTOMER is at the top of the class hierarchy and the specific sports are *subclasses*.

In an object-oriented setting, we might designate the entities like this:

CUSTOMER(customer_number, name, address)
CUSTOMER.GOLF(handicap, preferred_clubmake)
CUSTOMER.BASEBALL(position, preferred_batsize)

The inference in object-oriented programming is that GOLF is a subclass of CUSTOMER. Although not specifically stated, CUSTOMER.GOLF *inherits* all the attributes of CUSTOMER plus has attributes pertinent to GOLF. The example is one of specialization—the thinking process started with a class, CUSTOMER, and then specialized to specific sports.

The idea of classes in a database infers the ability to describe subclasses and superclasses with inheritance features.

As an example of a generalization, suppose we have a STUDENT entity that contains information about students. But, suppose we wanted to store information about all the people at an institution—not only students, but also staff and faculty. We might think of a superclass called PERSON that contains a subclass for STUDENT, another subclass for STAFF, and yet another subclass for FACULTY. Clearly, information about each of these subclasses of PERSON contains information pertinent to that subclass. Yet, the PERSON superclass entity would contain information common to all of these subclasses. PERSON may contain a name, address, and phone number, and when the STAFF subclass was defined, it would inherit those attributes of the superclass and define more attributes pertinent to STAFF. The superclass in a database is called a *generalization*, and the subclasses (STUDENT, STAFF, and FACULTY) are called *specializations*.

The concept of classes includes the use of simple attributes, as we have seen. In object-oriented programming, the concept of a class also includes actions that a class may perform. As with data typing, databases tend to focus more on attributes than procedural action.

10.3 VARIANTS

One way programmers in the past solved the problem of specializations was to create *variants*. Variants are record pieces that vary according to other parts of the record. To illustrate variants and their use in ER diagrams, consider this problem: Suppose we have an entity that has values that vary according to "the situation." For example, suppose we are modeling student-athletes, and each athlete plays some sport. We would, of course, record information about the student or athlete—a name, a unique identifier like a student number, and perhaps some other information. But then, we would like to record some information about the sport that the student-athlete may play. Let us suppose that we have an ATHLETE table with this type of data:

ATHLETE

student	student_no	other	sport	info
Baker	123456789	...	tennis	220, state rank 14
Adams	123456788	...	football	tackle, neck brace
Jones	123455676	...	golf	handicap 3

The *info* attribute has different values for different sports. These different values are called *variants*. While the introduction of variants in records seems to solve a problem of representing data, it causes database problems with storage and retrieval. In a database, one expects that all the information in a column of a table is consistent. Student numbers might contain nine digits; hence, all values in the student number column would contain a nine-digit number. With variants, this is not the case. The ATHLETE table contains inconsistent columnar information in the *info* column. This variant problem in a database has been solved in various ways over the years.

A solution to the problem of variants in records and varying attributes in entities in the ER diagram is to excise the variant and reference it back to the primary key of the "parent" information piece. We attack the problem in this way.

In ER diagrams, we recognize that we are actually storing information about two different, but related, things: a generalization called *athletes*, who have a name, ID, and so on, and specializations, which are sports (tennis, football, golf, etc.), each with its own different attributes. Since we are storing information about two things, why not create an entity called SPORTS and then relate the ATHLETE to the SPORTS entity? One SPORTS entity would not work because the SPORTS entity would be too general; we would want to store different information about different, specific sports. Furthermore, we want to store information about a sport as it pertains to each individual student-athlete.

Why then would we not create a series of weak entities—one for each sport—that depends on the ATHLETE? The answer is that we could do this, but there is a better way to look at this problem, which, as it turns out, will result in the same database as using a weak entity/relationship but gives us an alternative way to present the ER information with more expressive diagrams that include the concept of inheritance.

10.4 EXAMPLES OF GENERALIZATIONS OR SPECIALIZATIONS

Generalizations and specializations are categorizations of entities for which the specialization entity may result from generalizations containing variants. These variants are most easily handled by removing the variant from the generalization and treating it as a subclass entity and leaving the original, "fixed part" of the entity as a superclass or parent type. If we referred to the superclass as a *parent class*, then we would call the variant parts the subclasses, the *child classes*.

Pursuing the parent-child superclass/subclass idea a bit further, we can imagine the child class inheriting the characteristics of the parent class. Inheritance in this context means that the child class will have defined in it whatever attributes are defined in the parent class. In a relational database, the tying of the child to the parent (hence placing parent and child information together) is done using table combination operators called *joins*. In our sports example, we would consider the ATHLETE as a parent class and SPORTS as a child class so that when we define information about a sport, it is done in the context of maintaining the possibility of inheriting information from the parent, ATHLETE, via a join operation.

If we were designing the database for student-athletes, and we recognized that we would want to record a name, a personal identifier (ssno), address, and so on, we could be starting with the generalization (or parent or superclass). Then, we decide to record a player in a sport and some information about the sport itself. The player-sport is said to be a specialization of the ATHLETE class. This design approach may be characterized as *top down*.

If we had been designing the database and we started with sports, we might have had a TENNIS entity, a FOOTBALL entity, and so on for each athlete, only to recognize that these entities may be generalized into an ATHLETE entity (a superclass) with individual sports as subclass entities; this design approach might be characterized as *bottom up*. A generalization relationship specifies that several types of entities with certain common attributes can be generalized into a higher-level entity class, a generic or superclass entity.

Either way (bottom up or top down), we end up with one entity being a superclass (a parent) and the other being a subclass (a child) of the parent. Whether one needs to specialize or generalize in design depends on where one recognizes the problem.

To illustrate how we might handle this generalization-specialization, parent-child class situation, suppose we have defined our entity, ATHLETE, like this:

Entity: ATHLETE
Attributes: name, ssno, address, gender, weight, height.

The ER diagram for this entity is simple and straightforward. Then, in the course of database design, we decide to add information about sports that athletes play. We might attempt to draw a diagram like Figure 10.1 with a variant *sports flag*.

What is wrong with Figure 10.1? The problem is that we have attributes that have attributes that have attributes. Sports flag is not a composite attribute—it does not have component parts. So, instead of creating

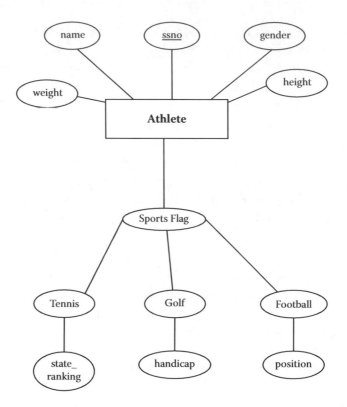

FIGURE 10.1
The **ATHLETE** with an attempt to add a variant attribute.

attributes with attributes, we will create entities for each specific sport and then relate these entities back to the **ATHLETE**.

Now, refer to Figure 10.2. Here, we created weak entities for each sport rather than use attributes of attributes. We have to make the sports weak entities because they have no primary key per se—they depend on **ATHLETE**. This diagram still does not tell the whole story because sports are not just weak entities, but rather they are in a sense "choices." If the sports were simply weak entities, then you would expect that all superclass entities were related to each subclass. This is not really the case. Plus, we want to honor the concept of inheritance.

The process of specialization is intended as a process by which the subclass inherits all the properties of the superclass. In EER terminology, the **ATHLETE** entity is called a superclass, and the sports entities are called subclasses. The attributes like handicap may be termed *specific attributes* as they are specific to the particular subclass.

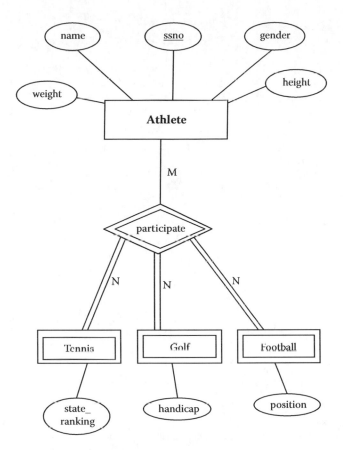

FIGURE 10.2
The ATHLETE shown as a strong-weak relationship variant attribute.

The sports entities, *specializations*, are depicted in the EER scheme as illustrated in Figure 10.3. In Figure 10.3, we made three sports entities unto themselves—information pieces that we will store information about.

First, in the ATHLETE entity, we include an attribute called sport. Sport is called a *defining predicate* as it defines our specialization(s). To this point, we have assumed that athletes play one sport, and the one sport has variant information in it. If an athlete were to play multiple sports, then the defining predicate must be multivalued. Referring to Figure 10.3, the defining predicate may be written on the line that joins the ATHLETE entity to the circle with an *o* in it. The circle with an *o* in it describes an "overlapping" constraint. *Overlapping* means that the subclass entities that are joined to the superclass may overlap; that is, a superclass entity may contain more than one subclass or specialization for a given ATHLETE.

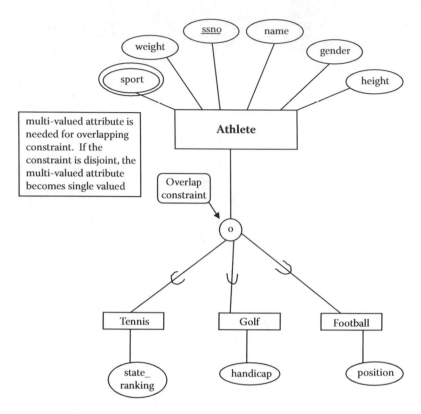

FIGURE 10.3
ATHLETE with superclass/subclass overlap relationship.

The overlap (*o*) in Figure 10.3 means that an athlete may participate in more than one sport.

If there were a *d* in the circle (in place of the *o*) in Figure 10.3, then the entities would not overlap: They would be *disjoint*. A *d* would indicate that athletes would participate in only one sport; that is, the athletes would play only golf, only tennis, or only football (but not any of the two together). If this were the case, then the small *o* would be replaced by a *d*, and Sport, the defining predicate, would be single valued. As a final note on this diagram, the participation of the superclass in the subclasses is optional. There is a single line joining the o/d designation that means that an athlete *may* participate in a sport—some athletes (or potential athletes) do not participate in a sport or sports.

An example of a disjoint constraint is shown in Figure 10.4. According to Figure 10.4, all the furniture in the database is a chair, a desk, or a table. In this case, there is no sense of overlapping subclasses. There is a

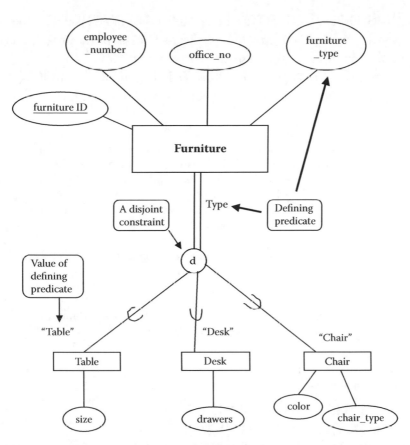

FIGURE 10.4
An office database with specialization entities, full participation, and disjoint relationship.

full participation designation from the **FURNITURE** entity to the o/d circle. Each piece of furniture *must* participate in a subclass. Contrast this to the partial participation in the **ATHLETE** example. The disjoint constraint specifies that if the subclasses of a generalization are disjoint, then an entity may be a member of only one of the subclasses or specializations. Further, the defining predicate for disjoint subclasses will be single valued.

In Figure 10.4, the name of the specialization is the name of the entity itself. If this is not the case, then the defining predicate may be repeated in the diagram for clarity.

Figure 10.3 shows a subclass symbol (⊂) between the predicate-defined entities and the disjoint/overlapping (o/d) constraint circle. "Tennis," "Golf," and "Football" *belong to* the defining predicate "Sport." The entities

TENNIS, GOLF, and FOOTBALL are subclasses of ATHLETE. The subclass symbol on each line that connects a subclass to the circle indicates the direction of the superclass/subclass or parent-child, inheritance relationship. In Figure 10.3, the subclass TENNIS, GOLF, or FOOTBALL (the specializations) would inherit from the parent, ATHLETE.

CHECKPOINT 10.1

1. What is a specialization? Give an example of a specialization.
2. What is a generalization? Give an example of a generalization.
3. What is a disjoint constraint? What symbol shows the disjoint constraint in EER diagrams?
4. What is an overlapping constraint? What symbol shows the overlapping constraint in EER diagrams?
5. What does the subclass symbol signify?
6. Why would you create a generalization/specialization relationship rather than creating a "weak entity"?
7. How does "inheritance" play into the superclass/subclass relationship? Discuss.
8. What is the difference between a generalization entity and regular entity as described in the previous chapters?

10.5 METHODOLOGY AND GRAMMAR FOR GENERALIZATION/ SPECIALIZATION RELATIONSHIPS

We need to revisit step 6 in the ER design methodology to include generalization/specialization relationships. The previous version of step 6 was:

> *Step 6. State the exact nature of the relationships in structured English from all sides, for example, if a relationship is A:B::1:M, then there is a relationship from A to B, 1 to Many, and from B back to A, Many to 1.*
>
> *For ternary and higher-order (n-ary) relationships, state the relationship in structured English, being careful to mention all entities for the n-ary relationship. State the structural constraints as they exist.*

We add the following sentence to step 6:

> *For specialization/generalization relationships, state the relationship in structured English, being careful to mention all entities (subclasses or specializations). State the structural constraints as they exist.*

The grammar that we propose for specialization/generalization relationships is similar to that we used in weak relationships. We add to the grammar to include the participation and the overlapping/disjoint (o/d) constraints: The grammatical description for weak entities was

For each **weak** entity, we do not assume that any attribute will be unique enough to identify individual entities. Since the **weak** entity does not have a candidate key, each **weak** entity **will** be identified by key(s) belonging to the **strong** entity.

In the case of the subclasses of ATHLETE, a first attempt to describe the subclass identified by a superclass becomes

For each sport, we do not assume that any sport attribute will be unique enough to identify individual sport entities. Since sport does not have a candidate key, each sport will be identified by inheriting key(s) belonging to ATHLETE.

So, a more complete EER diagram grammatical pattern would say

For each *specialization*, we do not assume that any attribute will be unique enough to identify individual entities. Since the *specialization* does not have a candidate key, each *specialization* will be identified by key(s) inherited from the *generalization*. Further, *specializations overlap [or are disjoint]*. [Explain the overlapping/disjoint situation.] The individual *specialization* is identified by a defining predicate, *attribute name*, which will be contained in *generalization*. If the specializations overlap, the defining predicate will be multivalued.

For Figure 10.3, the pattern becomes

For each sport, we do not assume that any attribute will be unique enough to identify individual entities. Since the sport does not have a candidate key, each sport will be identified by key(s) inherited from ATHLETE. Further, the sports overlap. Athletes may play more than one sport. The individual sport is identified by a defining predicate attribute, sport, which will be contained in ATHLETE. Since a person may play more than one sport, the defining predicate is a multivalued attribute. The sports we will record are GOLF, TENNIS, and FOOTBALL.

10.6 MAPPING RULES FOR GENERALIZATIONS AND SPECIALIZATIONS

In this section, we present mapping rules to map generalizations and specializations to relational databases. Generalizations and specializations can be mapped in several different ways, and rules to map generalizations and specializations to a relational database depend on several factors (Elmasri and Navathe, 2007): (a) the total/partial constraints of the generalization/specialization relationships; (b) the overlapping/disjoint constraints of the generalization/specialization relationships; (c) the number of attributes on the specializations; (d) whether the specializations are predicate defined; (e) how many specializations exist.

Table 10.1 provides a summary of the mapping rules for mapping generalizations and specializations and the situations in which they work best. Mapping rules 15 and 16 create multiple relations, and mapping rules 17 and 18 create single relations. In each case, there are relational database trade-offs with regard to the result.

In the next few sections, we explain each of the mapping rules and the trade-offs that result.

TABLE 10.1

Summary of Scenario in which Each Mapping Rule Works Best

Mapping Rule	Relations Created	Works Best with
• Mapping rule 15	• Multiple relations	• Total or partial participation • Disjoint or overlapping relationships
• Mapping rule 16	• Multiple relations	• Disjoint relationships • Total participation
• Mapping rule 17	• Single relations	• Only disjoint relationships • Can be total or partial participation • Not many attributes on specialization • Single type attribute
• Mapping rule 18	• Single relations	• Better for overlapping relationships but can be used for disjoint relationships • Many type fields—one for each subclass

10.6.1 Mapping Rule 15

As per Table 10.1, mapping rule 15 works well for either disjoint or overlapping scenarios. This rule would also work well if the specializations have many attributes.

> *Mapping Rule 15—Mapping generalizations and specializations with* disjoint or overlapping subclasses and with total or partial participation constraints (with few or many attributes on the specializations). **For each generalization/specialization entity situation, create one relation (table) for the generalization entity (if you have not done so already per the prior steps) and create one relation (table) for each specialization. Add the attributes for each entity to their respective relations. Include the primary key of the generalization entity in the specialization relations. The primary key of the specialization relations will be the same as the primary key of the generalization relation.**

So, using mapping rule 15, we create a separate relation for the generalization (superclass) as well as for each of the specializations (subclasses). Refer to Figure 10.3. The generalization/specialization relationship between ATHLETE and TENNIS, GOLF, and FOOTBALL would be mapped as follows:

ATHLETE(ssno, weight, name, gender, height, (sport))
TENNIS(ssno, state_ranking)
GOLF(ssno, handicap)
FOOTBALL(ssno, position)

Since ATHLETE in Figure 10.3 contains a multivalued attribute, ATHLETE now becomes

ATHLETE1(ssno, weight, name, gender, height)

and

ATHLETE-SPORT (ssno, sport)

The key of the generalization entity ssno is added to the specialization entities TENNIS, GOLF, and FOOTBALL as the primary key. And, since

ATHLETE in Figure 10.3 contains a multivalued attribute, ATHLETE-SPORT maps the multivalued attribute.

Showing some sample data, the relations would be

ATHLETE

ssno	weight	name	gender	height	sport
239-92-0983	140	Kumar	M	5.95	golf
398-08-0928	200	Kelvin	M	6.02	football
322-00-1234	135	Sarah	F	5.6	tennis
873-97-9877	165	Arjun	M	6.01	golf
876-09-9873	145	Deesha	F	5.5	tennis, golf

which would resolve to

ATHLETE1

ssno	weight	name	gender	height
239-92-0983	140	Kumar	M	5.95
398-08-0928	200	Kelvin	M	6.02
322-00-1234	135	Sarah	F	5.6
873-97-9877	165	Arjun	M	6.01
876-09-9873	145	Deesha	F	5.5

ATHLETE-SPORT

ssno	sport
239-92-0983	golf
398-08-0928	football
322-00-1234	tennis
873-97-9877	golf
876-09-9873	tennis
876-09-9873	golf

TENNIS

ssno	state_ranking
322-00-1234	23
876-09-9873	47

GOLF

ssno	handicap
239-92-0983	3
873-97-9877	1

FOOTBALL

ssno	position
398-08-0928	tackle
239-92-0983	quarterback
398-08-0928	full back

The only difficulty with this mapping is that it generates tables that are somewhat atypical in a relational database. In an ordinary relational database, one expects a table with a joining attribute. Here, the *joining attribute* is actually a table name rather than an attribute value. If the o/d constraint were *d* (disjoint), then the sport defining predicate would be single valued, the original **ATHLETE** table would have only one value for sport, and the decomposition of **ATHLETE** into **ATHLETE1** and **ATHLETE-SPORT** would be unnecessary.

10.6.2 Mapping Rule 16

Mapping rule 16 works best with disjoint subclasses and when the relationship is total between the generalization and specializations.

*Mapping Rule 16—Mapping generalizations and specializations with disjoint relationship constraints and total participation between generalizations and specializations. **Create a separate (subclass) relation for each specialization entity. Include the attributes for each specialization entity in their respective subclass relations. Also include the primary key and other attributes of the generalization entity in all the subclass relations. The primary key of the subclass relations will be the primary key of the generalization entity.***

To illustrate this rule, we map Figure 10.4 as follows:

TABLE(furniture_id, office_no, employee_number, furniture_type, size)

DESK(furniture_id, office_no, employee_number, furniture_type, drawers)

CHAIR(furniture_id, office_no, employee_number, furniture_type, color, chair_type)

Using this mapping rule 16, we create separate relations for each subclass, but we do not have a separate relation for the superclass entity. This rule works best with the disjoint relationship scenario in which the number of subclasses is very small and fixed. If this rule were used in the overlap relationship scenario, it would create redundancy in the database since all the attributes from the generalization entity would be rerecorded several times over. In the tables presented, we included the attribute furniture type, which is redundant to the name of the table itself. This was done to mirror the diagram and should be excised to produce the following:

TABLE(furniture_id, office_no, employee_number, size)

DESK(furniture_id, office_no, employee_number, drawers)

CHAIR(furniture_id, office_no, employee_number, color, chair_type)

Also, this is a good rule to use if the subclasses have too many attributes.

10.6.3 Mapping Rule 17

Although mapping rule 17 will work for both total and partial participation, it will work only for disjoint relationships and (a) if the specializations do **not** have many attributes and (b) if the specializations are predicate defined. Using this mapping rule, if the specializations have many attributes, then this mapping will create many null values. And, if mapping rule 17 were used with overlapping relationships, redundancy would be created in the database.

Mapping Rule 17—Mapping generalizations and specializations with disjoint relationships, total or partial participation constraints, and predicate defined with single type attributes. **Create a single**

**relation that includes the attributes of the generalization (super-
class) as well as the attributes of the specializations (subclasses) in
one relation. The primary key of the relation will be the primary
key of the generalization (superclass).**

In Figure 10.4, if we assume that furniture_type is the defining predicate, for example, a condition of membership is specified on furniture_
type as follows: furniture_type = "Table", then this is a defining predicate
of this specialization. In the EER diagram, the predicate-defined subclass
is shown by writing the predicate condition next to the arc that connects
the subclass to the relationship constraint circle. Also, the defining predicate name is placed on the arc from the superclass to the relationship
constraint circle. So, we would map Figure 10.4 as per mapping rule 17 as
follows:

FURNITURE(furniture_id, office_no, employee_number,
    furniture_type, size, drawers, color, chair_type)

This mapping rule will generate nulls for the nonparticipating attributes. For example, chairs do not have drawers; hence, if the furniture
type is "chair," there will be a null for the drawers attribute. Nulls are generally undesirable. There is a trade-off in the relational database here in
that on one hand nulls may be tolerated to reduce the number of tables,
but the purist approach would dictate that each furniture type have its
own table per mapping rule 15 or 16. Also, while this table configuration
looks plausible, it is not in the third normal form (3NF) and hence represents another database trade-off.

10.6.4 Mapping Rule 18

Mapping rule 18 will work for overlapping relationships but can also be
used for disjoint relationships. This mapping rule again uses the predicate
or flag for each specialization and assumes that such predicates or flags are
unique to the specialization. This rule would be used if there were numer-
ous overlaps within each generalization.

*Mapping Rule 18—Mapping overlapping relationships and gen-
eralizations/specializations with more than one flag. **Create a
single relation that includes the attributes of the generalization***

(superclass) and the attributes of the specializations (subclasses) and the subclass flag. The primary key of the relation is the primary key of the superclass.

With disjoint relationships, mapping rule 18 would create many null values when the entity is not a member of a particular specialization (subclass). Hence, this rule works best if there are many overlaps. This rule is also not recommended if the subclasses have many attributes since this will also cause many null values when these subclasses are not be used.

So, mapping Figure 10.3 as per mapping rule 18 and using flag predicates, we would have

ATHLETE(ssno, weight, name, gender, height, sport, tflag, state_
ranking, gflag, handicap, fflag, position)

Again, the problem with this arrangement is that the resulting table is not in 3NF. There are clearly transitive functional dependencies in the table with tflag → state_ranking and gflag → handicap and so forth. A normalization of this table would also generate the result as per mapping rule 15.

CHECKPOINT 10.2

1. How are the mapping rules for generalizations/specializations different from the mapping rules for weak entities?
2. Would it be wise to map Figure 10.3 using mapping rule 17? Why or why not?
3. Which mapping rules are good to use if there are too many attributes on the subclasses?
4. Which mapping rule or rules will not work well for overlapping subclasses?
5. When would you create an overlapping relationship?
6. When would you create a disjoint relationship?
7. Does mapping rule 15 create relations in 3NF? Discuss.
8. Does mapping rule 16 create relations in 3NF? Discuss.

10.7 SUBCLASSES OF SUBCLASSES

So far in this chapter, we have presented scenarios of one generalization class, that is, only one superclass. This superclass has had one or more subclasses. The subclasses could have one or more attributes. It is possible for subclasses to have subclasses and for there to be more than one set of subclasses. Here, we give examples of a specialization hierarchy, a specialization lattice, and shared subclass parents.

Subclasses of subclasses are shown in Figure 10.5. In Figure 10.5, the subclasses **HOBBY** and **PROFESSIONAL** are "part of" or "subclasses" of **FOOTBALL**. **HOBBY** and **PROFESSIONAL** would inherit attributes from **FOOTBALL**, which would inherit attributes from **ATHLETE**. (To simplify the EER diagram, attributes of the subclasses in the football tree are omitted.) So, of the athletes, some athletes play football, and of those who play football, some play football as a hobby, and some are professionals. Every instance of **HOBBY** will inherit from the subclass **FOOTBALL**; likewise, every instance of **PROFESSIONAL** will also inherit from **FOOTBALL**. In this case, every subclass is inheriting from only one other subclass. When a subclass inherits from only one subclass,

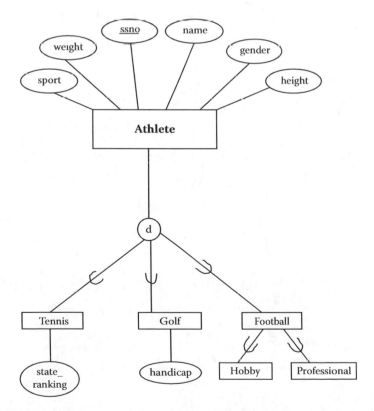

FIGURE 10.5
Specialization hierarchy.

that is, if a subclass has only one subclass as a parent, it is referred to as a *specialization hierarchy*. Figure 10.5 shows a specialization hierarchy with FOOTBALL as an example.

Another possible EER diagram could have more than one set of specializations. Suppose we have an athlete who plays various sports but is also viewed as having professional or hobbyist specializations. Also suppose that both sets of subclasses are overlapping. If a subclass has more than one subclass as its parent, it is referred to as a *specialization lattice*. Figure 10.6 illustrates such a specialization lattice. In Figure 10.6, we have the subclass *professional football player* that will inherit information from both the FOOTBALL subclass and the PROFESSIONAL subclass.

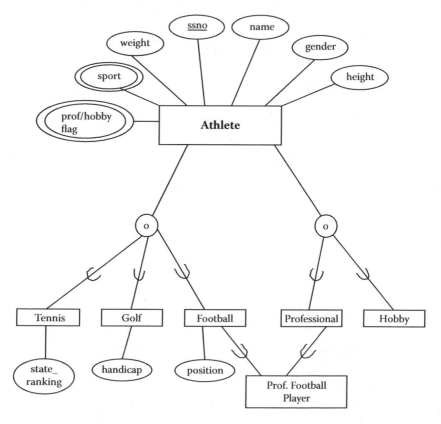

FIGURE 10.6
Specialization lattice, shared subclass.

A *shared subclass* is a subclass that has more than one subclass for its parents. PROFESSIONAL FOOTBALL PLAYER is a subclass of FOOTBALL as well as PROFESSIONAL and hence inherits from multiple subclasses. Every instance of a shared subclass inherits all the attributes of all its superclasses.

10.7.1 Mapping Rule 19

We present mapping rule 19 to map shared subclasses.

> *Mapping Rule 19—Mapping shared subclasses.* **In general, the same criteria that are used to determine which rule would be best for mapping generalizations and specializations can be applied to mapping shared subclasses. However, the rule that generates the best database is usually mapping rule 15.**

As an example of applying mapping rule 15, consider the mapping of Figure 10.6:

    ATHLETE(ssno, weight, name, gender, height, (sport),(prof/hobby
        flag))
    TENNIS(ssno, state_ranking)
    GOLF(ssno, handicap)
    FOOTBALL(ssno, position)
    PROFESSIONAL(ssno, agent,...
    HOBBY(ssno, title, budget,...
    PROFESSIONAL_FOOTBALL_PLAYER (ssno, team,...)

Here, we used mapping rule 15 to map Figure 10.6. In other cases, it could be appropriate to use one of the other mapping rules, 16–18. An important thing to note is that, since a shared subclass ultimately has only one superclass, the subclasses maintain the same key attribute. Also in this mapping there are multivalued attributes, which necessitates normalization for a relational database. To normalize these tables, there would have to be two more tables to deal with the multivalued predicates:

    ATHLETE(ssno, weight, name, gender, height, (sport),(prof/hobby
        flag))

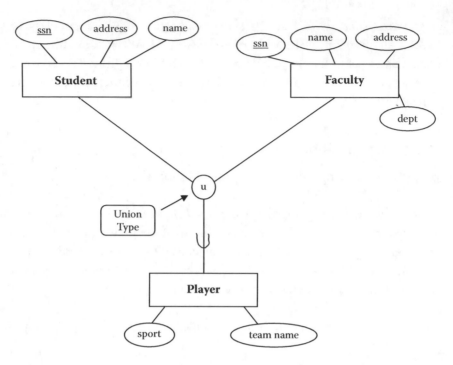

FIGURE 10.7
(a) A category or union type with same primary keys (partial participation).

becomes

    ATHLETE1(<u>ssno</u>, weight, name, gender, height)
    ATHLETE_SPORT(<u>ssno, sport</u>)
    ATHLETE_PROAM(<u>ssno, prof/hobby flag</u>)

10.8 CATEGORIES OR UNION TYPES

Thus far in this chapter, we presented examples with one superclass and several subclasses. Suppose the design of the database results in several superclasses, and a subclass inherits from the superclasses. Each superclass is an entity unto itself. When a subclass has more than one superclass from which it may inherit, it is referred to as a *category* or *union* type. Note that this is different from the previous section in that here we are

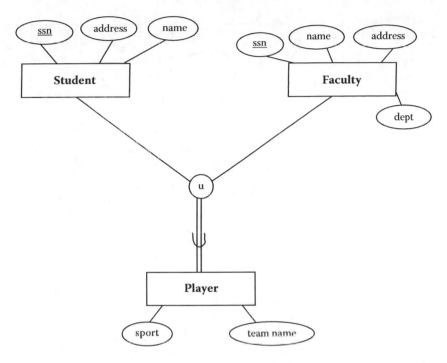

FIGURE 10.7
(b) A category or union type with the same primary keys (full or total participation).

discussing inheriting from more than one *super*class as opposed to more than one *sub*class.

Whereas a shared subclass always has only one superclass in its hierarchy, a category or union type can have more than one superclass. A category or union type will inherit information from any one of the superclasses; hence, the term *union* is used to describe the combination of information from whichever superclasses are the parents. Symbolically, we show the union type with a *u* in the circle connecting the subclasses to its super-classes, as shown in Figure 10.7a. Usually, the superclasses will have different keys since they are different entities, but there may also be scenarios for which a category or union type could inherit from two superclasses that have the same type key. For example, if we have a superclass called STUDENT, another superclass called FACULTY, and a subclass (category or union type) PLAYER, as shown in Figure 10.7a, the PLAYER category can be a subset of the union of the superclasses, STUDENT and FACULTY, and inherit the same key, ssn.

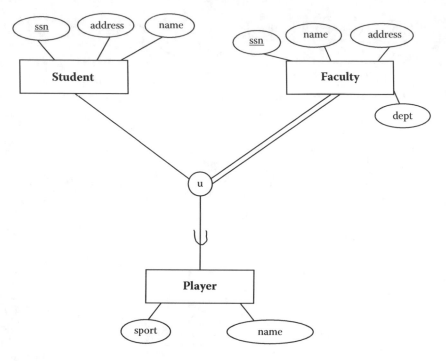

FIGURE 10.7
(c) Full participation between FACULTY and PLAYER.

Figure 10.7a says:

A player may be a *student* or *faculty member.*

A category or union type inherits all the attributes of the class or classes to which it belongs. So, if a player belongs to the STUDENT class (superclass), it inherits all the attributes of the student entity type, and if it belongs to the FACULTY class (superclass), it inherits all the attributes of the faculty entity type.

As another example of a union in an ER diagram, consider Figure 10.8a. Here, we have a bill payer, but the payer may come from several superclasses. PAYOR could inherit data from PATIENT, PRIMARY_INSURANCE, or OTHER_RESPONSIBLE_PARTY.

10.8.1 Participation Ratios in Categories or Union Types

Categories or union types can also have participation constraints. Reconsider Figure 10.7a. The category or union type PLAYER has

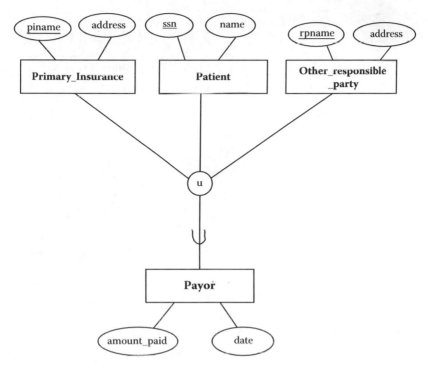

FIGURE 10.8
(a) A category or union type with different primary keys (with partial participation).

partial participation (single lines) from the circle with the *u* to the sub-class **PLAYER**. This partial participation would imply that **PLAYER** may or may not include student or faculty. There would be faculty and students who are not players.

If a category such as **PLAYER** has full participation, as shown in Figure 10.7b, this would imply that the category (or union type or sub-class) **PLAYER** holds at least one entity from the union of its superclasses **FACULTY** and **STUDENT**. Figure 10.7b implies that **PLAYER** includes at least one **FACULTY** or **STUDENT**. Note that this diagram represents one specific school. Further, this database is probably kept to keep track of players and not meant to keep track of everyone in the school. The diagram simply says we have a database of players, all of whom belong to either the **FACULTY** or **STUDENT** entity.

If there were double lines going from the **FACULTY** to the circle containing the *u*, as shown in Figure 10.7c, the player entity would include every faculty member, but not every student.

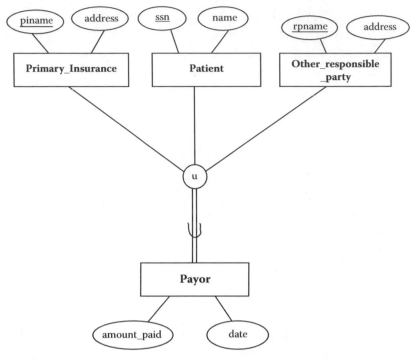

FIGURE 10.8
(b) A category or union type with different primary keys (with full or total participation).

In Figure 10.8b, there is full participation between PAYOR and the superclasses PATIENT, PRIMARY_INSURANCE, and OTHER_ RESPONSIBLE_PARTY. All payers are identified as parented by one of the superclasses. PAYOR would contain appropriate information in PATIENT, PRIMARY_INSURANCE, and OTHER_RESPONSIBLE_ PARTY by inheritance.

10.8.2 Mapping Categories or Union Types When Superclasses Have the Same Primary Keys

When subclasses are inheriting from superclasses that have the same primary key, as shown in Figure 10.7b, the mapping becomes simple since this primary key is just included in the subclass relation. We present mapping rule 20 to map categories or union types when superclasses have the same primary key.

Mapping Rule 20—Mapping categories or union types when superclasses have the same primary keys. **Create a new relation for** the subclass (or union type) and include the primary key of the superclass (or superclasses) in the subclass (or union type) as the primary key. Include the other attributes of the subclass in this relation. Create separate relations for each of the other super- classes and map them as you would map regular entities.

Figure 10.7a would map to

STUDENT(<u>ssn</u>, name, address)
FACULTY(<u>ssn</u>, name, address, dept)
PLAYER(<u>ssn</u>, name, sport)

10.8.3 Mapping Categories or Union Types When Superclasses Have Different Primary Keys

Since superclasses are generally different entity types, superclasses gener- ally have different primary keys. For example, see Figures 10.8a and 10.8b. If the superclasses have different primary keys, we would need to create a common key between the superclasses. This common key is referred to as the *surrogate key*.

We present mapping rule 21 to map categories or union types when the superclasses have different primary keys.

> *Mapping Rule 21—Mapping categories or union types when the super- classes have different primary keys.* **Create a new relation for the subclass (or union type). Create a surrogate key for this relation. The surrogate key will be the primary key for this relation. Include any other attributes of this subclass into this relation. Create sepa- rate relations for each of the superclasses and map them as you would map regular entities. Add the surrogate key to the super- class relations as a foreign key.**

Figure 10.8a would map to

PRIMARY_INSURANCE(<u>piname</u>, address, payor_id)
PATIENT(<u>ssn</u>, name, payor_id)
OTHER_RESPONSIBLE_PARTY(<u>rp_name</u>, address, payor_id)
PAYOR(<u>payor_id</u>, amount_paid, date)

In this mapping, payor_id is the surrogate key.

CHECKPOINT 10.3

1. Figure 10.7a says, "A player may be a student or a faculty." We show this as a union. Could we have shown this as a disjoint relationship? Discuss.
2. What is the difference between a disjoint relationship and a union?
3. How would you map a category or union type with the same keys on the superclasses?
4. How would you map a category or union type with different keys on the superclasses?
5. When would you create a generalization/specialization relationship, and when would you create a category or union type? Explain with examples.
6. A shared subclass inherits attributes from _____?
7. A category or union type inherits attributes from _____?
8. What is the difference between a shared subclass and category or union type?

10.9 FINAL ER DESIGN METHODOLOGY

So, our final ER design methodology has finally evolved to the presentation discussed next.

10.9.1 ER Design Methodology

Step 1. Select one, primary entity from the database requirements description and show attributes to be recorded for that entity. Label keys if appropriate and show some sample data.

Step 2. Use structured English for entities, attributes, and keys to describe the database that has been elicited.

Step 3. Examine attributes in the existing entities (possibly with user assistance) to find out if information about one of the entities is to be recorded.

(We change *primary* to *existing* because we redo step 3 as we add new entities.)

Step 3a. If information about an attribute is needed, then make the attribute an entity, and then

Step 3b. Define the relationship back to the original entity.

Step 4. If another entity is appropriate, draw the second entity with its attributes. Repeat steps 2 and 3 to see if this entity should be further split into more entities.

Step 5. Connect entities with relationships (one or more) if relationships exist.

Step 6. State the exact nature of the relationships in structured English from all sides, for example, if a relationship is A:B::1:M, then there is a relationship from A(1) to B(M) and from B(M) back to A(1).

For ternary and higher-order (n-ary) relationships, state the relationship in structured English, being careful to mention all entities for the n-ary relationship. State the structural constraints as they exist.

For specialization/generalization relationships, state the relationship in structured English, being careful to mention all entities (subclasses or specializations). State the structural constraints as they exist.

Step 6a. Examine the list of attributes and determine whether any of them need to be identified by two (or more) entities. If so, place the attribute on an appropriate relationship that joins the two entities.

Step 6b. Examine the diagram for loops that might indicate redundant relationships. If a relationship is truly redundant, excise the redundant relationship.

Step 7. Show some sample data.

Step 8. Present the "as designed" database to the user complete with the English for entities, attributes, keys, and relationships. Refine the diagram as necessary.

10.10 CHAPTER SUMMARY

In this chapter, we have described the concepts of generalizations and specializations, overlapping and disjoint relationships, shared subclasses and categories or union types. This chapter approached EER diagrams as discussed by Elmasri and Navathe (2007) and Connolly, Begg, and Strachan (1998). Some authors (e.g., Sanders, 1995) use a close variation of this model and call the specialization/generalization relationship an "IsA" relationship.

This chapter also concluded the development of the EER design methodology and mapping EER diagrams into a relational database.

CHAPTER 10 EXERCISES

Exercise 10.1

Draw an ER diagram for a library for an entity called *library holdings*. Include as attributes the call number, name of book, author(s), location in library. Add a defining predicate of *holding type* and draw in the disjoint, partial specializations of journals and reference books, with journals having the attribute *renewal date* and reference books the attribute *checkout constraints*. Map this to a relational database and show some sample data.

Exercise 10.2

Draw an ER diagram for computers at a school. Each computer is identified by an ID number, make, model, date acquired, and location. Each computer is categorized as a student computer or a staff computer. If it is a student computer, an attribute is *hours available*. If it is a staff computer, an attribute is *responsible party* (owner, if you will). Map this to a relational database and show some sample data.

Exercise 10.3

Present an EER diagram that has a union type, a disjoint relationship, and an overlapping relationship. Also include shared subclasses with different keys. Include primary keys and a minimal set of attributes and finally map this to a relational database. Write out the structured English to explain your diagram.

BIBLIOGRAPHY

Connolly, T., Begg, C., and Strachan, A. 1998. *Database Systems, a Practical Approach to Design, Implementation, and Management*. Harlow, UK: Addison-Wesley.

Elmasri, R., and Navathe, S. B. 2007. *Fundamentals of Database Systems*, 5th ed. Reading, MA: Addison-Wesley.

Sanders, L. *Data Modeling*. 1995. Danvers, MA: Boyd and Fraser.

Teorey, T. J., Nadeau, T., and Lightstone, S. S. 2005. *Database Modeling and Design: Logical Design*. San Francisco, CA: Morgan Kaufman.

CASE STUDY

West Florida Mall (continued)

So far in our case study, we have developed the major entities and relationships and mapped these to a relational database (with some sample data). Then, on reviewing step 7, which says

> *Step 7. Present the "as designed" database to the user complete with the English for entities, attributes, keys, and relationships. Refine the diagram as necessary.*

Suppose we obtained some additional input from the user:

A **PERSON** may be an owner, employee, or manager. For each **PERSON**, we will record the name, Social Security number, address, and phone number.

On reviewing these additional specifications, we came up with one new entity, **PERSON**.

Now, repeating step 2 for **PERSON**, we obtain the information as described next.

The Entity

This database records data about a **PERSON**.

For each **PERSON** in the database, we record a person's name (**pname**), person's Social Security number (**pssn**), person's phone (**pphone**), and person's address (**padd**).

The Attributes for PERSON

For each **PERSON**, there will be one and only one **pname** (person's name). The value for **pname** will not be subdivided.

For each **PERSON**, there will be one and only one **pssn** (person's Social Security number). The value for **pssn** will not be subdivided.

For each **PERSON**, there will be one and only one **pphone** (person's phone). The value for **pphone** will not be subdivided.

For each **PERSON**, there will be one and only one **padd** (person's address). The value for **padd** will not be subdivided.

The Keys

For each **PERSON**, we will assume that the **pssn** will be unique.

These entities have been added to the diagram in Figure 10.9.

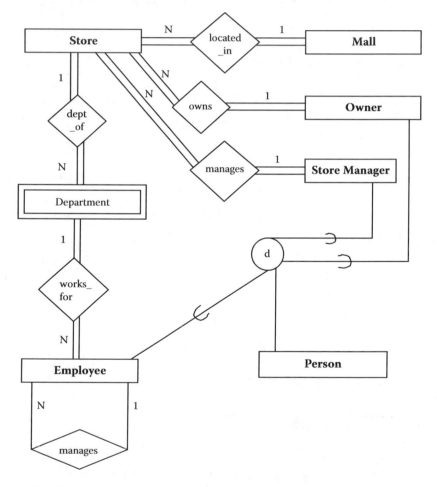

FIGURE 10.9
Final ER diagram of West Florida Mall.

Using step 6 to determine the structural constraints of relationships, we obtain the following:

As shown in Figure 10.9, there is a disjoint relationship between PERSON and STORE_ MANAGER, OWNER, and EMPLOYEE. This means that a person may be an owner, store manager, or an employee (a disjoint generalization/specialization relationship).

To map this relationship we would normally have:

MALL

name	address

STORE

sloc	sname	snum	mall_name	so_ssn	sm_ssn

OWNER

so_ssn	so_off_phone	pssn

DEPARTMENT

dname	dnum	snum

EMPLOYEE

essn	dnum	snum	dm_ssn	pssn

PERSON

pssn	pname	padd	pphone

Store-Manager

sm ssn	pssn	...

But since PERSON has the fields of Social Security number (pssn), name (pname), address (padd), and phone number (pphone), and since a person may be an owner, store manager, or an employee (a disjoint) generalization/specialization relationship, notice that we removed some of the attributes from the original entities. For example, in the EMPLOYEE entity, we no longer need to keep the ename field since this can be obtained from PERSON as long as we have the ssno of the employee. Also, since pssn is actually the same field as essn in EMPLOYEE, so_ssn in OWNER, and sm_ssn in STORE_MANAGER, we do not need to include pssn in EMPLOYEE, OWNER, or STORE_MANAGER again.

So, in summary, our relational database would finally develop to (without the data)

MALL

name	address

STORE

sloc	sname	snum	mall_name	so_ssn	sm_ssn

OWNER

so_ssn	so_off_phone

DEPARTMENT

dname	dnum	snum

EMPLOYEE

essn	dnum	snum	dm_ssn

PERSON

pssn	pname	padd	pphone

STORE MANAGER

sm_ssn	...

This ends our case study.

11

Relational Mapping and Reverse Engineering ER/EER Diagrams

11.1 INTRODUCTION

Throughout this book, we have developed rules for mapping entity relationship (ER) and enhanced entity relationship (EER) diagrams to a relational database. In this chapter, we present a summary of the mapping rules and then discuss reverse engineering—starting with the database and working backward to an ER/EER diagram. We often find that databases exist without an ER/EER diagram to accompany them. The ER/EER diagram is documentation; just as computer programs require documentation, so do databases. Therefore, we have included a section on reverse engineering. As we did previously, for reverse engineering we present a series of steps to develop an ER/EER diagram from tables and data.

11.2 STEPS USED TO MAP ER/EER DIAGRAMS TO RELATIONAL DATABASES

In this section, we present a summary of the steps that we have developed to map an ER/EER diagram to a relational database. In following these steps, the resulting relational tables should be close to the third normal form (3NF). It must be pointed out that these rules do not preclude the usual exercise of checking the resulting database to be absolutely sure it is normalized. If databases are not normalized, redundancy will likely be present. As much as possible, the steps should be followed in the order presented to promote correct mapping to result in tables as close to 3NF as possible. Here are the steps:

Step 1: Map all the strong entities in the ER diagram.

287

We start with mapping rule 1 to map strong entities:

Mapping Rule 1—*Mapping strong entities.* Develop a new table (relation) for each strong entity and make the indicated key of the strong entity the primary key of the table. If more than one candidate key is indicated on the ER diagram, choose one for the primary key.

Next, we have to check the mapping of the attributes in the strong entity. Since the mapping rules are different for atomic attributes, composite attributes, and multivalued attributes, we present each of the mapping rules separately. First is the mapping rule for mapping atomic attributes:

Mapping Rule 2—*Mapping atomic attributes.* For entities with atomic attributes, map the entities to a table and form columns for each atomic attribute.

In a relational database, all columns have to be atomic. If we have nonatomic attributes on our diagram, we have to make them atomic for mapping to the relational database.

For composite attributes, we achieve atomicity by recording only the component parts of the attribute. Our next mapping rule concerns composite attributes:

Mapping Rule 3—*Mapping composite attributes.* For entities with composite attributes, map entities to a table and form columns of each elementary (atomic) part of the composite attribute.

The mapping rule for multivalued attributes is

Mapping Rule 4—*Mapping multivalued attributes.* Form a separate table for the multivalued attribute. Record a row for each value of the multivalued attribute together with the key from the original table. The key of the new table will be the concatenation of the multivalued attribute plus the key of the owner entity. Remove the multivalued attribute from the original table.

At the end of this step, all the strong entities should be mapped.

Step 2. Map all the weak entities in the ER diagram.
For weak entities, we use mapping rule 11.

Mapping Rule 11—*Mapping weak entities.* Develop a new table (relation) for each weak entity. As is the case with the strong entity, include any atomic attributes from the weak entity in the table.

If there is a composite attribute, include only the atomic parts of the composite attribute and be sure to qualify the atomic parts in order not to lose information. To relate the weak entity to its owner, include the primary key of the owner entity in the weak entity table. The primary key of the weak entity table will be the partial key in the weak entity concatenated to the primary key of the owner entity.

If the weak entity owns other weak entities, then the weak entity that is connected to the strong entity must be mapped first. The key of the weak owner entity has to be defined before the "weaker" entity (the one furthest from the strong entity) can be mapped.

After the strong entities are mapped (as per step 1), it is important that the weak entities are mapped next since the key of the weak entity is the key of the strong (owner) entity *plus* the partial key of the weak entity.

Once all the strong entities and weak entities have been mapped, the next step is to map the relationships.

Step 3. Map the relationships.

The relationships can be mapped in any order. It is most convenient to begin by mapping binary M:N relationships. At this point, we should have tables for all the strong and weak entities. The next section involves adding attributes to these tables or creating new tables to house relationships.

Mapping Rule 5—Mapping M:N relationships. **For each M:N relationship, create a new table (relation) with the primary keys of each of the two entities (owner entities) that are being related in the M:N relationship. The primary key of this new table will be the concatenated keys of the owner entities. Include any attributes that the M:N relationship may have in this new table.**

Next, we will map the binary 1:1 relationships. Mapping 1:M or 1:1 relationships depends on participation constraints. Most of the rules that follow involve either (a) adding an attribute (a foreign key) to a table created by a previous mapping rule or (b) adding a new table in a process similar to mapping M:N relationships.

Mapping Rule 6—Mapping binary 1:1 relationships when one side of the relationship has full participation and the other has partial participation. **When one of the sides of the relationship has full participation and the other has partial participation, then store the primary key of the side with the partial participation** constraint on the side with the full participation constraint; this attribute is a foreign key (it is not underlined). Include any attributes on the relationship in the same table to which the key was added.

Mapping Rule 7—Mapping binary 1:1 relationships when both sides have partial participation constraints.

When both sides have partial participation constraints in binary 1:1 relationships, the relationships can be mapped in one of two ways:

Option 1:
Mapping Rule 7A. **Select either one of the tables to store the key of the other as a foreign key.**

This choice depends on semantics. Perhaps a safer choice for mapping this type of relationship is rule 7B:

Option 2:
Mapping Rule 7B. **Depending on semantics, you can create a new table to house the relationship that would contain the key of the two related entities.**

Mapping Rule 8—Mapping binary 1:1 relationships when both sides have full participation constraints. **Use the semantics of the relationship to select which of the tables should contain the key of the other. If this choice is unclear, then use mapping rule 7B: create a separate table to house the relationship.**

Now that the M:N relationships and binary 1:1 relationships have been mapped, the next step will be to map the common binary 1:N relationships.

Mapping Rule 9—Mapping binary 1:N relationships when the N side has full participation. **Include the key of the entity on the 1 side of the relationship as a foreign key on the N side.**

Mapping Rule 10—Mapping binary 1:N relationships when the N side has partial participation. **This situation would be handled just like a binary M:N relationship with a separate table for the relationship. The key of the new table would consist of a concatenation of the keys of the related entities. Include any attributes that were on the relationship on this new table.**

Partial participation is a problem because it leads to null values. If we put the key from the 1 side into the N-side table and if the participation is partial (not every row on the N side has a relationship to the 1 side), then there will be nulls in the database when it is populated. Therefore, it is better to create a separate table for the 1:N relationship and hence avoid nulls.

Finally, on the subject of 1:N relationships, we should look at Figure 8.2, where an M:N relationship was converted into two 1:N relationships. Note that the result of converting the M:N into two 1:N relationships will result in the same set of tables from 1:N mappings.

Our next step would be to map recursive relationships.

> *Mapping Rule 12—Mapping 1:N recursive relationships.* **Reinclude the primary key of the table with the recursive relationship in the same table, giving it some other role name.**

> *Mapping Rule 13—Mapping M:N recursive relationships.* **Create a separate table for the relationship (as in mapping rule 5).**

We will use mapping rule 14 to map *n*-ary relationships.

> *Mapping Rule 14—Mapping* n-*ary relationships.* **For each *n*-ary relationship, create a new table. In the new table, include the keys of the connected entities and any attributes of the relationship. Make the keys of the connected entities the concatenated primary key of the new table.**

Next, we map the EER diagram.

> *Step 4. Mapping generalizations/specializations.*

> *Mapping Rule 15—Mapping generalizations and specializations with disjoint or overlapping subclasses and with total or partial participation constraints (with few or many attributes on the specializations).* **For each generalization/specialization entity situation, create one table for the generalization entity (if you have not done so already per the previous steps) and create one table for each specialization. Add the attributes for each specialization to their respective tables (relations). Include the primary key of the generalization entity in the specialization tables. The primary key of the specialization tables will be the same primary key as the generalization table.**

> *Mapping Rule 16—Mapping generalizations and specializations with disjoint relationship constraints and total participation between generalizations and specializations.* **Create a separate**

(subclass) table for each specialization entity. Include the attributes for each specialization entity in their respective subclass tables. Also include the primary key and other attributes of the generalization entity in all the subclass tables. The primary key of the subclass tables will be the primary key of the generalization entity.

Mapping Rule 17—Mapping generalizations and specializations with disjoint relationships, total or partial participation constraints, and predicate defined with single type attributes. Create a single table that includes the attributes of the generalization (superclass) as well as the attributes of the specializations (subclasses). The primary key of the table will be the primary key of the generalization (superclass).

Mapping Rule 18—Mapping overlapping relationships and generalizations/specializations with more than one flag. Create a single table that includes the attributes of the generalization (superclass) and the attributes of the specializations or subclasses (including the subclass flags). The primary key of the table is the primary key of the superclass.

Mapping Rule 19—Mapping shared subclasses. The same criteria that are used to determine which rule would be best for mapping generalizations and specializations can be applied to mapping shared subclasses. That is, any of the mapping rules 15–18 can be used to map a shared subclass.

Mapping Rule 20—Mapping categories or union types when superclasses have same primary keys. Create a new table for the subclass (or union type) and include the primary key of the superclass (or superclasses) in the subclass (or union type) as the primary key. Include the other attributes (if any) of the subclass in this table. Create separate tables for each of the other superclasses and map them as you would map regular entities.

Mapping Rule 21—Mapping categories or union types when the superclasses have different primary keys. Create a new table for the subclass (or union type). Create a surrogate key for this table. This will be the primary key for this table. Include any other attributes (if any) of this subclass in this table. Create separate tables for each of the superclasses and map them as you would map regular entities. Include the surrogate key in the superclass tables as a foreign key.

CHECKPOINT 11.1

1. What is the first mapping rule?
2. Why is it good to first map strong entities and then map the weak entities?
3. What would you map after you map the weak entities?
4. How would you map weak entities of weak entities?
5. While mapping a binary 1:N relationship when the N side has full participation, why do we include the key of the 1 side of the table in the N side of the table? What would be wrong if we included the key of the N side of the table in the 1 side of the table?
6. Why would it be reasonable to map a 1:N binary relationship that has partial participation on the N side like an M:N relationship?

If the rules are followed, the resulting relational database should be at or close to 3NF. The next phase of mapping is "checking your work" by reviewing the table to ensure that you are at least in 3NF (refer to Chapter 3). In brief, checking for 3NF consists of the following steps:

1. **1NF**—Check that there are no nonatomic attributes in any table. Nonatomic attributes were dealt with in mapping rule 3 for composite attributes and mapping rule 4 for multivalued attributes.
2. **2NF**—Check that all attributes in all tables depend on the full primary key. Ask yourself, "Will I always get the same value for attribute Y when I have value X when X is the primary key?" X in this case could be a concatenated key, and you would be looking for partial dependencies.
3. **3NF**—Check for situations for which an attribute is in a table but that attribute is better defined by some attribute that is not the primary key. Recall that if the primary key in a table is X and X → YZW, then if Z → W is clearer than X → W, you likely have a transitive dependency and you would need to normalize.

11.3 REVERSE ENGINEERING

Having developed a methodology to develop ER/EER diagrams and map them to a relational database, we now turn our attention to the reverse engineering problem—the issue of taking a relational database and devising an ER/EER diagram. Often, in real-world situations, we find ourselves with a database and have no diagram to show how it was developed. There are several reasons why a reverse engineered diagram (RED) paradigm is useful.

The Reverse Engineered Diagram provides us with a grammatical and diagrammatic description of the database. Often, people use databases but do not understand them because there is no "big picture." By reverse engineering from the data and tables to the diagram, we can more easily express the meaning of the database in words. By having the ER/EER diagram of the relational database and the grammatical expression of the diagram, we can embellish the database and maintain meaning. The ER diagram can also aid greatly in the development of queries on the database.

While the expression *reverse engineering* might imply that we reverse the steps to create a diagram, we have found it easier to repeat the steps from the top (more or less) to discover which diagram would have been used to create the relational database. The process of reverse engineering is most easily approached by finding strong entities and then filling in the other parts of the database. There is one caveat here in that the steps presented assume that the database is in 3NF. If it is not in 3NF, then reverse engineering may aid in discovering why redundancy exists in the database and hence suggest some changes.

With ER diagrams and the elucidation process, we proposed drawing the diagram, adding English descriptions, and presenting the result to the user. Here, after this process of reverse engineering is completed, it is expected that the resulting diagram would be accompanied by an English version and presented to the users as well. The sense of this reverse engineering process is much like the original elucidation in that one proceeds and checks with users to be sure the analysts have it correct. The rules are provided as a guideline to move from no ER diagram to a more complete, documented database. The following rules are not to be considered rigid but rather a starting point toward "negotiating" a documented database. It is likely that the ER diagram will evolve, the database may change, and the users will govern the final product. For example, superclasses and subclasses can be mapped in several ways. It may be discovered that another mapping may have been better than the existing one. With no original ER diagram, many scenarios are possible once the big picture is presented.

We suggest the following rules to affect reverse engineering (Figure 11.1):

11.3.1 Reverse Engineering Rule 1. Develop Strong Entities

For tables with a one-attribute key, draw a strong entity R for that table and include all the attributes of that table in the entity R on the ER diagram.

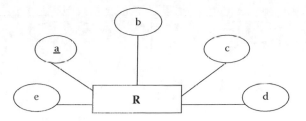

FIGURE 11.1
Reverse engineering strong entities.

For example, if you have a table R(a,b,c,d,e), a is the key. Create a strong entity called R and show a,b,c,d, and e as attributes with a as the key.

R

a	b	c	d	e

11.3.2 Reverse Engineering Rule 2. Look for 1:1 and 1:N (1:x) Relationships

As second, third, and additional strong entities are discovered, look for foreign keys in the tables. Excise the foreign keys from the previous entity diagram and create a relationship between the entities. Finding foreign keys in a strong entity most likely indicates a 1:x relationship (and x is most likely N).

For example, suppose you have two tables that are strong entities. Suppose you have R as in the previous section and another table, S, S(d,f,g). d is the key of S. Now, you observe that the key of S, attribute d, is also in table R. d is a foreign key in R. For the purpose of creating an ER diagram, remove d from the diagram for R and connect R and S by a 1:N or 1:1 relationship. The side that has the foreign key will be the N side of a 1:N relationship (see Figure 11.2a).

Here is another example of this situation:

A database has a list of items ordered by some customer:
ITEMS(item_no, description, price, order_no).

And, you have another table for orders like this:
ORDER(order_no, date, customer_no).

The order_no in the ITEM table is a foreign key since it is the key of the ORDER table. In this example, we assume item_no is a unique

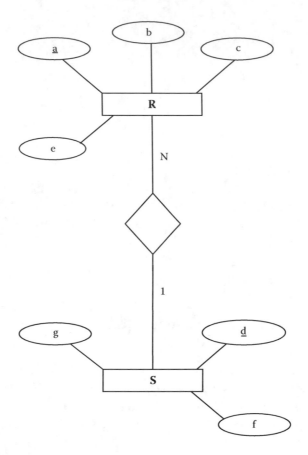

FIGURE 11.2a
Reverse engineering 1:N relationships.

identifier for the ITEM table. The ER diagram for this database is illustrated in Figure 11.2b.

In all cases of relationships, we will have to determine the cardinality and the participation constraints from the semantics of the database as well as the data itself. Sometimes the way that the tables are formed gives a clue. For example, reverting to the R and S tables, if the R and S tables are as the case suggests, then it is likely that the relationship is N:1, with the N side being R since R contained d, a foreign key. The data can be examined to determine the number of child entries that occur with parent entries that would indicate partial or full participation. Looking for nulls in the data is another clue to indicating the cardinality and participation constraints.

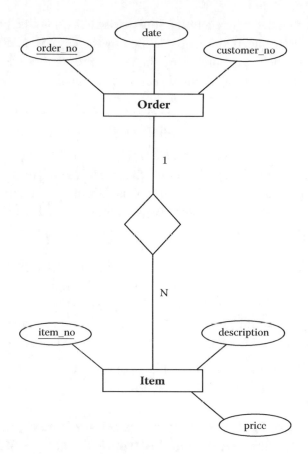

FIGURE 11.2b
Another example of reverse engineering 1:N relationships.

We must use the word *indicate* because only the true (albeit unknown) semantics and the data itself would "prove" the full/partial participation.

11.3.3 Reverse Engineering Rule 2a. Check for Attributes of the 1:x Relationship

In the ER diagram, if a foreign key is excised from an entity R because it is the key of S, you have to check to see whether any of the remaining attributes in R should stay with the entity R, should be placed on a relationship RS, or should be placed with S. Since step 2 is reverse mapping a 1:x relationship, it may be that an attribute from the 1:x relationship itself was placed with the foreign key when the original ER diagram was mapped, or it may be that an attribute was on the relationship itself.

You have to judge where a remaining attribute is more likely to belong. If it is likely that the attribute was defined by the key of an entity, put the attribute with the entity containing the key. If the attribute requires both keys for its identity, the attribute should be placed on the relationship RS.

Example 11.2

In the case discussed, we removed d from R in the ER diagram because d was the key of S. Suppose after we create S, we determine that e only makes sense if we define it in terms of both a and d, the keys of R and S. This would imply that e was an intersection attribute on the relationship between R and S and hence would be depicted as such, as shown in Figure 11.3a.

Reconsider the ORDER database example. If, in our ORDER database example, the items_ordered were uniquely identified by item_no, but the situation was that items were ordered repeatedly, then the date attribute would have to be identified by both the item_no and the order_no. In this case, Figure 11.2b would become Figure 11.3b.

This concludes the reverse mapping of obviously strong tables. We now look for weak tables and multivalued attributes.

11.3.4 Reverse Engineering Rule 3. Look for Weak Entities and Multivalued Attributes

Examine the tables for any concatenated keys to see whether they contain any of the keys of the strong entities. If they do, this could indicate a weak entity, a multivalued attribute, or a table resulting from M:N or higher-order relationship. Which of these it is may depend on nonkey attributes.

11.3.5 Reverse Engineering Rule 3a. Checking for Weak Entities

If there is a table in which there are attributes other than the concatenated key (which consists of a foreign key from a strong entity *and* another attribute—the partial key), then you probably have a weak entity.

For example, if you have a table

SKILL(<u>emp_no, skill_type</u>, date_certified)

The concatenated key is emp_no and skill_type. Here, emp_no is a foreign key, and skill_type is not; hence, skill_type would likely be a partial

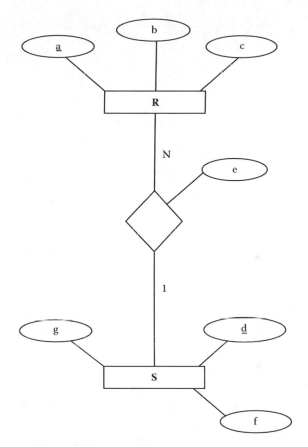

FIGURE 11.3a
Reverse engineering a relationship attribute.

key of a weak entity. Why a weak entity? This is because there is another attribute, **date_certified**, which means that we are storing information about skills for that employee. Here, **skill_type** is not a unique identifier for the information presented.

Place the weak entity on the ER diagram along with a relationship to its owner entity (Figure 11.4). The relationship is likely to be 1:N::strong (owner):weak(dependent)::partial:full. Examine the attributes in the weak entity to determine whether they would have come from the weak entity or the relationship between the weak entity and its owner. Here, **SKILL** is the weak entity, **skill_type** is the partial key, and **date_certified** is an attribute of the weak entity **SKILL**.

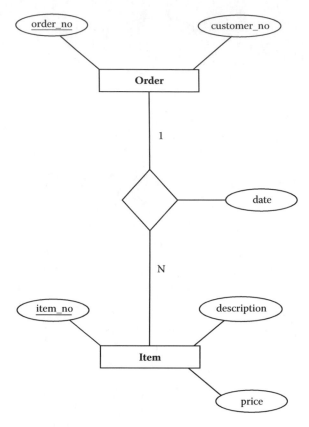

FIGURE 11.3b
Reverse engineering 1:N relationships with relationship attributes.

11.3.6 Reverse Engineering Rule 3b. Checking for Multivalued Attributes

If there are (a) no other attributes other than a concatenated key in a table; (b) part of the key is a foreign key from a strong entity; and (c) the other attribute is not a foreign key, then it is likely that this a multivalued attribute situation. The multivalued attribute would have been connected to the strong entity referenced by the foreign key. Place the multivalued attribute on the entity to which it belongs as a multivalued attribute (Figure 11.5).

For example, if we have the table

INSTRUCTOR (<u>ssno, degree</u>)

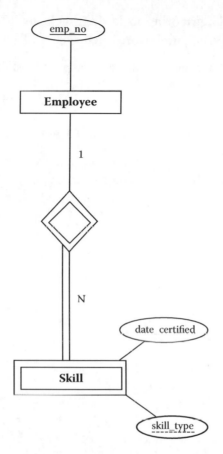

FIGURE 11.4
Reverse engineering weak entities.

Here, we have a concatenated key and no other attributes. Since ssno is likely the key of another entity, (say) PERSON and since degree is not a likely key, then degree must be a multivalued attribute. Why not a weak entity? If it were a weak entity, there would probably be more attributes— for example, we would be recording information about the degrees for that person, but we are not doing so in this case.

FIGURE 11.5
Reverse engineering multivalued attributes.

11.3.7 Reverse Engineering Rule 4. Check for M:N and *n*-ary Relationships

Examine the database tables with concatenated keys for multiple occurrences of primary keys.

11.3.8 Reverse Engineering Rule 4a. Check for the Binary Case

If there are two foreign keys in the concatenated key of a table, this is likely to be a table that occurred because of an M:N relationship. In the multivalued attribute case given, only one of the concatenated key attributes was deemed to be a foreign key. If the two foreign keys occur along with other attributes in a table, it is even more than likely that an M:N relationship exists. Place an M:N relationship between the two owner entities with foreign keys and include other attributes as relationship attributes (Figure 11.6).

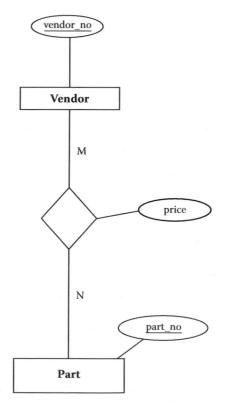

FIGURE 11.6
Reverse engineering M:N relationship.

For example, suppose you discover a table called PURCHASE that looks like this:

PURCHASE (<u>vendor_no, part_no</u>, price)

Suppose vendor_no is the key of an entity called VENDOR, and part_ no is the key of an entity called PART. *Parts* are *purchased* from *vendors*. These two foreign keys (primary keys of other entities) are a clear message that this is a table formed from an M:N relationship. It is possible that the cardinality could be 1:x, but the M:N relationship is most likely; the relationship can be deduced from the data. If, for example, there are multiple occurrences of parts for vendors and multiple vendors for parts, this is an M:N relationship. If for every part there are several vendors, but every vendor supplies only one part, then this would be VENDOR:PART::N:1.

11.3.9 Reverse Engineering Rule 4b. Check for the *n*-ary Case

If there are more than two foreign keys in a table participating as the concatenated primary key of the table, this is likely a table that occurred because of an *n*-ary relationship. There may well be other attributes in the table with three or more foreign keys. Place an *n*-ary relationship (*n* = number of foreign keys) between the *n* entities with foreign keys and include other attributes as relationship attributes.

For example, if you have the table

PURCHASE (<u>vendor_no, part_no, cust_no</u>, price)

The three foreign keys vendor_no, part_no, and cust_no imply a ternary relationship. The attribute price is likely an intersection attribute on the relationship. In this case, we would be saying that all three keys would be necessary to identify a price, as shown in Figure 11.7.

11.3.10 Reverse Engineering Rule 5. Check for Generalization/Specialization Relationships

There are several situations that indicate a generalization/specialization relationShip. Recall from Chapter 10 that there are a number of ways that a given EER diagram with generalization/specialization characteristics can be mapped to a relational database.

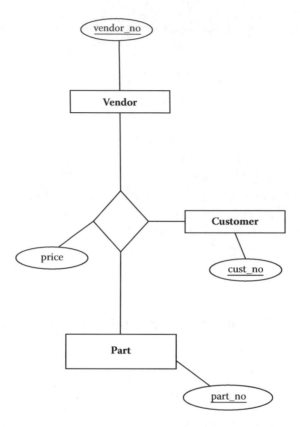

FIGURE 11.7
Reverse engineering the *n*-ary case.

11.3.11 Reverse Engineering Rule 5a. Check for Generalization/Specialization Relationships with Disjoint or Overlap Relationships with Total or Partial Participation Constraints

If the primary key of a larger table with a one-attribute primary key appears on other (probably smaller) tables as a one-attribute primary key, there is probably a generalization/specialization relationship (but note that this could also be a category or union type relationship; refer to reverse engineering rule 7 for reverse engineering the category or union type relationships). The larger table is most likely a superclass, so make this a strong entity/superclass (with the primary key). The smaller tables are the subclasses. The subclass entities will not have a primary key in the EER diagram but will be shown as overlapping or disjoint subclasses.

For example, if we had the following set of tables in a database:

M (m, a, b, c, f)
N (m, d, n)
O (m, o)
P (m, p, e)

we can see that m is the primary key in all the tables. Since M is the larger table, it is probably the superclass and N, O, P are subclasses that will inherit from M. This set of tables would map to Figure 11.8.

Next, we should try to determine if the subclasses are disjoint or overlapping. We do this by looking at the data. If the primary key appears on one subclass table at a time, that is, if a record or object appears to be in only one table at a time, then this is probably a disjoint relationship, so we would place a *d* in the circle joining the superclass entity to the subclasses entities. If the primary key appears on more than one subclass table at a time, that is, if a record or object appears to be in more than one subclass table simultaneously, then this is probably an overlapping subclass situation, so we would place an *o* on the circle joining the superclass entity to

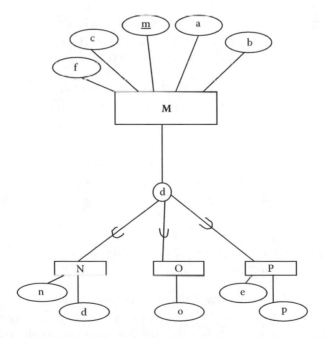

FIGURE 11.8
Reverse engineering a generalization/specialization relationship.

the subclass entities. If the subclasses overlap, then a multivalued attribute will be necessary in the superclass entity.

To try to determine if the relationship is total or partial, we again need the help of some actual data. If every primary key (or object or record) in the superclass table appears on at least one of the subclass tables, this is probably a total participation subclass/superclass relationship. But, if every primary key (or object or record) in the superclass table does not appear on at least one of the subclass tables, this is likely a partial participation relationship.

11.3.12 Reverse Engineering Rule 5b. Check for Disjoint Generalization/Specialization Relationships with Single-Predicate-Defined Attributes

If there is a single large table that appears to have predicate-defined attributes and values or nulls corresponding to the predicate-defined attributes, this is probably a disjoint generalization/specialization relationship with a predicate-defined attribute on the superclass. The superclass entity will have the primary key and the attributes that are not predicate defined. The subclasses will contain the attributes corresponding to the predicate-defined attributes.

11.3.13 Reverse Engineering Rule 5c. Check for Overlap Generalization/Specialization Relationship with More than One Flag

In the case of the overlap generalization/specialization relationship with more than one flag, flags are defining predicates. If there is a single large table that appears to have more than one flag and several values corresponding to the flags, it is probably an overlapping generalization/specialization relationship. The superclass entity will be the large table with the primary key and the attributes that do not correspond to flags. The subclass entities will be composed of the attributes that correspond to the respective flags.

11.3.14 Reverse Engineering Rule 6. Check for Shared Subclasses

To determine whether there are shared subclass entities, we need to follow reverse engineering rules 5a–5c, and we need data to help us determine if the subclasses are actually shared. If from the data we observe that the attributes have been inherited from more than one subclass, this would suggest that this is a shared subclass entity. The shared subclass entity would have one primary key—inherited from its subclasses.

11.3.15 Reverse Engineering Rule 7. Check for Categories or Union Types

If the primary key of a table appears on other tables as a primary key, there could be a category or union type of relationship in which the superclass entities have the same primary key (but this could also be a generalization/specialization relationship; see reverse engineering rule 5a). In this case, it might be difficult to decipher which are the superclasses in the category or union types. We might need the data to help us see which tables are inheriting from which tables; this will help us determine which are the superclasses and which are the subclasses.

If the primary key of a table appears on other tables as a foreign key, there could be a category or union type of relationship in which the superclasses have different primary keys; hence, a surrogate key was created, which was included in the other superclass tables as the foreign key. In this case, the superclasses would be the tables that contain the surrogate key as the foreign key (these superclasses would have their own primary keys), and the table that contains the surrogate key as the primary key would be the category or union type.

> CHECKPOINT 11.2
>
> 1. What hints would you look for to determine if a relationship is ternary?
> 2. What hints would you look for when you are trying to determine whether tables have weak entities and multivalued attributes included in them?
> 3. What hints would you look for to determine if there is a generalization/specialization relationship?
> 4. What hints would help you determine if a shared subclass exists?
> 5. What hints would help you determine if a category or union type of relationship exists?

11.4 CHAPTER SUMMARY

In this chapter, we presented a summary of the mapping rules (rules used to map ER and EER diagrams to relational databases) that we developed throughout the book and then discussed and developed a set of rules for reverse engineering to ER and EER diagrams from a relational database.

CHAPTER 11 EXERCISES

Exercise 11.1

1. Come up with an ER diagram for the following relational database:
   R (<u>a</u>, b, c, d, w)
   S (<u>d</u>, e, f)
   T (<u>c</u>, g, h)
   U (<u>c, d</u>, j)
   V (<u>d, k</u>)
   W (<u>a</u>, m, <u>o</u>, p)
   X (<u>a, d, c</u>, r)
   Y (<u>a, o, s</u>, t)

Exercise 11.2

2. Come up with an ER diagram for the following relational database:
   A (<u>a</u>, d)
   B (<u>b</u>, e, f, g)
   C (<u>c</u>, i, j, a, b)
   CL (<u>c, l</u>)
   AB(<u>a, b</u>, h)
   M (<u>b, m</u>, o, n)
   P (<u>b, m, p</u>, r, q)
   ABC (<u>a, b, c</u>, t)

Exercise 11.3

3. Come up with an EER diagram for the following relational database:
   A (<u>a</u>, b, o, s, t)
   C (<u>a</u>, c)
   D (<u>a</u>, d)
   E (<u>a</u>, e)

Exercise 11.4

4. Come up with an EER diagram for the following database:
   A (<u>a</u>, d, e, f, n)
   B (<u>b</u>, g, h, n)
   C (<u>c</u>, i, j, n)
   D (<u>n</u>)

BIBLIOGRAPHY

Elmasri, R., and Navathe, S. B. 2007. *Fundamentals of Database Systems*, 5th ed. Redwood City, CA: Benjamin Cummings.

12

A Brief Overview of the Barker/Oracle-Like Model

12.1 INTRODUCTION

There are many variations of entity relationship ER diagrams. One such model was introduced by Richard Barker (1990). The Barker model was adopted and modified slightly by the Oracle Corporation. In this chapter, we introduce the conventions used in the Barker/Oracle-like model as it applies to our ER Design Methodology. We depict major concepts of the ER diagrams of both Barker and Oracle. Our combined Barker/Oracle-like model is not meant as a primer on the "pure model" of either party, but the transition to the ER diagram of Barker or Oracle will be minor.

Why are we interested in the Barker/Oracle-like model, and why present it here? First, the Barker/Oracle-like model is common; it is used often in Oracle literature. The pedantic problem with the Barker/Oracle-like model is that one needs to understand relational database theory fully to understand why the Barker/Oracle-like model is done the way it is. We present the Barker/Oracle-like model here because the way it unfolds is a bit different from the Chen-like model. The Chen-like model focuses on modeling data, whereas the Barker/Oracle-like model adapts the data to the relational database concurrently with the design. Therefore, the ER design methodology for the Barker/Oracle-like model will develop differently from the Chen-like model. Further, the Barker/Oracle-like model will not have some of the conventions used in the Chen-like model. For example, the Barker/Oracle-like model does not directly use the concept of composite attributes, multivalued attributes, or weak entities, but rather handles these concepts immediately in light of the relational model. Since the Barker/Oracle-like model is so close to the relational model at the beginning, the mapping rules are trivial—the mapping takes place in the diagram itself.

12.2 A FIRST "ENTITY-ONLY" ER DIAGRAM: AN ENTITY WITH ATTRIBUTES

We start with developing a first, "entity-only" ER diagram in the Barker/Oracle-like model. To recap our example used previously in the book, we have chosen a "primary" entity from a student information database: the STUDENT. A *student* is something that we want to store information about (the definition of an entity). For the moment, we do not concern ourselves with any other entities.

What are the some initial attributes we used in the STUDENT entity? A student has a name, address, school, phone number, and major. We have picked five attributes for the entity STUDENT and have chosen a generic label for each: name, address, school, phone, and major.

We begin our venture into the Barker/Oracle-like model with Figure 12.1. A Barker/Oracle-like model uses soft boxes for entities (with the entity name in capital letters), and there is a line separating the entity name from the attributes (and the attribute names are in small letters). A Barker/Oracle-like model does not place the attributes in ovals (as the Chen-like model does), but rather lists the attributes below the entity name, as shown in Figure 12.1.

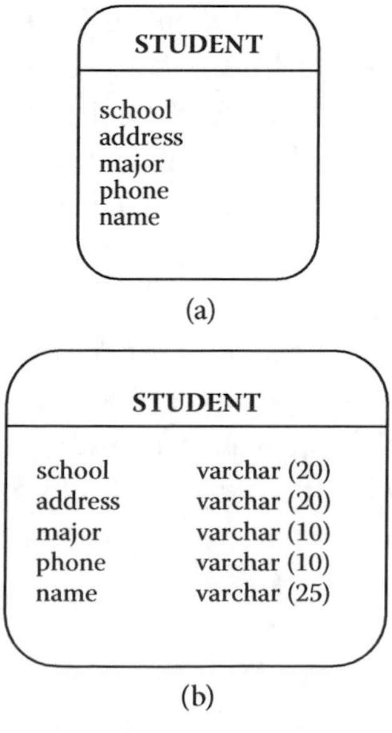

```
        STUDENT
    ┌──────────────┐
    │ school       │
    │ address      │
    │ major        │
    │ phone        │
    │ name         │
    └──────────────┘
         (a)


          STUDENT
    ┌──────────────────────────┐
    │ school    varchar (20)   │
    │ address   varchar (20)   │
    │ major     varchar (10)   │
    │ phone     varchar (10)   │
    │ name      varchar (25)   │
    └──────────────────────────┘
            (b)
```

FIGURE 12.1

Barker/Oracle-like notation of (a) an ER diagram with one entity and five attributes and (b) an ER diagram with one entity and five attributes with data types added.

Figure 12.1 shows an ER diagram with one entity, STUDENT, and the attributes name, address, school, phone, and major. In the Oracle-like version of the Barker/Oracle-like ER diagram, the data type is also listed (see Figure 12.1b).

12.3 ATTRIBUTES IN THE BARKER/ORACLE-LIKE MODEL

All attributes in a Barker/Oracle-like model are considered simple or atomic as in relational databases. The Barker/Oracle-like model does not have the concept of composite attributes. So, our Barker/Oracle-like adaptation will show parts of the composite attributes using a dot (.) notation, as shown in Figure 12.2.

12.3.1 Optional versus Mandatory Attributes

When designing a database, it is necessary to know whether an entity may contain an unknown value for an attribute. For example, in the STUDENT entity (shown in Figure 12.1), suppose that the address was optional. In other words, if data were recorded for a student on a paper data entry form, we could demand that the person fill out his or her name and student number but allow the person to leave the address blank (i.e., unknown). We would say that the name and student number were "mandatory" and address was "optional." A missing value is called a *null*. Hence, the mandatory attribute is said to be *not null*. *Not null* means that in **no** occasion would an instance of the entity exist without knowing the value of this mandatory attribute. In the Barker/Oracle-like ER model, we will show

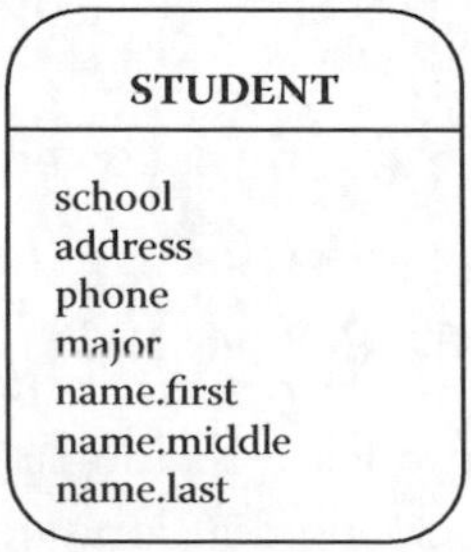

```
 _____
|      STUDENT               \
|                             |
|  school                     |
|  address                    |
|  phone                      |
|  major                      |
|  name.first                 |
|  name.middle                |
|  name.last                  |
 _____/
```

FIGURE 12.2
Barker/Oracle-like notation of an ER diagram with a composite attribute: name.

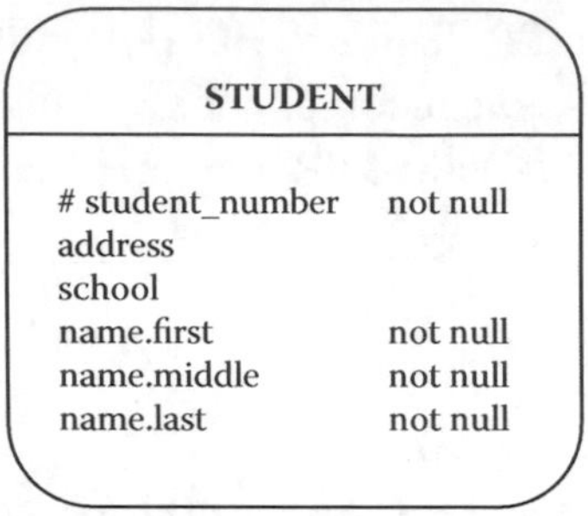

FIGURE 12.3
Barker/Oracle-like notation of an ER diagram with a primary key or unique identifier attribute and optional and mandatory attributes.

the optional attribute without the not null depiction and the mandatory attribute by adding the phrase *not null* to the description (as shown in Figure 12.3). A mandatory attribute could be a key, but it is not necessarily a key. Mandatory and optional attributes are usually not indicated explicitly in the Chen-like model.

In our Barker model, the primary key has a # in front of the name of the attribute (as shown in Figure 12.3). A primary key has to be a mandatory attribute in a relational database, but again, all mandatory attributes here are not necessarily unique identifiers.

CHECKPOINT 12.1

1. What do mandatory attributes (in the Barker/Oracle-like model) translate into in the Chen-like model? Discuss with examples.
2. What do optional attributes (in the Barker/Oracle-like model) translate into in the Chen-like model? Discuss with examples.
3. How are the primary keys shown diagrammatically in the Barker/Oracle-like model?

12.4 RELATIONSHIPS IN THE BARKER/ORACLE-LIKE MODEL

In the Barker/Oracle-like model, a relationship is represented by a line that joins two entities. There is no diamond denoting the relationship (as we saw in the Chen-like model). The relationship phrase for each end of a relationship is placed near the appropriate end (entity) in lowercase, as

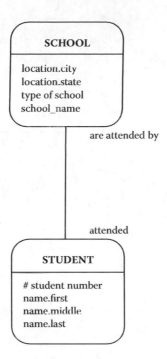

FIGURE 12.4
Barker/Oracle-like notation of the STUDENT entity with a relationship to the SCHOOL entity.

shown in Figure 12.4. In this model, from the STUDENT entity to the SCHOOL entity we would say (informally),

Students attended schools

And, from the other direction, from the SCHOOL entity to the STUDENT entity, we would say,

Schools are attended by students.

12.5 STRUCTURAL CONSTRAINTS IN THE BARKER/ORACLE-LIKE MODEL

In the Barker/Oracle-like notation, the cardinality of 1 is shown by a single line leading to the entity. In Figure 12.5, a single line joins the two entities, so this is a 1:1 relationship between the STUDENT and AUTOMOBILE. This means that one student may be related to one and only one automobile, and one automobile can be related to one and only one student.

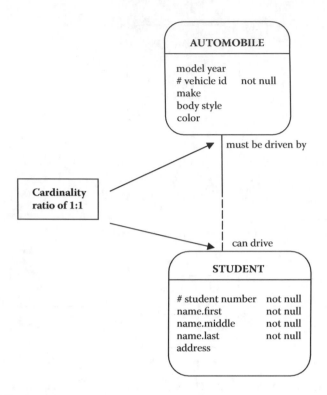

FIGURE 12.5
A 1:1 relationship in the Barker/Oracle-like notation.

The dashed line leading to an entity signifies optional (partial) participation of an entity in a relationship. In Figure 12.5, the STUDENT entity is participating optionally in the relationship, but the AUTOMOBILE entity is not participating optionally (the latter relationship is mandatory).

An enhanced grammar from the STUDENT entity to the AUTOMOBILE entity would be

A student may drive one and only one automobile

And, from the AUTOMOBILE entity to the STUDENT entity it would be

An automobile must be driven by one and only one student.

A continuous (solid) line coming from the AUTOMOBILE entity (as shown in Figure 12.5) signifies mandatory (full) participation of that entity in a relationship. A dashed line coming from the STUDENT entity (as shown in Figure 12.5) signifies optional (partial) participation. Again, according to Figure 12.6, students **must** occupy dorms, but a dorm **may** have students.

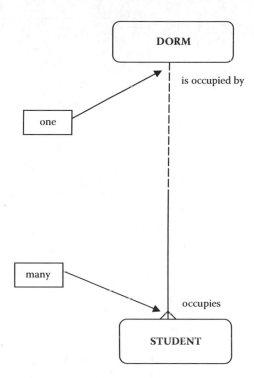

FIGURE 12.6
A 1:M relationship in the Barker/Oracle-like notation.

A cardinality of M (many) is shown by a "crow's-foot" structure leading to the respective entity. Figure 12.6 is an example of a 1:M relationship between DORM and STUDENT. The exact grammar for Figure 12.6 would be

A dorm may be occupied by zero or more students

and

A student must occupy one and only one dorm.

CHECKPOINT 12.2

1. How is the optional relationship shown diagrammatically in the Barker/Oracle-like model?
2. How is the many relationship shown diagrammatically in the Barker/Oracle-like model?
3. Show the following using the Barker/Oracle-like notation:
   a. A movie theater must show many movies, and movies must be shown in a movie theater.
   b. A movie theater may show many movies, and movies may be shown in a movie theater.

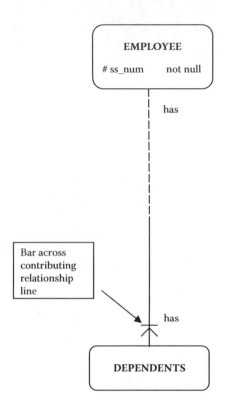

FIGURE 12.7
Unique identifier (to include a weak entity relationship) shown by placing a bar across the
contributing relationship line(s).

12.6 DEALING WITH THE CONCEPT OF THE WEAK ENTITY IN THE BARKER/ORACLE-LIKE MODEL

The Barker or Oracle models do not have a concept of the "weak entity,"
and the weak entity notation is also not used in Oracle literature. We
extend the concept of the unique identifier in a relationship to include
the weak entity. In the Barker/Oracle-like model, the unique identifier
in a relationship may be diagrammatically shown by a bar cutting across
the contributing relationship, as shown in Figure 12.7. In Figure 12.7, to
uniquely identify a dependent, one needs the employee's social security
number. This means that the DEPENDENT entity cannot independently
stand on its own and hence is a weak entity. However, here the weak entity
would be mapped as per the mapping rules discussed in Chapter 7.

12.7 DEALING WITH THE CONCEPT OF MULTIVALUED ATTRIBUTES IN THE BARKER/ORACLE-LIKE MODEL

The Barker or Oracle models do not have the concept of the "multivalued" attribute. Multivalued attributes can be shown as in Figure 12.8, which shows that a student may have attended many schools.

In the Barker/Oracle-like model, the foreign key is shown in the appropriate entity, whereas in the Chen-like model, foreign keys are not

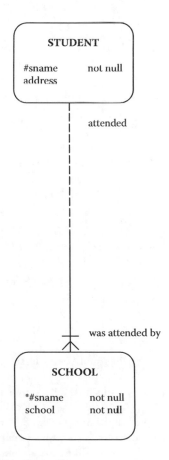

Note: "*" shows a foreign key

FIGURE 12.8
The multivalued attribute and the foreign key.

"discovered" until the database is mapped. We signal a foreign key with an asterisk (*) in front of the attribute (see Figure 12.8). An instance of this database shown in Figure 12.8 is

STUDENT

sname	address
Sumona Gupta	111 Mirabelle Circle, Pensacola, FL
Tom Bundy	198 Palace Drive, Mobile, AL
Tony Jones	329 Becker Place, Mongotomery, AL
Sita Pal	987 Twin Lane, North Canton, OH
Neetu Singh	109 Bombay Blvd, Calicut, CA

SCHOOL

sname	school
Sumona Gupta	Ferry Pass Elementary
Sumona Gupta	PCA
Sumona Gupta	Pensacola High
Tom Bundy	Mobile Middle School
Tom Bundy	St. Johns
Tony Jones	Montgomery Elementary
Tony Jones	Montgomery Middle
Tony Jones	Montgomery High
Sita Pal	Tagore Primary School
Sita Pal	Nehru Secondary School

As you can see, the multivalued attribute is mapped to tables as it is depicted in the Barker/Oracle-like notation. In the Chen-like model, the multivalued attribute is kept in the diagram and then mapped using the mapping rules (see mapping rule 4).

CHECKPOINT 12.3

1. Does the Barker-like model or the Oracle-like model have the concept of the weak entity? Discuss.
2. Show the following using the Barker/Oracle-like notation: For a student, we are trying to store the student's name, address, phone, books (that is, books that the student borrows from the library). Map this to a relational database and show some sample data.
3. Does the Barker/Oracle-like notation have the concept of the multivalued attribute? Discuss.

12.8 TREATMENT OF FOREIGN KEYS

In the original Barker model, foreign keys are not marked. In the Oracle model, foreign keys are included in the respective relations. For example, Figure 12.9 says

> *A student may drive many automobiles*

and

> *An automobile must be driven by a student.*

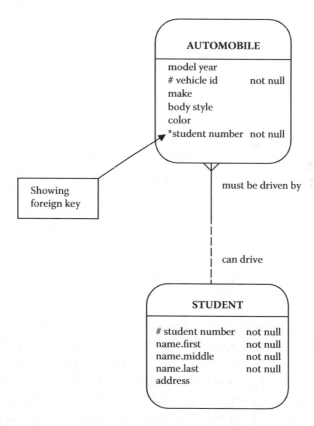

FIGURE 12.9
Barker/Oracle-like notation showing foreign key.

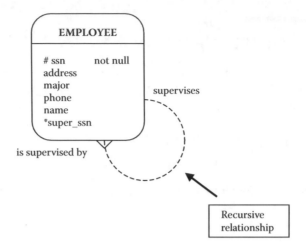

FIGURE 12.10
Barker/Oracle-like notation recursive relationship.

The primary key from the STUDENT relation (the 1 side), student num-ber, is included in the AUTOMOBILE relation (the N side). In our Barker/Oracle-like model, we precede the foreign key with an asterisk (as shown in Figure 12.9).

12.9 RECURSIVE RELATIONSHIPS IN THE BARKER/ORACLE-LIKE MODEL

Recursive relationships in the Barker/Oracle-like model are drawn as shown in Figure 12.10. Again, the dotted line in the relationship shows an optional relationship, the solid line would show a mandatory relationship, and a "crow's-foot" would show a many relationship. The relationships are named as shown. Figure 12.10 shows that an employee may supervise other employees, and an employee may be supervised by one and only one supervisor. Note the foreign key super_ssn in the EMPLOYEE rela-tion itself.

12.10 MAPPING M:N RELATIONSHIPS

Finally, we discuss one important aspect that is treated differently in the Barker/Oracle-like model: an M:N relationship. In the Barker/Oracle-like model, all M:N relationships are resolved into two 1:M relationships with an intersection entity in the middle. In the Chen-like model, the M:N may be presented as two 1:M relationships.

Figure 12.11 is an example of an M:N relationship in the Chen-like format. In the Barker/Oracle-like model this would be shown as in Figure 12.12.

CHECKPOINT 12.4

1. How are recursive relationships shown in the Barker/Oracle like model?
2. Why is it difficult to show M:N relationships in the Barker/Oracle-like model?
3. How are the foreign keys treated in the Barker/Oracle-like model?
4. How are recursive relationships shown in the Barker/Oracle-like model?

12.11 CHAPTER SUMMARY

This chapter briefly discussed some of the main features of the Barker/Oracle-like model. The one-entity diagram, with attributes, was presented. The idea of optional versus mandatory attributes was discussed. Relationships and structural constraints were briefly discussed in the context of the Barker/Oracle-like model, and although the Barker/Oracle-like notation does not use the concept of the weak entity and multivalued attributes, we showed how these concepts can be shown diagrammatically in the Barker/Oracle-like notation. An example of the depiction of the recursive relationship in the Barker/Oracle model is illustrated. Finally, the chapter showed how to map an M:N relationship into two 1:M relationships. Mapping rules were also discussed in the context of the Barker/Oracle-like notation.

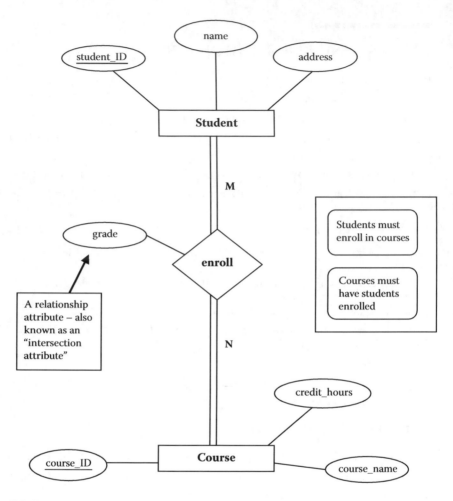

FIGURE 12.11
An ER diagram of an M:N relationship in the Chen-like model.

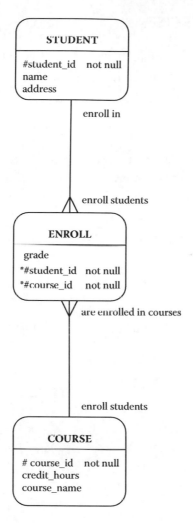

FIGURE 12.12
Barker/Oracle-like notation of an M:N relationship broken into two 1:M relationships.

CHAPTER 12 EXERCISES

Exercise 12.1

1. Redraw Figure 8.17a using the Barker/Oracle notation. Map this to a relational database and show some sample data.

Exercise 12.1

2. Redraw Figure 8.7 using the Barker/Oracle notation. Map this to a relational database and show some sample data.

BIBLIOGRAPHY

Barker, R. 1990. *Case*Method, Entity Relationship Modeling*. Reading, MA: Addison Wesley.

Hay, D. C. 1996. *Data Model Patterns*. New York: Dorset House.

Rodgers, Ulka. 1991. *ORACLE: A Database Developer's Guide*. Englewood Cliffs, NJ: Prentice-Hall.

Siau, K. 2004. *Advanced Topics in Database Research*. Hershey, PA: Idea Group.

Glossary

A

Attribute: Property used to describe an entity or relationship.

B

Binary relationship: Relationship between two entities.

C

Candidate key: An attribute or set of attributes that uniquely identifies individual occurrences of an entity type.

Cardinality ratio: Describes the number of one entity that is related to another entity.

Category: When a subclass has more than one superclass that it may inherit from; also referred to as union type.

Composite attribute: An attribute composed of multiple components, each with an independent existence.

D

Database: A shared collection of logically associated or related data.

Degree of a relationship: The number of participating entities in a relationship.

Derived attribute: An attribute that gets a value calculated or derived from the database.

E

Entity: "Something" in the real world that is of importance to a user and that needs to be represented in a database so that information about the entity may be recorded. An entity may have physical existence (such as a student or building) or it may have conceptual existence (such as a course).

Entity set: A collection of all entities of a particular entity type.

Entity type: A set of entities of the same type.

F

First normal form (1NF): The domain of all attributes in a table must include only atomic (simple, indivisible) values, and the value of any attribute in a tuple (or row) must be single-valued from the domain of that attribute.

Foreign key: An attribute that is a primary key of another relation (table). A foreign key is how relationships are implemented in relational databases.

Full participation: All of one entity set participates in a relationship.

Functional dependency: A relationship between two attributes in a relation. Attribute Y is functionally dependent on attribute X if attribute X identifies attribute Y. For every unique value of X, the same value of Y will always be found.

G

Generalization: The process of minimizing the differences between entities by identifying their common features and removing the common features into a superclass entity.

H

Hierarchical model: All data are arranged in a top-down fashion.

I

Identifying owner: The strong entity on which a weak entity is dependent.

Identifying relationship: A weak relationship.

K

Key: An attribute or data item that uniquely identifies a record instance or tuple in a relation.

M

Mandatory relationship: Same as full participation; all of one entity set participates in a relationship.

Many to many: Many tuples (rows) of one relation can be related to many tuples (rows) in another relation.

Many to one: Many tuples (rows) of one relation can be related to one tuple (row) in another relation.

Mapping: The process of choosing a logical model and then moving to a physical database file system from a conceptual model (the ER diagram).

Multivalued attribute: An attribute that may have multiple values for a single entity.

O

One to many: A relationship in which one tuple (or row) of one relation can be related to more than one tuple (row) in another relation.

One to one: A relationship in which one tuple (or row) of one relation can be related to only one tuple (row) in another relation.

Optional participation: A constraint that specifies whether the existence of an entity depends on its being related to another entity via a relationship type.

P

Partial key: The unique key in a dependent entity.

Partial participation: Part of one entity set participates in a relationship.

Participation constraints (also known as optionality): Determines whether all or some of an entity occurrence is related to another entity.

Primary key: A unique identifier for a row in a table in a relational database; a selected candidate key of an entity.

R

Recursive relationship: Relationship among entities in the same class.

Regular entity: *See* Entity.

Relation: A table containing single-value entries and no duplicate rows. The meaning of the columns is the same in every row, and the order of the rows and columns is immaterial. Often, a relation is defined as a populated table.

Relationship: An association between entities.

Reverse engineering: The process of going from relational tables to a logical model (or ER diagram).

S

Second normal form: A relation that is in first normal form and in which each nonkey attribute is fully functionally dependent on the primary key.

Shared subclass: A subclass that has more than one subclass for its parents.

Simple attribute: Attribute composed of a single value.

Specialization: The process of maximizing the differences between members of a superclass entity by identifying their distinguishing characteristics.

Specialization hierarchy: A subclass inherits from only one subclass.

Specialization lattice: A subclass has more than one subclass as its parent.

Strong entity: An entity that is not dependent on another entity for its existence.

Structural constraints: Indicate how many of one type of a record is related to another and whether the record must have such a relationship. The cardinality ratio and participation constraints taken together form the structural constraints.

Subclass: An entity type that has a distinct role and is also a member of a superclass.

Superclass: An entity type that includes distinct subclasses that are required to be represented in a data model.

T

Table: Same as relation; a tabular view of data that may be used to hold one or more columns of data; an implementation of an entity.

Third normal form: A relation that is in second normal form and in which no nonkey attribute is functionally dependent on another nonkey attribute (that is, there are no transitive dependencies in the relation).

U

Union type: A subclass has more than one superclass it may inherit from; also referred to as a category.

Unique identifier: Any combination of attributes or relationships that serves to uniquely identify an occurrence of an entity.

W

Waterfall model: A series of steps that software undergoes, from concept exploration through final retirement.

Weak entity: An entity that is dependent on some other entity for its existence.

Index